Received on

NOV 1 4 2019

Green Lake Library

D0959161

NO LONGER PROPERTY
SEATTLE PUBLIC LIBRARY

IT'S NOT OVER UNTIL YOU WIN

IT'S NOT OVER UNTIL YOU WIN

My Lifetime of Experiencing the Miracles of God

MARILYN HICKEY

It's Not Over Until You Win: My Lifetime of Experiencing the Miracles of God
Copyright ©2019 Marilyn Hickey

Marilyn Hickey Ministries
P.O. Box 6598
Englewood, Colorado 80155
1-888-637-4545
marilynandsarah.org

Published by: Marilyn Hickey Ministries
Distributed by: Thomas Nelson

Edited by Diane Reiter and Michelle and Solomon Ofori-Ansah

All rights reserved. No part of this publication may be reproduced, distributed, or transmitted in any form or by any means, including photocopying, recording, or other electronic or mechanical methods, without the prior written permission of the publisher, except in the case of brief quotations embodied in critical reviews and certain other noncommercial uses permitted by copyright law. For permission requests, write to the publisher with correspondence addressed "Attention: Permissions Coordinator," 2150 E. Continental Boulevard, Southlake, Texas, 76092.

Unless otherwise noted, all scripture quotations are taken from the New King James Version® of the Bible. Copyright © 1982 by Thomas Nelson. Used by permission. All rights reserved.

Scripture quotations marked (NIV) are taken from the Holy Bible, New International Version®, NIV®. Copyright © 1973, 1978, 1984, 2011 by Biblica, Inc.™ Used by permission of Zondervan. All rights reserved worldwide. www.zondervan.com The "NIV" and "New International Version" are trademarks registered in the United States Patent and Trademark Office by Biblica, Inc.™

Scriptures are taken from the English Standard Version® (ESV®). Copyright ©2001 by Crossway, a publishing ministry of Good News Publishers. All rights reserved.

ISBN: 978-1-7327904-7-6

Printed in the USA

This book is dedicated to . . .

My amazing family; specifically, my daughter, Sarah, and my son-in-law, Reece, along with my wonderful grandchildren who have loved me unconditionally;

My incredible team of loyal and hard-working staff members who have faithfully helped me cover the earth with the Word;

My friends and partners who have prayed unceasingly and given sacrificially to open the doors and provide the resources for me to minister to millions of people in over 137 nations around the world.

Table of Contents

Foreword ix

Introduction xi

Chapter 1: From Dust to Romance 1

Chapter 2: Saying "Yes!" 19

Chapter 3: A Partner for Life 41

Chapter 4: The Fight for My Family 69

Chapter 5: Breaking Barriers 97

Chapter 6: Passion and Purpose 129

Chapter 7: Miracles and the Underground 159

Chapter 8: I Love Muslims, and Muslims Love Me 193

Chapter 9: Wrestling with Terror 219

Chapter 10: Don't be Buried with the Mantle 247

Acknowledgments 265

Endorsements 266

Foreword

It is a great honor to write the foreword for my friend Marilyn's life story. She is an amazing, beautiful woman of God, and I am blessed and inspired by her diligence and steadfast determination to go all the way with God in everything He's called her to do.

Marilyn has a special, very sincere love for people of all different cultures and ethnicities, which speaks loudly of God's heart for the world. She's a living example of what it means to love others as Jesus loves us—selflessly, putting their best interests and needs above her own. Many times, she's prayed fervently for people in various countries and it has opened up opportunities for her to personally go to those places and share the truth of the Gospel. These situations have also set the stage for God to do astounding miracles through Marilyn's ministry.

Your life will change as you learn of Marilyn's wholehearted devotion to live for God and her unshakeable faith that has taken her all over the world to share the Gospel. Her experiences will inspire everyone who reads her story to believe God can and will do what He says He will do as they walk out His plan for their lives.

I believe reading this book will restore your faith in miracles and open your heart to believe that with God, all things are possible. Your faith will be strengthened, and you may end up doing amazing things yourself.

—Joyce Meyer, best-selling author and Bible teacher

Introduction

It was a very dangerous time in a very dangerous nation. A man with a gun was stationed outside the door of my hotel room 24/7 for protection because 32 suicide bombers had taken an oath to blow up the stadium with thousands of people, my entire team, and me in it. The government of that country had uncovered the plot, but they had not found or arrested all of the suicide bombers. The majority of those men, determined to kill me, were still out there. That is why the government officials told me that they could not allow me to continue with the evening healing meetings we had been working on for over a year. They felt the situation was extremely volatile, massively dangerous, and too explosive. And they were right! Every logical instinct inside of me said to get out of there, quickly. But with God, it's not over until you win.

A few years earlier I had been in a different nation, teaching leaders of churches. The meetings had been set in the dark of night with nothing more than the glow of lanterns to illuminate those of us who were gathered. Some of the leaders had come from hundreds of miles away, mostly on foot, to receive encouragement and instruction from the Word of God. There was a sweet anointing as we opened the Scriptures, but each person who had come to receive had done so at great personal risk. It wasn't overly dangerous for me. Yes, I could be arrested and detained, but there wasn't much more that could be done to me. But for the leaders I was teaching, it was exceedingly dangerous. If we were discovered, they could be arrested, tortured, thrown in prison, or killed. But with God, it's not over until you win.

More recently, I was standing before the massive brick wall that marks the separation between Israel and Gaza. The vicious twists of barbed wire at the top of the wall were vivid reminders that this was a region where violence erupted often, frequently without warning. The heavily armed guards were vigilant and alert. Many would ask what I was doing there, who did I think I was, and how in the world did I think I was going to make it through the checkpoints and walk into Gaza? But I knew that I was supposed to go into that dangerous and war-torn area with the love of Jesus. Even though my paperwork had been carefully and accurately completed, I had been waiting for hours to receive permission to be processed through the checkpoints and walk the mile-long, dust-covered road into Gaza. It was getting later and later and the cut-off time for getting in was quickly approaching. Once again, I had to remind myself that with God, it's not over until you win.

More times than I can count, the Lord has put a country on my heart and prompted me to pray earnestly for that nation. Then He has led me to go there in order to share the good news of the Gospel and the healing power of Jesus Christ with those who would receive it. But many of those times, I have faced closed doors. The doors weren't just closed, they were seemingly locked, barred, and barricaded against me. Visas were denied again and again or promised but never given. Often it looked like the very thing God had called me to do was totally impossible. But with God, it's not over until you win.

What is the most difficult situation you are facing in your life right now? Does it seem hopeless, with insurmountable odds and innumerable obstacles? Does it seem impossible for you to succeed? I am inviting you to come with me as I detail the life I have lived. At times, I have experienced devastating defeats. Other times, I have tried and failed only to try and fail again. I have even stepped out, full of faith, and run straight into solid brick walls that would not budge. Yet, through it all, I can look back and say that I have truly enjoyed a lifetime of experiencing the miracles of God. My prayer is that you, too, will stand in faith in the midst of seemingly impossible situations and see for yourself that it's not over until you win.

Jesus is the most radical gift God could ever give. John 3:16 says, *"For*

God so loved the world that He gave His only begotten Son . . ." My prayer for you is that you would know the unconditional love of your heavenly Father and that His love would become even more real to you as you read this book; and ultimately, that you would know Jesus Christ more intimately as your personal Lord and Savior. As you will see, I have been blessed to walk a very supernatural life. Throughout this book, you will read about the specific journey I took in order to learn about the power of the Holy Spirit operating in the lives of believers. As I share those experiences, I pray that you would be encouraged to believe God for miracles in your life as well. I also realize that some of my experiences with the Holy Spirit may be foreign to you or outside the realm of your experience. Let me encourage you in this way: Do not get hung up on any experiential differences. In any area where you have questions, search the Bible for answers. John 16:13 says that He is the *"Spirit of truth"* and that He came to *"guide you into all truth."* No matter what you may be facing today, with your heavenly Father's love, Jesus Christ as your Lord and Savior, and the Holy Spirit leading and guiding you, it's not over until you win!

Chapter 1

FROM DUST TO ROMANCE

I WAS ALWAYS A DREAMER. Often, when I was young, I would look up at the sky and watch the airplanes fly by. I was fascinated by them. I was awed by how small they looked in the air, and always wondered where they were going. How did they fly? What kind of people were on those planes? I daydreamed about what the people were doing and the wonderful destinations to which they were traveling. I enjoyed reveling in those imaginary travels and would think to myself with a smile, *One day I will be on one of those planes!* Of course, it seemed foolish, almost impossible, an unrealistic hope for a girl who lived in the dusty neighborhoods of a little Texas town during the Great Depression. I never even remotely imagined that one day I would fly in thousands of planes and minister to millions of people in 137 nations of the world.

My life began in a very ordinary way. I was born on July 1, 1931, Marilyn Allene Sweitzer. I was the brown-haired, brown-eyed, firstborn child of Mary Alice and John Sweitzer, born in the small town of Dalhart, located in the northern corner of the Texas Panhandle. The Lone Star State in the 1930s was not a very pleasant place to live. Dalhart was in the center of the Dust Bowl, where long periods of drought and dry, swirling dust storms made life challenging. I remember days where the gritty particles of dust were everywhere. They filled our eyes, ears, and nose, and made it almost impossible to see, hear, or breathe. We took extra safety precautions because of the dangerous dust storms. When we traveled, we kept a big can of water in the trunk of our car so that if there was a dust storm, we could put wet cloths over our mouths to enable us to breathe through the dust.

Perhaps the scariest time of my childhood was being caught in a dust storm with my family. I was about three years old. We had driven to my grandparents' farm for a visit, which was something we regularly did as a family and I enjoyed immensely. That day, we were about to leave for home when we spotted thick storm clouds in the distance coming toward us. Quickly, my dad rushed us into the car and drove as fast as he could toward home. The dust storm caught up to us, making the ride slow and tedious. We kept wet cloths over our mouths the whole way. By the time we made the 15-mile journey home, the sky was so dark with dust that it felt like night, even though it was the middle of the day. After parking the car, we had to feel our way to the house since it was too dark with dust to see anything at all.

My Family

Dad was a typical American worker, a pioneer in every sense of the word. He was a very hard-working family man who always made sure we had our basic needs met. We did not have a lot of life's creature comforts during those days of the Great Depression. However, I never felt that there was anything I needed as a child that I did not have. We had enough food to eat, and I felt loved. The house where I grew up was very special to me. My dad built it himself, a little three-room house with a garage, painted in a beautiful beige. Dad was very good with his hands and because of that, as difficult as the times were, we didn't feel the lack as intensely as many other families did. Indeed, in so many ways, they were good times, too.

A person can dream all they want, but if they are not willing to work hard, those dreams will never become realities.

I had lots of family near Dalhart. My mother, Mary Alice Moore, had been one of 11 children, and most of her siblings lived close by. My grandparents, who also lived in Dalhart, had a total of 22 grandchildren! So, I always had family around. As a little girl, I loved being with my grandmother. One of my earliest memories is of me sitting on my grandmother's lap as she dipped a homemade biscuit in coffee and fed it to me. She said to my mother, "This child is too thin; you need to feed her better." I never felt I was too thin, but my grandmother certainly did, and she didn't hesitate to tell my mother her thoughts.

I have delightful memories of farm life with my grandparents. I didn't live there, but I might as well have, as I made frequent visits to the farm. My grandfather and my uncles would leave the house very early to work the land, and my grandmother would work all morning to make lunch, the biggest meal of the day. I loved being in the kitchen with her. She would let me sit on the counter and "help" her cook and bake; prepping the food was exciting, too. There were always such sweet aromas coming from my grandmother's oven. I also have very fond memories of chasing the chickens and turkeys, helping my grandmother gather eggs, and watching my uncles milk the cows. My grandparents were extremely hard workers, and they definitely passed that value down to me. I learned, at a very young age, that it is important to work hard. A person can dream all they want, but if they are not willing to work hard, those dreams will never become realities.

While my family was the source of many of my good habits, my love for people of all races, which started when I was young, must have been a gift from God. Love for diverse cultures and people was definitely not something that I always saw in my extended family or in the people around me. Dalhart was in the South. And I grew up during an era of extreme racial prejudice and discrimination. In fact, some of my relatives were very negative about black people, and their attitude bothered me a lot. Even as a child, I would get outright angry about racial discrimination; I didn't understand it or like it. I loved all people, but that made me appear as a troublemaker in the eyes of my relatives. My uncles would laugh at me and make fun of the way I felt. Their ridicule might have hurt my feelings, but it didn't change me. God had given me a love for all people, and it didn't matter to me if others made fun of me because of it.

When I was about five years old, my father got a new job that took us to San Angelo, Texas. It was hard saying goodbye to Dalhart because it was all I had known up to that point. I was nervous about leaving behind the familiar, and venturing into that which was new and different. We moved just before my first year of school began. At that time, San Angelo didn't have a kindergarten class, so I started first grade. I had such a great desire to excel and a fear of not doing well that I was easily overwhelmed. During those overwhelming times, my mother was an immense support to me. I would complain, "Mom, on Friday there is a spelling test, and I don't know what to do!" Mother's response was always the same, "You were a smart baby; you will do well." Her response to me was reassuring and gave me courage. It did not matter what my fears were or how often I thought I might not do well academically; she would encourage me by saying, "You were a smart baby!" She was actually saying that since I had been smart when I was a baby, I was smart at that point, too! After a while, I began to believe it.

With my parents' encouragement, I did well in school. I liked the challenge, and I liked getting good grades because of how it made me feel. It was rewarding to get A's, and it made my father happy. My father, John Allen Sweitzer, was a very quiet man, but very caring. He would smile with joy if I got an A, and I loved that. His response to my good grades inspired me to put in my best effort. I wanted to please him, so I worked even harder to get A's.

As I went through grade school, my parents' German household rules were deeply instilled in me. We had three very specific rules: work hard, be disciplined, and learn to provide for yourself. And that's exactly how I lived. When I was 11 years old, I began buying my own clothes. One of my first jobs was gathering baskets of apples that had fallen off trees. I would work for hours to fill one basket. I got paid five cents per basket, so it was worth the hard work! I believe those rules, along with my family experiences as a young child, were instrumental in developing a resilience in me that lasted throughout my young and late adulthood. My childhood experiences taught me to never give up, even when things looked impossible.

My younger brother, David, was born shortly after we moved to San Angelo. While his birth brought joy to my family, I, unfortunately, was not particularly fond of him. This was especially true when he was very young. Since he was several years younger than me, I didn't feel like we could have any fun playing together. Yet, he always wanted to play with me, my friends, and my dolls. I wasn't interested in sharing my friends with him, and my dolls were totally "off-limits" because when he played with my dolls, he often broke them, which made me so unhappy with him. At first, I didn't quite understand the whole sibling thing. To me, he was just a pesky little brother. Fortunately, by the time I turned 11, we started to have a better relationship. I think he finally grew old enough that I could appreciate him, and we started enjoying our times together.

David was much smarter than I was and performed better academically. He became an electrical engineer and did quite well. As adults, even though we lived in different states, he in Texas and I in Colorado, we remained close and talked often. Unfortunately, David struggled with mental health issues most of his life. During his difficult years, my mother stood for his salvation: she prayed for him and believed that he would know that God loved him, that he would accept the truth that Jesus died for him and pray

---

She instilled that same perseverance in me, a determination to never give up until God gives me the victory . . .

---

for Jesus to forgive him of his sins. My mother also prayed and asked God to fill David with the Holy Spirit. This is an experience talked about in the second chapter of Acts, where the followers of Jesus were filled with the Spirit of God and began to see the power of God operate through their lives. During his 60s, David received salvation and the filling of the Spirit. It happened in the late 1990s when he went to see my mother on her death bed. During that visit, she prayed for him, and he was saved and filled with the Spirit. After that, he was mentally and emotionally healthy until his death in 2012. My mother had refused to give up on him, and that tenacity produced results. I know that she instilled that same perseverance in me, a determination to never give up until God gives me the victory, which has enabled me to see amazing breakthroughs in my life.

My dad was originally from Pennsylvania, but he had suffered from asthma when he was younger, so he moved to Texas because of the warm climate. At the beginning of World War II, when I was 10, we moved to Sewickley, Pennsylvania where my dad helped build ships as part of the war effort. My mom liked Pennsylvania. She thought the area was beautiful, and particularly refreshing with its countless variety of plants, flowers, and trees. She also loved that Pennsylvania had four true seasons, and she loved the gorgeous colors all around us when the leaves changed in the fall. We lived in Sewickley until after the war ended in 1945. Those years were very tough for everyone because of the war and the shortages that resulted from it. I remember planting victory gardens so we would at least have vegetables to eat. As I look back, I can see that even in the midst of the struggles, God was working to shape His purpose for my life. This work was most evident in my education, social development, and friendships.

My First International Friend

Pennsylvania had very good schools. The teachers were devoted and engaging, and that sparked a hunger in me for learning. I did well academically, but the larger impact on my development extended beyond the four walls of the classroom. Pennsylvania, even at that time, was much more diverse than Texas. In so many ways it was very cosmopolitan. There was a large international population, including many people who were Polish or Italian, which exposed me to people from various ethnicities and backgrounds. The different cultures and languages were intriguing to me, and I loved being able to socialize with people from different countries. I befriended several children in my class who were very different from me, and I loved it!

My first "international" friend was an Italian immigrant. Her name was Clorinda Flora. I really took to her and thought her accent was captivating. Before Clorinda, I had never met anyone from another country. I felt especially drawn to her. The attraction might have been because in many ways she was an outsider and I could identify with her. During that period of my life, I often felt isolated and lonely myself, and it was evident that neither Clorinda nor I were in the popular crowd. I liked the fact that we were different from each other, and I didn't mind being different from the others around us.

I enjoyed hearing Clorinda tell stories about her life in Italy and her adventures near the Mediterranean Sea. For a dreamer like me, I had hit a gold mine. I would ponder her stories and wonder about life in Florence, Venice, and other parts of the world. Clorinda's family loved me, too. Whenever I visited her home, her family would cook authentic Italian food for me, which was so good! I loved hearing her family converse in their native Italian. I thought their conversations sounded so beautiful. Even though I was very young, my friendship with Clorinda taught me to appreciate the beauty of diversity. Our friendship grew throughout elementary school, as did my love of languages and desire to see the world.

Connected to Him

At that time, I felt very drawn to God and wanted to be connected to Him, even though the denomination that I had been raised in was quite liberal and did not encourage much in the way of a personal relationship with the Lord. Despite that lack of encouragement, my heart was pulled in such a way that I felt like I needed to know more about God. One day, I prayed a simple prayer in my heart to Him; I said, "I want to be where You are. Where are You? Should I go to the Methodist church, or the Catholic church, or the Baptist church? I want to be where You are." He replied to my heart with a crystal-clear message. He said, "I am in the Word." That seemed strange at first, but it also made sense to my heart. Even though our church had not emphasized reading the Bible in personal devotions, my mother had always said the Bible was the Word of God and had all the answers. The example set by my mother and the clear message from God convinced me that I needed to read the Bible.

I began reading my Bible each day, and every night I knelt on the floor of my second-story bedroom and prayed the Scriptures. Outside, there were several sturdy pine trees that seemed to shelter my window. The beauty of the surroundings, together with the tranquility of prayer, made that a very peaceful place. Although I enjoyed those times immensely, I never had even an inkling that those actions were laying the foundation for my life's work and future success. The seemingly innocent love that had developed for the Scriptures and prayer laid the foundation for a passionate, life-long discipline of Bible reading that literally changed the course of my life and shaped my destiny.

I don't understand why, but in the beginning, I loved reading the book of Isaiah. I read Isaiah all the time and began to take some of the promises from that book and actively believe for them to become a reality in my life. I also began to read the book of Psalms. Psalm 139 quickly became one of my favorites. Everyone should read and memorize Psalm 139. It teaches us that nobody is an accident and that everyone on this earth is a divine appointment.

We are not always aware of the challenges and dangers
ahead of us, but God is, and He will prepare and fortify us so
that we can walk in His grace through those challenges.

A Dark Time

Despite all the positive experiences that took place during my years in Pennsylvania and the wonderful truth I was learning from the Word of God, there was a very dark side to my life as well. It easily could have overshadowed all the joyful experiences, the friendships at school, and the deep spiritual work that was taking place in my life. Looking back, I believe I survived that dark time because of my deep foundation in the Word of God. In my heart, I knew that God loved me, even though my negative experience caused me to question that truth. Since then, I have learned that we are not always aware of the challenges and dangers ahead of us, but God is; and He will prepare and fortify us so that we can walk in His grace through those challenges.

My dark experience started when my family first moved to Pennsylvania. In the beginning, we lived with my aunt and uncle. Unknown to anyone else at that time, my uncle began sexually molesting me when I was only 11 years old. I didn't know the facts of life or really understand what he was doing, at the time. I only knew that I didn't like it. It confused me because when he wasn't sexually abusing me, he was very nice to me. In fact, he was nice to everyone. He was loved by so many people who thought he was the nicest person in the world. His popularity only added to my turmoil. After each incident of abuse, I felt ashamed and guilty, and blamed myself for what was happening. Because he was so well-liked by everyone, I felt that the abuse had to be my fault. I thought, *If I weren't doing something wrong, this wouldn't be happening.* It was a totally devastating and extremely confusing time in my life. Shortly after I turned 12, the abuse suddenly stopped, and we moved out of their house. Even though the abuse had stopped, I plunged into depression. I thought that there was something desperately wrong with me, and I wanted to end my life. I even tried to commit suicide.

That entire year was intensely sad and extremely difficult. I thought I was completely alone. It felt as though God had abandoned me.

My emotional distress didn't begin to get better until I started the seventh grade. During that school year, I started receiving positive feedback because of my good grades and began to pull out of the devastating downward spiral. The encouragement that I received from my academic success pulled me out of depression. My accomplishments at school brought some initial healing and enabled me to take my eyes off the abuse and move forward.

As I excelled academically and as the years went by, I completely blocked all the memories of the sexual abuse. In fact, I completely forgot about it until many decades later. I was unaware of the devastating ways it had affected me over the years. But, when I was in my early 70s, more than 60 years after the abuse, I was infected with parasites during a ministry time in Kazakhstan. The parasites made me extremely ill; I lost 20 pounds and became very weak. Nine months went by before the doctors diagnosed the problem. In the meantime, I became weaker and weaker. My situation seemed hopeless because no one seemed to have any answers as to what was plaguing me. I had to cancel all my trips and speaking engagements. I shook all the time, trembling clear down to my bones. I became very depressed, was down physically and mentally, and didn't want to live.

At that time, I had some friends who were counselors, and they recognized the horrible, debilitating depression that had been plaguing me. They offered to meet at my house to pray for me. That prayer meeting was life-changing and life-saving! At the beginning of our time together, they prayed that the Holy Spirit would bring to my mind anything of which I needed to be aware. It was like a light bulb had been turned on and suddenly I remembered the abuse that had been hidden for decades. Until that moment, I had no idea that the sexual abuse I experienced early in life had never really been healed. But after we prayed, God reminded me that for an entire year after the abuse had ended, over 60 years earlier, I had wanted to commit suicide.

God spoke to me and said, "You thought I abandoned you, but I was there the whole time." He showed me how He had stopped the abuse, taken me out of the situation, and given my family a different place to live. He also reminded me that I had been able to attend junior high school right after that, finishing at the very top of my class. I realized that God had been with me all along, leading me out of danger.

After I received that word from God, I cried for three days, my heart was healed, and joy returned. I was so happy to be alive! God had healed me when I didn't even know that I needed it. That healing experience radically changed me. After that night, I could help people more effectively. Prior to that healing experience, I wasn't very compassionate with people. If someone was having a hard day, I would feel like telling them, "Take a rubber band, put it around your head, and snap out of it!" I couldn't understand why they couldn't get their attitude and feelings lined up with the Word of God and "make themselves better." I didn't know how horribly wrong I was!

After God healed my heart and filled me with joy, I understood people's hurts so much better. I began to love the book of Ecclesiastes more than ever before. I could see many promises from Ecclesiastes coming to pass in my life. Ecclesiastes 3:11 says, *"He has made everything beautiful in its time."* And He did!

For over 60 years, I had put the entire abuse experience out of my mind—it seemed as though it didn't even affect me. But God had not forgotten it. At the right time, He brought it back and said, "Now is the time for total healing." I realized that in many ways, I had carried on as if nothing had happened. I forgave my uncle and even went back to Pennsylvania for his funeral when he died of a heart attack. I spent time with his wife, Aunt Ethel. But the suicidal part of me, the part that felt abandoned by God and wanted to die, had not been healed. That night, at a life-saving prayer meeting, God healed me. It was His perfect time!

God Uses People

As I look back over my childhood, I realize there were several people who made a profound impact on my life. The first of these was my Aunt Ethel. She had a way of making me feel like I was the most important person in her life. She did that for so many people. She was the most hospitable person I have ever known. If she had the means to do it, she would have fed the world. Where I grew up in Pennsylvania, the people

I learned that the real adventures and rewards were with people, and I made them my life's pursuit.

could sometimes be snobbish, but Aunt Ethel was different. She always held her arms open for the needy. In fact, I remember two men in our neighborhood who needed help, but no one cared about them because they appeared a little strange. They probably were, but that didn't stop my Aunt Ethel. She made soup for them and left it in an area where they could find it, so they always had something to eat. She was constantly willing to help in any way she could. I believe she inspired me to be more caring and generous toward others, especially the "untouchables" of society. God used her example to help me have a bigger heart for people: a heart that was moved with compassion and wasn't nervous about reaching out and offering a helping hand, even in the most desperate of situations. Many times, we have compassion for people but we don't do anything to help them because we are afraid. Aunt Ethel taught me that I had to do more than feel compassion; I had to do something to help.

Aunt Ethel was caring. She had a strong personality, with a very positive disposition and outlook on life. She was not afraid to take a stand. She was way ahead of her time in many respects. In an era when most women had accepted their roles as subservient to men, Aunt Ethel was a revolutionary. She didn't believe that women, because of their gender, had to have smaller ambitions than men. When I told her that I wanted to be a foreign ambassador, she said, "You can be anything you want to be." She would always tell me that God had given me a "strong mind." I never questioned her belief in me. I just soaked it in. In fact, she pushed me to master languages, especially Latin. It was from her encouragement that I developed a love for the romance languages. Yet, it was never just the languages; it was the people, places, and the nations represented that sparked in me a burning passion. From my aunt's example, I learned that the real adventures and rewards were with people, and I made them my life's pursuit.

I was in the seventh grade when I first took Latin. I had a wonderful Latin teacher, Mr. Hawes. He was a Harvard graduate, with an obvious love for Latin, who also loved to play chess. Latin was hard at the beginning, but I was determined. Mr. Hawes always pushed me to learn more and more. He would often make me cry because he worked me so hard. One day, he told me, "If you didn't have the ability, I wouldn't be pushing you." After that, I stopped being negative about how hard it was and just worked harder. Eventually, I fell in love with Latin. That experience with Mr. Hawes deepened my desire to learn other languages. So, I added French to my Latin courses, and eventually studied Spanish and Greek as well.

During my junior year of high school, at the age of 16, I was offered a scholarship to a Methodist summer camp in Jumonville, Pennsylvania. I was excited to go because it was a "camp," but I did not know that attending the camp would change me and set me on a different course—a better course for my life than I could have ever imagined. As I look back at that summer, I know it was a divine setup. We were at the camp for four days, and all the other girls in my dorm were different from me. They had something I didn't have, but I didn't know what it was. They talked to me about God all week. I learned more about God each day. On the last day, I had a life-changing encounter. The minister that evening was a youth pastor. At the end of his sermon, he asked, "Do you have Jesus in your heart?" It was the first time I had heard anyone mention that you could have Jesus live inside your heart. I thought, *I don't. I know about Him, but I don't have Him inside.* The minister then invited everyone who didn't have Jesus in their heart to come to the front. I thought, *I love Him; I want Him.* Without a second thought, I went up to the front and prayed a simple prayer to receive Jesus as my Lord and Savior.

Transformation Through Jesus

The very moment that I received Jesus into my heart, I was transformed. For three days, I was so filled with love and joy that I wanted to hug the trees! When I got home from camp, my mother said, "I don't know what's wrong with you; you are so joyful!" I could not stay out of the Bible. I finally had the Author in my heart, and I desperately wanted to know Him more. For years, I had read the Bible, but suddenly, something had changed. The Bible had become personal; it had become the "living Word of God" in my life. I knew that God had been drawing me closer to Himself for years but praying that prayer and asking Jesus to live inside of me as my Lord and Savior made all the difference in the world. That life-changing experience also marked the beginning of the supernatural work of God in me. I had so much to learn, but little by little I began to see God do miracles in my life. I was beginning to realize that God is a good heavenly Father, Who has abundant blessings for His children.

Everything was wonderful. I read the Bible every day and grew stronger in my walk with the Lord. I was awed by His love and filled with joy and peace. As I enjoyed each moment of each day with Him, I didn't know that once again everything in my life was about to get upended. Big changes, and even bigger challenges, were directly ahead of me.

Moving to Colorado

That fall, my father's asthma flared up. He had fought it many times in the past, but this time, the effects of the asthma were life-threatening. His doctors told us that we had to move someplace where the air was healthier. It was at that time that we moved to Denver, Colorado. I was 16 and a junior in high school. I wasn't excited about attending a new school with new teachers and new kids, but I was determined to make the best of it. Even still, I wasn't prepared for the enormity of the change. In Pennsylvania, my high school had 400 students, but when we got to Denver, my new high school, South High, had over 2,000 students. There were more students in my junior class than there had been in my entire high school in Pennsylvania.

I felt completely lost in the crowd. I didn't know anyone in the school, and it seemed like everyone else knew each other well. Many of the kids had gone through years of school together, so I was definitely an "outsider." Not having many friends at school, especially at first, made the transition even more difficult. Fortunately, I had another great Latin teacher. Again, he motivated me to excel in and appreciate languages even more. His encouragement and my subsequent success in mastering languages helped me adjust to my school and new life in Colorado. It also prepared me for the amazing, supernatural future that God had planned for me.

By the time I graduated from high school, I had taken six years of Latin, several years of French and Spanish, and even some Greek! My desire to be a foreign ambassador had blossomed into a life-long career goal. I loved the thought of traveling and even living in other countries because I wanted to experience the uniqueness of the people and their cultures. As the question of college and further study came up, I was very confident of the direction I wanted to go. I had decided to go to a university and pursue a degree in foreign languages.

Years before I ever attended a university, when I told my dad that I wanted to go to college, he said, "Great, but I'm not paying for it. Get scholarships and work your way through." And that's what I was determined to do! I worked hard in high school to get good grades and earn scholarships. During my first year of college, I did have scholarships, but I also worked during the day, lived at home to save money, and attended night classes at the University of Colorado.

My first year of college was hard. It was difficult to take classes and work full-time, but it proved beneficial. I was able to save enough money to transfer to the University of Northern Colorado and live on campus for the last three years of college. I went home on weekends and worked at a clothing store to help cover the rest of the cost. I was able to finish college and graduate without any debt. Of course, a university education was not as expensive then as it is now, but graduating debt-free is still quite a testimony to the faithfulness of God.

My First Small Group Bible Study

College also introduced me to another avenue for spiritual formation that had a tremendous impact on my life. When I transferred to the University of Northern Colorado, I found that most of the girls in my dorm were Lutherans. They held a Bible study in the dorm each week. I had never heard of small group Bible studies before, so it intrigued me. I decided to join them and fell in love with that way of studying the Bible. The girls in the Bible study had such an impact on my life that I even attended their Lutheran confirmation classes. I was never officially confirmed, but despite not being an official Lutheran, I became the president of the Lutheran Student's Association at the University of Northern Colorado.

Looking back, I realize that those wonderful Bible studies were much more than a group of young adults gathering to learn the Bible. God was definitely using them to equip me with a system for spiritual life development that I would need in the future. Over the years, Bible study groups became an integral part of my ministry. I am so grateful to God for the experiences I had with those girls, learning and growing together in our knowledge of God.

In 1953, I graduated with honors with a Bachelor of Arts in Collective Foreign Languages from the University of Northern Colorado and was immediately hired to teach Spanish and English at a high school in Pueblo, Colorado. I loved my job, enjoyed my students, and relished the day-to-day challenges of teaching, but I could not get away from my dream of being a foreign diplomat. I planned to get my master's degree, study French, Italian, or Spanish, and eventually become a foreign ambassador. I was 22 years old, and had my life planned out. Only later did I realize that God had a plan that was even better than mine.

Chapter 2

SAYING "YES!"

THE PAIN AND HURT WE suffer in life often become the crucible God uses to mold us into agents of transformation in a hurting world. Even though I was a relatively happy child, my upbringing wasn't perfect. There were dysfunctional elements, negative events, and hurtful situations in my home that might have left lasting scars and sidetracked my life if it had not been for the grace of God. It is not only the sweet but also the sour and bitter experiences that became the backdrop of the canvas on which God painted my life.

My father struggled for years with mental illness and depression. Though he had been loving to me when I was a small child, as the years went by, his despondency grew worse and he became more and more verbally and physically abusive. Unfortunately, my brother David received the brunt of it. Dad turned his anger and frustration toward him and hit him at the slightest provocation. For some reason, I was spared his physical anger, until one very bad day. I am not sure why he was so upset, but my father came at me with ferocious anger. I knew he was about to hit me, but, my five-foot, four-and-a-half-inch frame would not cower. I was trembling on the inside, but I stood my ground, looked at him boldly and declared, "If you hit me, you will never be safe again." He was obviously taken aback. He gave me a baffled look, then turned and left the room. After that, he never came after me again. I don't know where those words came from, or what they might have meant, but they were definitely filled with authority. I believe God used that verbal declaration to protect me. I could not fight back physically, but I could take a stand spiritually.

Both of my parents grew up in a liberal church and continued those teachings in our home. They were moral people and certainly religious, but not very spiritual or exuberant. They attended church and tried their best to live a good life. Their faith was personal but not necessarily practical. As my dad's depression intensified and our home life deteriorated, the pressure of that situation led to a shift in our home.

Mom's Introduction to the Holy Spirit

When I was 19 years old, my mom grew frantic. Father's erratic behavior and violence became increasingly unbearable for her. For years, Mom had been tough, dug in, and soldiered on; however, things had reached a tipping point. She desperately needed a respite. One day, as she prayed and searched for help, she turned on the radio and heard a Spirit-filled pastor in our city preaching a message. He belonged to the Assembly of God church, which was drastically different from the type of church Mom and I attended. However, the minister's message struck a chord of hope in her, and Mom did not allow tradition or pride to stop her from getting the help she needed. She started attending that Assembly of God church, searching for answers. It was at that church that my family's journey into the Spirit-filled life began. The Bible talks about a specific point in Christian history where the Holy Spirit first filled the followers of Jesus and empowered them to share His love and truth with miracles, signs, and wonders, and it teaches us how that same experience is available to Jesus's followers today. Mom was the first person in our family to experience the dramatic filling of the Holy Spirit; but because of her wonderful journey, all of my family and the lives of many other people have been deeply impacted.

A genuine encounter with the Holy Spirit changes a person's life. The initial results of encounters with the Spirit can range from mild to extreme. Over my lifetime, I have seen many drastic spiritual transformations, but, as radical changes go, Mom's was most definitely at the top of the list. When Mom became Spirit-filled, the difference in her was resounding, and we felt it immediately. She did not just attend church occasionally or ritually on Sundays, she went to church as often as the doors of the church were open. Her personal devotion to God gained greater depth, and she prayed and spoke scriptures in ways she had never done before. What had been a quiet, private, and rather dull Christian life suddenly morphed into a very public and vibrant expression of faith. In just a short time, it had become too strange for the family. None of us could understand what Mom was doing or why, and we fought to turn back the clock.

David and I were appalled by Mom's new spiritual fervor and felt ashamed. He was still living at home, while I attended college and was home only on weekends. The first weekend I was home, I was shocked to see the new addition to the family home, Bible verses everywhere! Mom had posted scriptures all over the wall above the kitchen sink. I gasped as though it were profane graffiti. David sniggered, "Wait until you see the bathroom. You haven't seen anything yet!" And he was not exaggerating. The bathroom was covered almost wall-to-wall with scriptures that Mom would speak as she got ready in the morning. The whole situation was mind-boggling; we had never seen anything like it before. We wondered, *Is she insane, desperate, or just madly in love with Jesus?* It wasn't until years later that I discovered the answer to those questions for myself.

My mom wanted to share her new-found joy with us, and none of our disapproval or criticism stopped her. Moreover, she managed to convince me to attend some of the church services with her. I was not comfortable with the whole experience at all. I squirmed in my seat as the singers, speakers, and congregation members continued their exuberant displays. It was definitely a culture shock. I really tried, but I could not adjust to their style of worship. They were simply too loud and too emotional for me. "They even clapped their hands," I criticized. Interestingly and sadly, one of my main objections was that they allowed women to speak! I had never seen that before, and it rocked me to the core.

My mom sat on the second row, so that meant that I had to sit close to the front, too. One Sunday service, a female preacher came down from the platform into the congregation. She looked at me and said, "Sister, you have too much of Jesus. Let Him flop over on me; splash on me." And I thought, *I am not your sister!* I was naïve about the lingo and jargon and thought she was being disrespectful; in reality, she was just seeing Jesus in me. Her approach, sincere as it might have been, completely turned me off to the Spirit-filled world for quite a while. Little did I know that one day I would be a woman speaking in many churches, and the things that I had frowned upon would become things I love and cherish.

Sometimes tragic events or impossible situations cause us to lean into God in a new way. That is exactly what happened with Mom. She had been diagnosed with a cancerous tumor in her breast and was given little hope for survival. Nevertheless, she was convinced that God would heal her. She didn't care what the doctors said. Her family, including all 10 of her siblings, thought she had gone "over the top" in her religious beliefs. They all believed that she would die from breast cancer. My dad, brother, and I didn't have much faith either. We felt helpless in the face of that monster, and began to grieve, even though she was still living. Through all the negativity and skepticism, Mom's faith in a healing God was never shaken. She just kept praying and believing for her miracle.

Healed of Breast Cancer

One day, Mom was watching evangelist Oral Roberts on television, and he said to the audience, "Put your hand on the television, and God will heal you." I was in the room with her, and I saw her stand up to walk over to the television as he had instructed. Appalled, I told her, "Don't do that!" I thought it was a crazy thing to believe that God would heal her through a television evangelist, and I couldn't allow my mom to be fooled by him. However, when Mom set her mind to do something, nothing could stop her. She continued to walk over to the television, put her hand on Oral Roberts' hands, and prayed in faith that she would be healed. When the prayer ended, she walked to the couch and sat down. It did not look or feel as if anything spectacular had happened, but God had moved miraculously in response to her faith.

Don't ever let petty things keep you from obeying God and receiving your miracle. Decide today that nothing is more important than seeing the answers to your prayers!

The next time Mom saw her doctors, they were astonished. She had been completely healed—the tumor was totally gone, and no cancer remained in her body! What a miracle! It was wonderful to see my mom receive a miraculous answer to prayer. We were so happy for her and so relieved that God had given us more time with her. Her healing was an amazing supernatural event that no one could deny. She lived to be 90 years old and never had any recurrence of breast cancer. Her healing was total and irreversible. It was quite remarkable and has been a point of inspiration ever since. Thank God, Mom didn't listen to me! I wonder what it is that makes some of us so resistant to the voice of the Holy Spirit. What did Mom stand to lose by putting her hands on that television screen? And yet, I protested in the strongest terms. The things of the Spirit may sometimes seem foolish (see 1 Corinthians 2:14). They may not be considered cute or cool, but they hold the key to our deliverance and victory. Don't ever let petty things keep you from obeying God and receiving your miracle. Decide today that nothing is more important than seeing the answers to your prayers!

It would seem natural that such a miraculous healing would elicit gratitude, as well as faith. And yes, I was grateful to have my mom healed, but it did not cause me to be a believer in the supernatural. It would take a lot more than that miracle to change my mind. I was very analytical, even cynical at times. It would prove to be very hard to convince me that God wanted to work supernaturally, but the seed had been sown. Mom's healing was verifiable and undeniable, and it had become a point of reference from which I could not escape. The good news is, God used that miracle. Eventually, many of Mom's siblings received Jesus's love and salvation as did their children and grandchildren. Even though she had to stand up to their unbelief (and mine!), she saw her family come to understand the reality of God's power and presence.

Mom had fought and conquered so much. She had overcome hard times, and she beat cancer, but there was still a darkness that lingered in our home because of my father's mental health. As Mom's spiritual walk with God grew stronger and more vibrant, my father's moods and behavior grew darker and more dangerous. He would do vicious things.

He hated that Mom was Spirit-filled and attended church, and he tried to forbid her from walking out her faith. He would scream, "You can't read the Bible, and you can't go to that church!" I didn't quite understand it, but he was more concerned about the type of church she was attending than anything else. Despite his ranting and raving, the light in Mom continued to shine brighter than ever. It could not be snuffed out.

One night, when I went home, I could tell that my father was extremely upset. He was in the kitchen, pacing back and forth and cursing. He turned to me and asked angrily, "Where is your mother?" I knew she was at church, but I was scared to tell him because of how angry he was. So, I responded, "I don't know." He retorted, "I know where she is; she is at church, isn't she? I told her that if she ever went back to that church, I would kill her." It was not the first time that Dad had been angry or made threats, but at that moment it felt more serious, and I was really afraid for my mom. So, I sat down in the kitchen to wait, hoping he would calm down before Mom returned. Instead, he grew more and more agitated.

When Mom finally returned, my dad's anger had reached a delirious intensity. He yelled, "Where have you been?" Strangely, Mom wasn't bothered by his temper at all. Calmly and confidently, she replied, "I have been at church." Dad blurted out, "I told you that if you went to that church again, I would kill you." Then, he lunged over to the cabinet, pulled a huge butcher knife out of the drawer, and started toward Mom. Expecting the worst, I began crying and screaming at him to stop. I was convinced that he had totally lost touch with reality and that he was definitely going to kill her, but Mom showed no apprehension whatsoever. She maintained her composure, and then, suddenly, the tables turned.

With intensity in her voice, Mom spoke up, "Drop that knife in Jesus' name!" She spoke with authority, yet without any display of anger. She said, "You are not going to touch me." Instantly, like a big log, my father fell on the floor with the knife still in his hand. He looked up at her, and moaned, "I can't get up." He was stuck on the floor. He couldn't move. Staring right back at him as he lay on the floor, Mom replied, "If you ever try to keep me from reading the Bible or going to church, you will never get up again." He responded with a hint of desperation in his voice, "I won't do it ever again." At that, he suddenly changed. He wasn't stuck on the floor any longer. That night, peace flooded our home; I knew that my father wouldn't harm her ever again. My fear went away because I saw God's awesome power protect us. Sadly, the battle for Dad's peace of mind raged on.

Shortly after that incident, things came to a head, and my father was admitted to a mental hospital. The prognosis did not look good. The doctors advised us that his chances of coming back home were nonexistent. The only known treatment for his mental illness was electric shock therapy, and it caused the patients to lose their memory. So, there was really no hope of his making a complete recovery. In spite of the gloomy prognosis, Mom believed that my dad would be healed. Truthfully, I was skeptical. Even though I knew God and I had seen Him miraculously heal Mom's body, I had a hard time believing that He could heal my father. I didn't have a good attitude, and I didn't encourage Mom in any way. Looking

> My attitude was all wrong, but it didn't stop God from hearing Mom's prayers and answering those prayers in a powerful way. It was important for me to learn that God's power is not stopped by the negative attitudes around us.

back on this, I realize that my attitude was all wrong, but it didn't stop God from hearing Mom's prayers and answering those prayers in a powerful way. It was important for me to learn the lesson that God's power is not stopped by the negative attitudes around us. Mom had walked this path before with her physical health, and she had a powerful testimony of her miracle. Mom refused to accept that this was the end of the road for my dad. She continued in faith, praying and fasting for him, believing that he would be released from the hospital. Her faith did not waver, and her hope did not decrease as the months went by.

Dad's Healing

Mom was persistent in prayer for about a year, and then God sent an answer. William Branham, a well-known traveling evangelist, came to Denver to hold a meeting, and Mom was determined not to miss it. It was a packed crowd, but I believe that Mom's tear-filled prayers had become a memorial before God. She would not be passed over. Mom did not know that God had a prophetic word for her that night, but she went to the meeting expecting God to help her. Prophecy is a gift from the Holy Spirit where a specific insight or "word" is given to a person to build up, encourage, or comfort that person. Out of a crowd of hundreds, Branham called Mom out to receive a prophetic word. He pointed to her and said, "You think your husband is demon-possessed, but he's not. He has had a complete mental breakdown. Take the handkerchief that you are crying on, put it on his body, and he will be fine." Those words came with power, and Mom put all her faith in them. Shortly after the meeting, she took the handkerchief to the hospital and pinned it to my father's pajamas.

Within a few days after Mom pinned the handkerchief to his pajamas, my father completely recovered from the mental breakdown. His mind was clear, and his emotions were peaceful. He wasn't irrational or plagued by the effects of mental illness. That was a total miracle because for the entire year before that day, there had been no change in his condition. We had been given no hope for his recovery. We were all beyond relieved when he came home from the hospital. He wasn't just a little better, he was completely healed. His mind was at peace. Within a year after being released from the hospital, Dad received salvation and was water baptized. It was a complete turnaround! After his healing and salvation experience, he lived eight more years. During that time, he was filled with more peace and joy than he had known at any previous time in his life.

My father died in December of 1975. It was comforting to know that he was in heaven, but his passing was still very hard on Mom. Even though there were years in their marriage where he had been abusive to her, she still grieved for over a year. She seemed to be stuck in that state of grief and depression, and she did not know how to break free from it. I felt for her and was worried but wasn't sure how to help. I did not want to appear inconsiderate or unfeeling, unintentionally dishonoring my father's memory. However, I knew that she needed to release her grief and move on. The time to mourn had come and gone, and it was now time to be comforted (see Ecclesiastes 3:4).

If it is prolonged, grief can become an idol that stands between us and the comforting arms of our good and gracious God. I pray that, like your sins, you will hang all your griefs on the Cross and begin to experience the life of joy that Christ has for you.

One day, the Lord spoke to my heart and said that it was the right time to minister to Mom and help her resolve her grief. I had no idea how to do that because grief seemed like such a personal issue. It felt like the subject of grief was beyond my expertise. However, God gave me an insight to share with her. So, I decided to gently confront the issue. I went to Mom's house with the intention of helping her push past the grief.

God had given me a series of questions to ask her. I started with, "Are you born again?" "What do you mean?" she asked. "Are you born again?" I insisted. "Yes," she replied, with a half-smile of confusion. "Are you Spirit-filled?" I asked. "Yes," she replied, still unsure of where I was going with my questions. I continued, "Did Jesus take your sins and your sicknesses?" "Yes, you know He did," she said. "And your griefs?" I asked. She paused as a knowing look spread across her face. She said, "Yes." At that point, I wanted her to really think about and receive the truth of what she had just said, so I asked her gently, "Then why are you carrying them?" She immediately understood exactly what I had been trying to say. She knew the truth: Jesus had carried her grief for her (see Isaiah 53:4). She needed to accept that truth and release the grief to God. She did not have to be buried in grief anymore. Before I left her home that night, I prayed a prayer and asked God to release her from grief, and from that day on, she was completely free.

You see, it is quite natural to grieve whenever there is a loss of someone or something precious. It is part of being human, and it happens to all of us. It can even be healthy and helpful in bringing much-needed closure. So, there is a place for healthy grieving. However, if it is prolonged, grief can become an idol that stands between us and the comforting arms of our good and gracious God. Furthermore, grief can become a barrier between us and the people we hold dear, a chasm between us and the good things that remain in our lives. So, no matter how painful and hard a loss is, we must endeavor to move to the other side of it. We must be careful not to allow ourselves to be taken captive by it. I pray that, like your sins, you will hang all your griefs on the Cross and begin to experience the life of joy that Christ has for you.

Unlike Mom, I did not face a burden of grief when my father passed. However, there was a hidden fear about his condition that haunted me for quite a while. I harbored the thought that one day I might experience a nervous breakdown like my father. That thought started to take over my mind at a point in my life when I was facing some very hard trials. I was exhausted and didn't think I could make it. I cried out to God, "God help me! Help me! I am having a nervous breakdown just like my father!" God replied, "You are just like your Father; that's true. I am your Father, and I have never had a nervous breakdown, so you won't either!" Before that day, without even realizing it, I had internalized the picture of me becoming like my father and having a nervous breakdown. By revealing the truth about Him being my heavenly Father, God freed me from that fear, and I never faced any anxiety about my earthly father or my own mental health again.

I did not know that I desperately needed the power of the Holy Spirit in my life if I was going to fulfill the purpose that God had for me.

Amazing miracles had taken place in my family that should have convinced me that God's creative, healing, delivering power is still active on the earth today. First, Mom recovered from breast cancer when everyone expected her to die. Then, God miraculously stopped my dad from killing her in his murderous rage. Finally, God healed and restored Dad's mental health when the doctors had given us no hope at all. Additionally, I had been taught from the Bible that God was a triune God, one God but three distinct persons: Father, Son, and the Holy Spirit. I had read in Acts where Jesus promised His followers that they would be filled with power when the Holy Spirit came upon them (see Acts 1:8). I had also read in Acts where the 120 people in the Upper Room were filled with the Holy Spirit and began speaking in unknown tongues (see Acts 2:4). But none of the miracles I had witnessed, nor the scriptures I had read, caused me to seek a deeper relationship with the Holy Spirit, the third Person of the Trinity. I did not want the "Spirit-filled experience." I was tolerant of it because I had to be; yet, I had no interest in experiencing it personally. I felt that it was okay for my mom, but it was not okay for me. I was satisfied. I was a Christian, loved God, and read my Bible, and that was enough for me. I did not know that I desperately needed the power of the Holy Spirit in my life if I was going to fulfill the purpose that God had for me.

Before I met my husband, Wally, I dated a man who was not a Christian. I had just graduated from college and was very naïve. Mom was not at peace with the relationship. She felt that something was wrong with it right from the start, so she began to "pray him out" of my life. I did not think Mom's prayers could come between my boyfriend and me, but they did. Before she started praying, I used to hear from that man regularly, but when she started praying, he suddenly stopped contacting me. There were no phone calls, no cards, and no visits from him. When I repeatedly tried to call him, I could not reach him. It hurt my heart to have him dump me like that—until I found out that he was a married man! Wow! I had made a divine escape, thanks to my praying mother. I was very glad not to be in that relationship, but I was still lonely. I knew Mom had prayed him out of my life, so I called her and asked her to be sure to pray someone *into* my life, too! Mom's prayers were as effectual as ever. Within three weeks, I met Wallace (Wally) Hickey, who became my husband for 57 years.

Meeting Wally

When we first met, Wally was radically on fire for God. He had been saved as a teenager but had drifted off and became an entertainer, living a very wild life. In his 20s, he came back to the Lord and was filled with the Spirit. His rededication to God and his becoming filled with the Spirit transformed his life. He was so hungry for God that he wanted to be in church as much as possible. Not too long after his rededication, he met my mother. Mom and her friends had been praying for me to be filled with the Spirit because even though I was a Christian, I wasn't any more committed to God than a fly. My mom admired Wally for his unreserved devotion to God, and she thought he could have a positive influence on me. So, she began to look for ways for Wally and me to meet.

One weekend, I visited Mom's house to spend time with her and my grandmother, but Grandma was sick, and Mom was too busy to spend any time with me. That created the opportunity Mom's friends and prayer partners had been looking for. Apparently, they were in on the matchmaking too! They invited me over for dessert and without a second thought, I accepted. I needed the company and didn't even consider that there could be ulterior motives behind their offer. Little did I know that they had a hidden agenda. It was all a setup for Wally and me to meet.

My first impression of Wally was, *You're too religious, but you are so good looking!* He was tall and very handsome. I was instantly attracted to him. That night, Wally invited me to church, my mom's church. I didn't care for Mom's church that much, but I wanted to spend time with Wally, so I went. From that point on, Wally and I started spending more and more time together. While I wasn't thrilled about a Spirit-filled church and had not personally been attending church that frequently, I knew that if I wanted to spend more time with Wally, I would have to go with him to church. I did make my stance about his type of spirituality clear. I told him, "Don't push me to speak in tongues. I don't want to do that." He never did. He was such a gentleman. We just enjoyed the friendship. After about seven months of dating, Wally proposed, and I accepted. He gave me a beautiful engagement ring, and I was so happy! It was one of the most memorable days of my life. I was thrilled! I had found love, and I was engaged to be married.

After Wally and I got engaged, reality hit. There was a real question about compatibility. Even though getting together with Wally had been Mom's idea, she was not happy about the relationship. She told me, "I don't know if you should marry Wallace Hickey. He is so spiritual, and you are not. I am afraid you will ruin him." That was something that bothered Mom immensely. I didn't agree of course; I loved Wally, and I knew that we would be fine. What I didn't know was that Wally was also having second thoughts.

One day, Wally called me and said that he was fasting. "Why are you fasting?" I asked. He replied, "I am fasting for you." Not quite understanding the gravity of the situation, I responded, "You don't need to fast for me; I am born again, so you don't need to fast for me." But he was resolved, "I want you to be a committed Christian. Marilyn, before I was born again, I served the devil with all my heart. Now, I am going to serve God with all my heart, and I am not going to marry a woman who is half-hearted. So, I am on a three-day fast for you to develop a greater hunger for God." Surprised at this, I asked, "Do you want your ring back?" hoping he would say, "No." His reply shocked me. He was ambivalent and said, "I don't know. I am fasting and praying." My heart dropped. I loved Wally, and wanted to marry him, but I didn't want to be as "wild and radical" for Jesus as he was. I went to bed that night deeply troubled.

Meeting the Holy Spirit

For the next three nights, I couldn't sleep. I was a teacher at Grant Junior High School in Denver, and the job was quite challenging. It required a lot of energy from me, and without good sleep, my job was almost impossible. The first night God dealt with me about surrendering to His will and becoming Spirit-filled, but I wasn't interested. The second night I couldn't sleep again, but I still wouldn't surrender to what God was speaking to my spirit. By the third day, I was not functioning well at school. I was almost dizzy from the lack of sleep. The third night, God said to me, "I have dealt with you and dealt with you about being filled with the Holy Spirit, and for four years you have said, 'No.' I am not going to deal with you about this anymore. If you turn down this opportunity to be filled with the Holy Spirit, I will show you what you will do. You will never marry Wallace Hickey. You will move to California. You will get your master's degree, and you will have a good life. You will marry a Christian, and you will go to heaven. But if you surrender, I have something so wonderful for you that you cannot imagine."

That broke my heart. I began to weep, and I cried out to Him, saying, "God, whether I marry Wallace Hickey or not, I want all You have for me. I want to be filled with the Holy Spirit. Do what You want with me because I want to be what You want me to be." That night, I committed everything to God, and said, "I want to be Spirit-filled." Within 24 hours, I was.

The next day, I went to a special evangelist's meeting. I did not hesitate to walk down to the altar to receive prayer to be filled with the Holy Spirit. I was beyond ready. That meeting was an old-fashioned, Spirit-filled meeting. The people prayed loudly. But I was not going to let that bother me one bit. That was my date with the Holy Spirit. One man was even screaming at me, "Sister, do you really want to be filled with the Holy Spirit?" I thought to myself, *Yes, if you go away and quit screaming at me, I'll receive it.* Fortunately, he settled down. After that, I received. I was filled with the Holy Spirit and began to speak in tongues (see Acts 2:4). The ability to speak in tongues is seen throughout the book of Acts and is explained in 1 Corinthians 14 as a special prayer language given by the Holy Spirit that enables a person's spirit to pray as the Holy Spirit directs. There at that meeting, I only spoke in tongues a little bit at first; but as I drove home later that night, my prayer language started to flow, and I spoke in tongues for the entire drive home. A new day had dawned!

When I got Spirit-filled, I really got Spirit-filled. I was all in. From then on, Wally and I went to church all the time. Church offered a very refreshing atmosphere, and we just couldn't get enough of it. We read Christian books; we listened to tapes from different ministers; we did whatever we could to get more of the Word of God. I was so hungry for God. It is the most joyful experience, and it never stops. I understood then what had happened to Mom and Wally, and I finally understood why a person would want to share that experience with others. Being filled with the Holy Spirit is a game-changer, and it launched me into a completely different orbit of the Christian walk. If you are on the fence about the Spirit-filled experience, I can certainly understand because I was there too. But, I challenge you to search the Bible and allow God to speak to your heart. He loves us with an unconditional love whether we are filled with the Holy Spirit or not, but I would have missed out on so much in my life if I had not received all that He had for me. I was Spirit-filled in November, and Wally and I were married one month later, on December 26, 1954.

More Divine Healings

Soon after the wedding, just when I was beginning to settle into married life, Mom had another health crisis. She was diagnosed with a brain tumor. That was Mom's second bout with cancer, but the victory came much more quickly because this time, she wasn't standing in faith alone. This time, she had a more mature, Spirit-filled daughter she could lean on. I was on fire for God, and I believed strongly that God would heal her. In addition to Wally and me, there were so many others whose lives Mom had touched by her love and service to God. They were all standing in prayer with her. There was no way the devil was going to win. A bunch of us went up to the mountains for a vacation and turned it into a prayer retreat. I spoke the Word of God over that tumor, and then I told her, "Go back to the doctor and get another test." A couple of days later she went back to the doctor. When they ran the test, there was not even a shadow of a tumor on the scan. We could not stop praising God. He had done it again, and I was part of it! My faith was growing.

Another divine healing encounter happened around that same time. Early in our marriage, I was told by a doctor, "You have an enlarged heart; there is nothing you can do about it." The doctor's words became a death sentence for me. "You will never be able to be active; you will have to live with this heart issue for the rest of your life. There is no hope for recovery." Those words started to tear down my faith, and the devil continued to assault my mind with fear, reminding me that my father had experienced a heart attack, and saying that I would, too! During that time, I was so blessed to have Wally by my side. When my shield of faith was down, his was up, and he helped me fight back. Ecclesiastes 4:9–10 says, *"Two are better than one . . . for if they fall, one will lift up his companion."* Wally encouraged me and prayed for me. We stood on Isaiah 53:5, which says, *". . . by His stripes we are healed,"* and Psalm 103:3–4, which says that He forgives all our iniquities, heals all our diseases, redeems our life from destruction, and crowns us with lovingkindness and tender mercies. We continued to believe that God would give me a new heart. Within a couple of months, I received my miracle healing, but it happened in the most unusual place.

Despite the diagnosis, we did not back down. We continued our routine. We worked, went to church, prayed, and believed for a miracle. One night, Wally was speaking at a homeless mission, one of the outreaches we did with our church in Denver at the time. Those types of services were usually a little difficult. Many of the people there just wanted a sandwich, but they had to sit through a service in order to get that sandwich. It was not the type of service that I would have considered "spiritual enough" to receive a creative miracle, like a new heart.

So, there I was, in what I considered an "unspiritual service," and I felt a warmth go all over my body. It felt special, and I just knew that something supernatural had happened. I was so excited. On the way home, I told Wally, "I have a new heart. You know, God has spare hearts, and He gave me a new one." Wally agreed with me that something good had happened. It really was Wally's faith and strength in the face of the

We need to make sure we don't get caught judging how, when, or where we might encounter God's healing power in our lives.

doctor's diagnosis that gave me the ability to believe that my miracle had occurred. When I returned to the doctor for an exam, he was shocked and amazed. "I don't know what happened, but you have a wonderful heart!" I was thrilled. I had personally experienced the power of our God. I was learning that He is a wonderful God Who is not bound by fears, limitations, or prejudice. He can heal wherever He wants. He is sovereign. Since that time, about every two years I go in for a check-up, and they always say, "Oh, you have the most outstanding heart." You see, heart problems ran in my family, but I'm no longer in that family. I have a new Father and a heavenly family. My heart is healed because of Who He is! Whether in a traditional healing service or at an outreach to a homeless shelter, God's presence and power are at work. He can heal in any environment whether we consider it spiritual or not. We need to make sure we don't get caught judging how, when, or where we might encounter God's healing power in our lives.

I was about to learn a powerful lesson—we can all experience and enjoy God's best, but we have to be fully surrendered to Him. Even though I was born again, filled with the Holy Spirit, and very active in church and ministry, there were certain aspects of my ambitions that I had not yet surrendered to God. I had released my dream of becoming an ambassador,

---

I was about to learn a powerful lesson—we can all experience and enjoy God's best, but we have to be fully surrendered to Him.

---

but I had not embraced the remote possibility of going into ministry. In fact, I was very adamant about one thing—I did not want to be married to a minister. That was because I still wanted to travel the world and I felt that being a minister's wife would constrain me considerably. Ministry was the last thing I wanted to do so I made sure to double check with Wally on that issue while we were still dating.

Married Life and Wally's Call Into Ministry

Before we married, I asked Wally, "You aren't called to be a minister, are you? I don't have any desire to be a minister's wife." At that time, Wally worked for a successful recording label in Denver and did well as a businessman. I had settled into teaching foreign languages and loved the opportunity to help expose students to other languages and cultures. Wally replied, "No, not that I know of." So, that left me at peace, and I knew I didn't have to worry about being confined to a small, local church with no hope of experiencing other cultures. During the first couple of years of our marriage, we were active in our church, and I loved it. We sang in the choir and taught Sunday school, but I told Wally, "I do not ever want to be in the ministry." "Don't worry," Wally replied, "it won't happen."

For several years, we lived as faithful Christians and served in the church the best way we could. Neither Wally nor I had a clue about what God had planned for us. However, three years into our marriage the Holy Spirit began to stir our hearts. Wally came up to me and said, "I feel like I am failing God." I didn't understand so I asked him, "How could you be failing God? We go to church three times a week. We teach Sunday school. We teach a Bible study for teenagers. What else is there?" He replied, "I don't know, but I feel like I am failing God." After spending some time in prayer, Wally realized that God wanted him to be a minister. It completely shocked him, but interestingly, I wasn't surprised as much as he was. For some reason, I had developed a gut feeling that God would call him to ministry. It was never on my agenda to be a pastor's wife or to become active in ministry, but I truly wanted to follow God. Additionally, I knew that I couldn't fight Wally's call into ministry or I would be fighting against God. A calling is simply the divine plan that God has for each of us. It is His assignment for our lives. God has a personal and unique plan for every individual. No one is an accident. Truthfully, I think I accepted Wally's calling because I loved him and wanted to be supportive, but I never thought I would have a call of my own.

You see, Wally had always been so supportive of me. Actually, he always believed in me more than I believed in myself. His love and support of me made it possible to adjust to our new reality of being called into ministry. Still, we had no idea what adventures God was preparing for us. Our lives had just begun, and God was going to open the windows of heaven and release His wonders into our lives. Living a Spirit-filled life had totally transformed me, but it was a package deal with Wally included. My marriage to Wally Hickey radically changed my life. I had a very long and fruitful marriage for over 57 years. Words cannot fully express how grateful I am to God for bringing Wally into my life.

Chapter 3

A Partner For Life

As partners go, I was blessed with the best. Wally was a very special man in so many respects. He was the complete package of lover, friend, husband, father, mentor, and minister, and I know that my life was better because of him. Of all the things that were pivotal in my life, perhaps there was none as influential as my marriage to Wally. The things that made him special lay in the unique circumstances surrounding his life and upbringing.

Born May 7, 1925, in Genoa, Nebraska, Wallace Hickey was the second youngest child of six siblings: Alice, Cecil, Richard, Lois, Wally, and Shirley. Wally's mother, Mamie, was an orphan who came through the Midwest on the "orphan trains" in the early 1900s. The "orphan trains" were part of a U.S. government resettling program that operated from 1853 to 1929. The trains took orphaned or abandoned children from large and congested cities on the east coast to farming communities in the West or Midwest that desperately needed workers. Wally's mother traveled by train from Canada to Kansas where she lived with a family and worked as their maid until she met and married Albert Hickey.

Before I met him, Wally had experienced his own share of life's tragedies. Two of his siblings had died. Wally's oldest brother, Cecil, had been killed in action in World War II. His younger sister, Shirley, was killed in a horrific accident when Wally was just 11. They were burning a heap of trash in their front yard, and Shirley, who was only four years old at the time, was playing around it when her dress caught on fire! Wally ran to her rescue. He rolled her on the ground to put out the fire, but it was too late. Despite his best efforts, she was burned so badly that she died. That incident scarred him emotionally. Wally didn't talk about it much, but he always felt so badly that he couldn't save her. Understandably, any 11-year-old would be traumatized by such a tragic event. It's only because of the grace of God that he was able to pull through. As an adult, Wally was always tender and compassionate, and I wondered if the childhood calamity he experienced made that natural bent stronger in him, or if his kindhearted nature was the reason the tragic event affected him so deeply.

In many ways, Wally was a prodigal during his early twenties. He served in the army in WWII. After he was discharged, he enrolled in Nebraska Wesleyan College, where he graduated with a degree in music. After college, Wally asked Jesus into his heart, but he became an entertainer and fell into wild living. He had not received any strong discipleship or Bible teaching, so he had no real foundation for his Christian walk. That was the most tumultuous season of Wally's life. One day, some friends witnessed to him, and he recommitted his life to Christ and was filled with the Holy Spirit. His dramatic conversion was a pivotal experience that completely changed his life. Shortly after that, we met, began dating, and eventually married.

After Wally and I married, we visited his family a couple of times a year. I was truly blessed to have incredible in-laws. Wally's parents were so hospitable to everyone. His mother, Mamie, was one of the sweetest people I have ever met. In their little hometown in Nebraska, everyone loved to go to Mamie's house to eat. She was a phenomenal cook, and Wally and I enjoyed some of his favorite dishes every time we were at their house. Wally's parents also used to visit us. We made such wonderful memories with them. I always looked forward to when they would come to stay with us, usually for eight or nine days at a time. Mamie would tell me, "Now get all of your things that need mending or a button, and I will take care of it for you." She was very precious, and she loved me as a daughter.

The Hickeys were beyond sweet. They were very supportive and gave Wally and me room to grow and discover the path that God had for us. They didn't understand the Spirit-filled experience and thought we were crazy for speaking in tongues, but they really appreciated Wally's stand for God and respected him for the change that had occurred in his life. At one point, Wally's parents attended one of his evangelistic meetings in Nebraska. It made quite an impression on his mother, Mamie, and she was very complimentary. On one of their visits to Colorado, Wally's brother, Richard, and his family came to our church. It was a stretch for them, but they loved us, and we loved them. We allowed each other to love God in our own ways.

Supporting Wally in His Call

The way God calls people and positions them to fulfill their callings is a mystery. We can never really predict it and shouldn't even try. Three years into our marriage, Wally felt called to the ministry. As I mentioned earlier, I had resisted the idea for a while, but God warmed my heart, and by the time Wally announced he was called, I was ready. After we discussed it, I knew it was the right thing to do, and offered him my full support. But the picture was still incomplete. There were questions of "where" and "how" his calling would happen: What kind of ministers were we going to be?

Who were we going to work with? And, how was it all going to pan out? Those were some of the questions Wally and I grappled with.

Never discount any door of opportunity. What may look
unpromising at first, may hold the key to a great future.

In 1957, Wally and I officially plunged into ministry. My aunt, Adlyn Moore, was a big piece of the divine puzzle. It began right in my hometown of Dalhart, Texas. It was quite an inauspicious beginning, but if there's one thing I have learned over the years, it was to never discount any door of opportunity. What may look unpromising at first, may hold the key to a great future.

Aunt Adlyn, who was Mom's sister-in-law, was visiting us in Denver. In one of our conversations with her, Wally mentioned that he felt called to the ministry. We didn't quite anticipate her response because we had just been sharing our thoughts with her with no expectations at all. But, as is so often the case, God's hand was at work. Without a moment's hesitation, Aunt Adlyn said, "Well, I am going to ask my pastor if you can preach at our church." And just like that, the door for ministry opened.

Aunt Adlyn attended the First Assembly of God church in Dalhart, Texas, which had a membership of about 60 people. That small congregation became the birthplace of our ministry. The pastor was a kind man named Fred Ball. Because Aunt Adlyn talked to him, he invited us to minister in the church. It was quite a shock when we heard the news. It was Aunt Adlyn's faithfulness and years of building relationships with the pastor and the people in the church that gave us the open door. Even though Wally was new to public speaking, Pastor Ball gave him his pulpit. That was a big deal! Pastors didn't just yield their pulpits to younger men starting out in ministry, but God had opened the door, so we traveled to Dalhart to hold four days of special meetings at the church.

It is an unbelievable feeling to see God use your life to make a positive difference in the lives of other people.

Aunt Adlyn had done her part, and now it was time for us to deliver. Wally had not preached from a church pulpit before, but he had been in plenty of meetings and had learned a lot from sharing in Sunday school, prayer meetings, and other small venues. Most importantly, he knew how to seek God. So, Wally fasted and prayed all day, every day, and preached at night. Wally was a very disciplined man, and that came in handy. My tasks were simple: getting the word out and evangelism. Every day, while Wally prayed at Aunt Adlyn's home, I went with a team from the church into the neighborhoods, knocked on doors, and invited people to the meetings. Sometimes the people invited us into their homes, and we prayed with them. The results of the door-to-door personal invitations were outstanding.

It is an unbelievable feeling to see God use your life to make a positive difference in the lives of other people. Before we arrived, the church was on life support and had not seen anything significant happen in four or five years. With God's help, Wally and I were able to bring new life into it. When people came to our meetings, many of them received salvation and were filled with the Holy Spirit. It was an incredibly successful series of meetings. We saw lives transformed and people restored. We were essentially duplicating ourselves and birthing real disciples. The services were very encouraging and gave Wally and me a glimpse into how life in ministry would look and feel for us. God had given us a blueprint.

The decision to go into full-time ministry was finally released in us after we finished those special meetings and returned home to Denver. Wally had been unleashed through the experience in Dalhart. In his heart, there would be no more back and forth with the decision to be in full-time ministry; it was time for a deep dive. There was nothing holding him back. I was on that page with him; the prospect of full-time ministry was very exciting to us.

Wally and I were members of an Assembly of God church in Denver, Colorado and had served there faithfully for years. Our pastor, Charles Blair, was so enthused by the results of the meetings in Dalhart that he advised Wally to apply for his licensure with the Assembly of God denomination. So, Wally applied and eventually received his ministry license. After that, we started traveling to small Assembly of God congregations to speak. To get the invitations to speak, we wrote letters to Assembly of God churches throughout Colorado and offered to preach. Our emphasis at that time was evangelism and revival. When the churches invited Wally to speak, we always had results because Wally fasted and prayed during the day and God showed up in powerful ways at the meetings each night.

Wally and I weren't just partners in life; we were partners in ministry, too. Wally wanted to travel, and I wanted to be part of it with him. I liked teaching, but I liked the call on his life even more. So, I resigned from teaching full-time and became a substitute teacher. This afforded me the flexibility I needed to travel and minister with him but still provided us with a small source of income. We also supplemented our income by renting out a room in our home. My father had said, "Whatever you do, buy a house." So, Wally and I owned a small home, and we rented out a bedroom to supplement our income. We loved traveling together in our beautiful green Chevy. It was a cute little two-door car with just enough room in the trunk for our luggage. We purchased it second-hand, but it was in good condition. It helped us get around the beautiful hillsides of

Colorado, preaching and ministering. We always had great memories of that very special time in our lives.

A few years later, E.R. Foster, the pastor of First Assembly Church in Amarillo, Texas called us. He was a big name in that area, and his church had about 500 people. Back then, that was a megachurch! He needed help and wanted Wally to become part of his team as the Assistant Pastor and Worship Leader. Wally prayed and felt led to accept the offer. When we visited Amarillo to check out the situation, we realized that the house they planned to provide for us was horrible. It was a dumpy little place that had been taken over by bugs. There were cockroaches everywhere. Yuck! That was probably the last place I wanted to be, but I still agreed to go. Wally and I were partners, and despite the infestation of bugs in the small cramped house, we had been offered a very big opportunity. So, we said, "Yes" to the offer, chased out the cockroaches, painted the house, and prepared for a new phase of ministry.

At that time, we had been married for about four years, living our dream as full-time pastors. Almost as soon as we arrived, they asked me to teach a young married couples' class. I thought, *Young married? I am young married!* But back then, they married very young in Texas, so I was considered a "marriage expert" at the ripe old age of 27! It was quite a challenge, but I took over the little class and believed for the best. I hoped to somehow make at least a small difference. I was like the little boy with five loaves and two fishes, wondering how in the world I could make a difference in the lives of 5,000 men (see John 6:1-14). I found out that God could multiply my effectiveness by giving me deeper insight into the Word of God.

Revolutionized by the Word

The revelation I needed came through the ministry of Kenneth Hagin, Sr. He came to minister at a Foursquare church near us, and Wally and I decided to attend. Brother Hagin taught about the Word and how it could work for you. What he shared was completely new to me. I had never heard anything like his teaching before. I had always believed in the importance of reading the Scriptures and leading a life of obedience to the

---

The practice of speaking God's Word, which began over 60 years ago, has become a cornerstone in my life. We need the Word. We need to read it, speak it, and do it!

Word of God. Hagin went beyond that, as he explained the importance of speaking the Word. He said that it wasn't enough to just read or follow the Word, we had to speak the Word. As I listened to him, I was inspired with a new thought, *If the Word works that way for him, it will work that way for me, too!* I became a believer in confessing the Word. I started speaking the promises of God over my problems every day. I would consider a problem or need in my life and then find specific scriptures where God promised to solve the problem or meet the need. Then I would speak those scriptures out loud every day. It worked! I began to see more miracles in my life. The promises of God were becoming more than words on a page; they were becoming a reality to me. The practice of speaking God's Word, which began over 60 years ago, has become a cornerstone in my life. We need the Word. We need to read it, speak it, and do it!

When you give the Word of God preeminence in your life
and speak it over every situation, it allows God to change
and mold your life in ways you cannot even imagine.

Up to that point, my life and ministry had been influenced by many things, but my world was about to be revolutionized by the Word. As I renewed my thinking about my daily interaction with the Word of God, I embraced the truth that speaking scriptures over my life would change my circumstances. That revelation, along with God's mercy and grace, has produced astonishing results. It's been over 60 years now since I first learned the importance of that truth, and I still speak scriptures every day. I like to read my Bible and confess scriptures every morning while enjoying a cup of coffee. When you give the Word of God preeminence in your life and speak it over every situation, it allows God to change and mold your life in ways you cannot even imagine.

After learning about this truth from Pastor Hagin, I decided to pay that revelation forward; so, I began teaching it in my young married couples' class. It was revolutionary for them, and we saw amazing success in their lives. As people spoke the Word over their circumstances, they experienced miraculous breakthroughs, healings, and life changes. I fell in love all over again with teaching the Bible. Whenever you teach the truth of the Word, you see transformation. As we saw transformation, more and more people began to join us until eventually I had over 100 people in that one class! At the same time, Wally was preaching, leading worship, and working as the Assistant Pastor. Over a two-and-a-half-year period, God caused the church to grow from 500 to 600 members. It was a true success story, and we were thrilled to be a part of the team God used to help people understand the power of His Word.

Success does not always equal fulfillment, and Wally was not fulfilled. Yes, Wally and I were in full-time ministry and God had blessed the work. As far as numbers go, we had exceeded any targets the church had established, and the members of the church had grown spiritually beyond what we could have imagined. We had seen God restore many lives and heard the testimonies of the tangible miracles that people experienced. We knew God had called and anointed us to do what we were doing because there was no way we could have done any of it in our own strength, but Wally felt stuck. Before he was a pastor, he felt great satisfaction as an evangelist. He experienced so much joy seeing people led to salvation and becoming Spirit-filled, that he desperately wanted to go back into evangelism. So, in 1960 we resigned from the church, said goodbye to Pastor E.R. Foster, and returned to Colorado. At that point, we didn't know that God would call us to be evangelists and pastor a local church, but we knew that we wanted to do everything He was calling us to do.

Learning to be Flexible

We must always remain flexible as we walk with God because it isn't always possible for us to see the whole picture. The Bible says, "*For My thoughts are* not your thoughts, *nor are* your ways My ways,*' says the* Lord *. . .*" (Isaiah 55:8). After returning to Denver, we saw this truth dramatically illustrated in our lives. Wally and I arrived in Denver, intending to jump back into our evangelism ministry. We were not burned out from pastoring, but church planting was off our radar. We saw it as something that we might do in years to come, but we did not see it as something that would happen any time in the near future. However, God had other ideas. We soon faced a need in our community that, try as we might, we could not shake off so easily.

Before we returned to Colorado, some friends of ours started a little church in Denver. They were a young couple whom we had led to Christ, so it was very rewarding for us to know that they had launched into ministry. We had not expected to work alongside them when we returned to Denver, but they unexpectedly asked us, "Would you help us pastor the church until you can get back into evangelism?" It felt reasonable, and it seemed like the most Christian thing to do, so we agreed to help. Our plan was to help them until they found a permanent pastor. The church was called, The Full Gospel Chapel.

Wally and I got to work. The first Sunday we had 22 people. We looked very common, and it didn't feel like much was going to come from our ministry. We held our service in a rough, little, storefront building. If you had seen it, you would have thought, *I don't want to go there!* At the same time, there were people who were not very kind to us. Some, who had known us when we attended Calvary Temple and taught Sunday school years earlier, couldn't get past seeing Wally as a salesman and me as a schoolteacher. They said, "Who are Wally and Marilyn to teach us anything? They are just babies in the ministry. They don't know enough." It seemed like a lot of people did not want to attend our church because they thought we were too young and too immature. We were definitely disrespected in our own hometown, and that was difficult to overcome.

Pastoring the church was supposed to be a temporary arrangement, but as time went on it became clear that we were the ones God had sent to pastor that group of people. Despite all the opposition we faced, we were resilient and pressed forward. Wally and I had a passion for evangelism, to reach the lost—those who did not know the love and salvation of Jesus. We had done it successfully in other ministries. It just made sense for us to apply the same principles we had learned to our own church. So, we activated our door-to-door evangelism "playbook" and worked it diligently.

What we did was simple. We went into homes and invited people to church. During that same time, I taught a soul-winning course at the church. As part of the class, I challenged the participants to join in my neighborhood outreach. Regardless of the response from my class, I was determined to go where people lived to invite them to church. The Bible refers to this as the *"highways and hedges"* (Luke 14:23), and I was excited to go where the people were located. Even when I had no company, I would still go out by myself. That meant that sometimes I walked the streets and approached houses on my own. Looking back, it was probably not the most prudent thing to go by myself into unfamiliar places, and I would not advise anyone else to do that unless they hear a direct command from the Lord to do so. Wisdom would say to always make sure you have someone with you, but I was young and naïve, and God protected me.

As exciting as those outreaches were, there were always a few homes where I hated to go. I detested going to houses with dogs. I look back at myself and laughingly say that it was the beginning of my "rebuking dogs ministry!" Quite truthfully, when I saw signs that said, "Beware of Dog," my instincts told me to go back home or at least to skip that house! Instead, I mustered my courage and approached the house anyway. Many times, the dog would start to charge at me, barking loudly with bared teeth. But because of God's help, and the courage He gave me each time, I refused to be intimidated. Even though I was trembling on the inside, I often looked the dog in the face and commanded in a loud voice, "Get out of my way, in the name of Jesus!" During those years of knocking on doors, not one dog ever bit me!

God really helped us during that time, and our hard work began to bring results. After a year of intense community outreach, we saw an increase. We still only had about 50-60 people in attendance at church, but at least we were growing. Unfortunately, those precious people were also some of the most needy and difficult that I've ever tried to help. Dealing with difficult people really stretched our faith and theology. We constantly had to ask God for wisdom, and at times we were emotionally and physically exhausted from the strain of their problematic situations. At one point I said, "God, I am so tired of all these issues! Could we just have some normal people?" His response was Hebrews 5:14. It says, *"But solid food belongs to those who are of full age, that is, those who by reason of use have their senses exercised to discern both good and evil."* God said, "I am allowing you to see what is real and what isn't real in order to help you gain wisdom for the future." He was saying, "I am teaching you with the Word how to help different people in seemingly impossible situations."

We encountered many interesting cases in those years of pastoring. One of the strangest happened during a regular evening church service. That night, a woman in the service began to cluck like a chicken. Wally was preaching, and every time he opened his mouth she would go, "Cluck." It was distracting and annoying, and nobody was paying attention to Wally's message. Everyone was too busy watching the lady who was clucking. Another time, a woman called and said, "I am having a mental breakdown. Would you come and pray for me?" We went to her house and met a petite 27-year-old woman with two little boys. As we talked with her, she started shaking. When Wally said, "Bonnie, we are going to pray for you," a demon started talking through her. The voice coming out of her no longer sounded like her voice, and her face was distorted and her body stiff. All I could think at that moment was, *I am going out the door!* Wally's response was totally different and much more helpful. He said, "We are moving too fast; let's pray, leave for now, and come back later." That is exactly what we did. It took three times, but Bonnie finally got free.

Prayer Brings Success

I have learned over the years that if ministry is to be successful, it must be backed by the prayers and support of people who have spiritual maturity and insight. We needed people like that right after we ministered to Bonnie because as soon as Bonnie was free, Wally suddenly fell into a terrible spell of depression. It was totally unlike him. We didn't exactly know what to do, but the older and wiser people around us knew that it was a backlash from that encounter with the demonic. One older woman in the church was especially bold. She prayed and took authority over the attack, in the name of Jesus. When she prayed, Wally was totally set free. The Bible says that the enemy comes *"to steal, kill, and destroy"* (see John 10:10). That is what he had tried to do to Wally, but because of the power of God operating through that woman's prayer, Wally was set free. Even though we were still relatively inexperienced in ministry, we were learning and growing. As we followed God and ministered to the people, it was comforting for us to have praying, spiritually-seasoned individuals in our lives.

Do not initiate anything that you are not
willing to saturate in prayer.

Our church grew because people were hungry for the preaching and teaching of the Word of God and desperate for the move of the Holy Spirit. Those were two things that Wally and I were very determined to have. People needed to experience the power of God changing their lives, healing their bodies, and setting them free. Many times, we experienced the tangible presence of the Holy Spirit in our services, and it felt like we were ringing a bell for people who had serious issues or who had been driven out of other churches because they needed too much help. God supernaturally met them with answers to their greatest needs, which caused our church to grow. We were still in the broken-down storefront building, but it was packed with more people than it could hold. We continued to attract new people because the Word of God and the ministry of the Holy Spirit gave people hope.

Prayer was also a real foundation for our ministry. It didn't take us long to learn that we could not initiate anything if we were not willing to saturate it in prayer. As the church increased in numbers, we increased the number of prayer meetings. We had young people at our house for Friday night prayer, we had early morning prayer, and we had Monday evening prayer. When Wally selected the 5 a.m. slot for us to pray in the mornings, and my alarm went off at 4:30 a.m., I groaned out loud because I seriously didn't know if I could make it. But I knew that both my husband and God wanted me to go, so I began to claim Hebrews 11:6, which says that God is a *"rewarder of those who diligently seek Him"*—even at 5 a.m.! That year, God answered literally hundreds of prayers. We kept a journal of prayer requests and made notes in the journal when we saw Him answer those prayers. We truly saw a supernatural outpouring of God's faithfulness, mercy, and grace as He changed lives and circumstances right before our eyes. Wally's Monday evening prayer meetings were also very powerful. He started those meetings because he had such a huge heart to intercede for the lost; he wanted people to know Jesus. His Monday night prayer meetings continued for decades. I believe that a heart for the lost and the willingness to pray helped us build a strong church, especially in the early days when things were sometimes a little crazy.

When the church increased to about 80 people, we desperately needed more space. So, we moved to a bigger storefront building, where we faced even more growing pains. We held Sunday school in the basement, which always got flooded. We had to go in early and sweep the water out so the children could have class. Then things got more interesting. Somebody told us that if we put mothballs out, they would remove the moisture.

So, we did. After that, the smell of the mothballs was so strong that the children started crying! I can look back now and laugh but believe me, no one was laughing at the time.

I have been amazed at the wonderful things God has done through my ministry over the years, but the foundation for so many of those miracles was laid by the great men and women who influenced my life. Kenneth Hagin, Sr. taught me how to meditate on and speak the Word. Oral Roberts impacted my entire family and me with his faith and vision. He also, along with several other Voice of Healing evangelists, birthed in me a love for the supernatural and faith for divine healing. T.L. and Daisy Osborn motivated me to pray over nations, and John Osteen inspired me with his love and compassion for people. But in all reality, the person who had the greatest influence on me and my ministry was my dear husband, Wallace Hickey. It was as though I had my own in-house mentor and personal trainer.

Equally Anointed

Wally was very forward thinking and always way ahead of his time. When Wally looked at me, he didn't only see a woman, wife, or mother, he saw someone who was equally anointed and a fellow minister of the Gospel. Wally could see enormous potential in me. It's as though he was looking through the eyes of God, and that enabled me to believe in myself. Wally always went beyond the vital pat on the back or verbal encouragement. He strived to help develop me and gave me the opportunity and room to flourish. When I could not see success in myself, Wally saw it and worked hard to enable me to be used by God.

He said, "Do it anyway. That's how you overcome your fear, by doing it."

In spite of the growth in our church, I struggled with self-confidence. I was shy and had no desire to speak in front of people. However, each service had a time slot for people to share their testimonies and Wally wanted me to tell everyone about the wonderful things God was doing. I told him that I didn't want to get up in front of people and do that, but Wally pushed back. He said, "Do it anyway. That's how you overcome your fear, by doing it." Wally was persistent, and always believed in me more than I believed in myself.

Wally didn't just push me forward, he also pushed past the traditional and cultural norms of the day. After I began having success in teaching Sunday school, he said, "You need to preach every other Sunday from the pulpit. I'll preach one, you preach the other, then I'll preach one, etc." That was unheard of at that time! Not only was it rare for a pastor to share his pulpit, but to allow a woman to speak from the pulpit was radical. That was my husband. He didn't worry about what other people thought; he just wanted to follow God. He always pushed me to do more and be more than I ever thought I could.

The Happy Church

Every church has its own uniqueness that makes it stand out from the rest. As our church grew, we developed a reputation in the city as being the "happy church." Wally and I didn't initiate that name; it came from members of the Catholic community around us who joined us for some of our services. Every time we talked to them, they said, "Oh, you are from the happy church!" It may have been because we were so joyful, but also, I think it was because of our worship. Wally was our worship leader, and they thought our worship was always upbeat and happy, so they deemed us the "happy church." The name stuck, and we eventually made it official by changing our name to The Happy Church.

Our church stood out in our community because of our emphasis on the Holy Spirit and the Word. Usually a church's distinction reflects its leadership, and this was certainly true with us. My role was in emphasizing the importance of the Word of God. My passion for the Bible spilled over onto the congregation as I stepped out and taught from the pulpit. Wally loved anything and everything involving the Holy Spirit. So, as a church, we highly valued the Word and embraced divine healing and the gifts and manifestations of the Holy Spirit, which were very evident in our services.

If you open your church or yourself to the dynamics and power of the Holy Spirit, you will be amazed at the results. We saw this in one of our Friday all-night prayer meetings. It was after midnight when everyone at the church witnessed an incredible supernatural occurrence. God had given Wally a new song, and as he sang it, we all heard someone in the balcony with a gorgeous voice singing along with such harmony that it was unbelievable. Everyone ran up to the balcony to see who was singing with Wally, and shockingly, there was no one there! It had to have been an angel singing with him because there was no one else around. It was incredible! It makes me think with awe of the sights and sounds the shepherds must have heard on the night the angels visited them in Bethlehem to announce the birth of Jesus (see Luke 2:8–20).

Our church was happy and supernatural, but we were also committed to deeply loving and caring for the people God brought to us. Wally was a merciful, compassionate, and protective pastor. He would always tell me, "Remember to be merciful." My answer would often be, "But I want to correct them!" He would say, "Be merciful instead." Early in our ministry, we had a guest speaker who preached at our church. He was apparently dealing with some personal issues, and from the pulpit, seemed to take out his anger on the "captive" audience. That did not sit well with Wally at all. On the way home Wally said, "That man's words hurt people, and I will never again give him an opportunity to attack them." That speaker was never invited back again. Wally always encouraged me to teach with mercy. While it never came as naturally to me as it did to him, I took his advice to heart.

We need to allow the gifts of the Spirit to operate in our lives, but we need to do so with wisdom. As much as he loved the things of the Spirit and prophesied in a heartbeat, Wally was also down-to-earth and very practical. He believed in giving to Caesar what was Caesar's and to God what was God's (see Matthew 22:21). He was always a good steward of the money God gave to us. We consistently and faithfully gave our tithes, 10 percent of our income to the church. In addition, Wally made sure that we saved 10 percent. Furthermore, he was careful with how we spent our money, which sometimes was difficult for me. Most of the time I agreed with our frugality, but on occasion, there was something I wanted or needed that wasn't in our usual budget. One very funny story comes to mind . . .

Wearing Faith Never Looked So Good

When Wally and I were first pastors at our little church, we were on a very tight budget. I was in downtown Denver, and I saw a beautiful fur coat in a shop window. I have always liked fur coats, and I had even bought one for myself during the early part of my teaching career. But fur coats were definitely not in our budget during those early years of our ministry. I thought, *We don't have any children yet, so we might be able to afford it; I am just going to look at it.* When I looked at the price tag, I instantly knew that it was way too expensive. Then, I made the mistake of trying it on; I looked so gorgeous in it that I was sold. I immediately thought, *I am going to buy it.*

When I took the fur coat home, I knew Wally would question me about it, so I had my strategy ready. When he saw me, he asked, "What's in the box?" I said, "I am not going to tell you until I try it on, then you can talk to me about it." After I tried it on, he said, "How much was it?" I replied, "I won't tell you until you tell me if you like it." So, he said, "I like it; how much was it?" When I told him, he exclaimed, "You are usually very careful with your money. What made you buy that coat?" I said, "The devil." He replied, "Why didn't you say, 'Get behind me Satan?'" I said, "I did. But then the devil said, 'It's pretty in the back too,' so I bought the coat."

That's a silly story, but it shows how much I like nice clothes. You know, it can be easy to think that God doesn't care about things like that, but we need to know that He cares about everything, even those things that seem frivolous, like my love for fur coats. Sometime later, I told Wally, "I would like a dark brown, full-length mink coat." His answer was, "Well, don't think I am going to buy it!" I replied, "I know. I am believing that God will provide it." It actually became a joke between us. He would say to me when I traveled, "Did someone give you a full-length, dark brown mink coat?" I would always say, "Not yet, but God is going to give me one!" I am not sure how serious I was, but I knew I wanted it!

At that time, there was a man in our church who owned a pawn shop in our city. He knew that I wanted a dark brown, full-length mink coat. One day, when I returned home, Wally said, "You're going to get something today that you have been believing for." "Is this a joke?" I asked. Then I saw it. Sal, the man who owned the pawn shop, was there with a dark brown, full-length mink coat, exactly like the one I knew I wanted. Surprised, I asked him, "Where did you get it?" He said, "A woman brought it into my shop. It's brand new, but she didn't like it. So, I told her, 'I have a pastor's wife that will like it,'" and he brought it to me! After that, I started actively believing for fur coats.

Years later, I visited Hungary for a ministry trip, and my hosts took us into Romania. At that time, the Iron Curtain was still in place and the church was completely underground. We stopped for lunch at a little café and next to the café there was a shop with beautiful black Persian lamb coats. Of course, I had to try one on! I asked, "How much does this cost?" They said, "Only communist officials are allowed to buy things like this." I thought, *Too bad! I love this coat.* Six months later I received that coat in the mail! Somehow my friends in Hungary had gotten it out. When I returned, they bought me a second full-length coat. And recently, they gave me yet another one! It's amazing how God cares about things like that. I don't live an extravagant life and never have, but certain things seem to matter to me, and God cares about those things, too!

It wasn't always easy to have a practical husband, as my fur coat story shows. At times, I felt he was unnecessarily tight with money. For instance, there were several years where I felt it was time for us to have a bigger house. Our house was too small to entertain, and we often invited people from church to our home. We knew we could afford a new one, but Wally would say, "No, God gave us this house." I would always reply, "He has more than one!" One day, God said to me, "Leave him alone. If you quit looking to him for a house, I can provide it." So, I didn't say anything else to Wally about it. Six months later he said to me, "I've always talked us out of getting another house, but now I am ready." Even then, we weren't extravagant, but our new house gave us space to bring people home from church and host them well. That's marriage . . . it may take some time to get on the same page, but if you trust God, you will get there, and it's worth the wait!

God's Provision

In our personal lives and ministry, Wally and I experienced God's provision in phenomenal ways. I attribute that to God's love and faithfulness, and to the fact that He helped us trust Him as a loving heavenly Father Who always provides for His children. When we first started our church, we were in desperate need of a new car. The one we were driving was on its last leg, and we knew it wouldn't be long before we had to replace it. Over time, we had managed to save $1,000 to buy another one, but before we had an opportunity to buy our new car, we attended a meeting led by T.L. and Daisy Osborn. They were raising money for their building, and during the meeting, Wally felt led to give them the $1,000 we had saved. I was so upset with Wally. I said, "Why did you do that?" He said, "God told me to. He will provide a car when we need it." I was frustrated and desperate. To make matters worse, shortly after Wally gave our $1,000 in that offering, we loaned our old and tired car to someone who wrecked it. At that point, we were totally desperate. We even had to borrow a car or ask for a ride to get to church. That was really embarrassing! Fortunately, God intervened.

Within a couple of months, John Osteen spoke at our church. He was a great speaker and moved in the prophetic. He had no idea about our car situation, but he said to Wally during one of the services, "I see the letters C-A-R over your head. Do you need a car?" My husband replied, "Kind of. I guess." I mumbled to myself, "Kind of! We are so desperate it's pitiful." Then without us saying one thing, Osteen raised an offering for us. It was overwhelming, amazing, and encouraging all at once because they gave us an offering that completely paid for a new car. During our ministry, we saw miracle after miracle like that. God helped us to trust Him, and He met our needs because of His unending faithfulness. We were learning to trust Him in greater ways as we saw that saving, giving, and receiving were all a part of our provision from Him.

Pastoring The Happy Church was a faith journey for Wally and me. We started out so small, but we believed God for growth. In addition to the door-to-door ministry, prayer meetings, and our church services, we took part in special city-wide evangelistic meetings in the Denver metro area. Each time we participated in those meetings, we made sure we were part of the follow-up team after the meetings. One such event was organized by Oral Roberts. At the end of it, we were given a list of people who had responded to the altar call. We followed up with people and ended up with three new families who joined our church. In that way, our church grew family by family.

In the early 1980s, we began to grow out of our building. That was good news. God was blessing us. We had worked very hard, prayed, and reached out to people in our community, and God was causing growth. To accommodate that growth, we began to look for a new building. We were especially excited about a building we found on Alameda Street in Denver and wanted to buy it. Before we looked at it, Wally said, "As we walk through the building, pray and say, 'In Jesus' name, every place that our feet touch belongs to us'" (see Joshua 1:3). We stretched our faith and believed God for a bigger building that could accommodate the growth God was sending to us.

> While it is important to seek advice and counsel from godly men and women whom you trust, it is more important to listen to God, do what He tells you to do, and stand in faith for His promises to come to pass.

At that time, one of our favorite ministers was a prophet named Dick Mills. He taught the Word and prophesied scriptures to people. The prophecies usually spoke about the circumstances they were encountering, and the things God was doing in their lives. At an earlier time, he prophesied Isaiah 54:2 (NIV) to us: *"Enlarge the place of your tent, stretch your tent curtains wide, do not hold back; lengthen your cords,*

strengthen your stakes." He said that our church would have two cords: an outreach and a local church. That was shocking at the time because we didn't see other people doing outreaches from local churches. We had always done outreach, but it was part of the church rather than something separate. Nevertheless, his prophecy was very encouraging to us.

We had always put a lot of weight on the things Dick Mills had said to us, but his response to our bid for the Alameda Street building was not as encouraging. He said, "There is no way you can afford a church this size. You are just small-church pastors." Some of his friends, who were also ministers, agreed with him. They said, "You just don't have a strong enough ministry to support a building that size." Their comments were from hearts of genuine concern, but their words were not from a position of faith. Those negative words should have discouraged us, but instead, our excitement continued. Despite the naysayers, we purchased that building, which seated 400 people, and we began to reach more lost people than ever before. While it is important to seek advice and counsel from godly men and women whom you trust, it is more important to listen to God, do what He tells you to do, and stand in faith for His promises to come to pass.

During that time, the Charismatic Renewal was in full swing across the United States and there was a lot of excitement in the body of Christ. It was a time when God was drawing people closer to Him and many people were getting saved and filled with the Holy Spirit. We invited guest speakers like Charles and Francis Hunter and George Otis, Sr. to minister in our church, and saw God move in powerful life-changing ways. Presbyterians and Lutherans came to our church because they liked our worship style and the move of the Spirit. People who wanted to know more about God and wanted to see Him work in their lives came, too. We also invited people who didn't know anything about God to come to our services. I had a burning desire to reach people who didn't know God with

God's love and bring them into the church; but, I knew we were missing opportunities—we weren't reaching as many people as God wanted us to reach. So, I prayed and asked God to show me how to reach more people. The Lord said, "Lost people are not going to come to you. You have to go to them." I replied, "Will You give me a way?" That's when He began to show me about reaching people through home Bible studies.

Teaching Home Bible Studies

While I was still pondering my questions on how to reach the lost, God gave me the answer. A couple brought their children to our Vacation Bible School. They didn't even attend our church, but our location was close to their house, so they took advantage of it. To my surprise, the wife asked if I would consider teaching a Bible study, and she offered to host it in her home. I had never considered that before, but I thought it would be exciting. In the beginning, there were only seven women, but it quickly grew and then multiplied. That particular Bible study lasted for seven years in that home. What a glorious experience! Home Bible studies are one of the most powerful tools I have ever seen God use to reach people.

The thing that set the home Bible studies apart was that they were outside the four walls of the church. I started with daytime meetings and then added evening meetings as well. I had so much favor and fun with the women who came. We would meet over a cup of coffee, a cookie, and a Bible; and women would learn about the love of God and accept Jesus in their hearts. God gave me such success that I even started holding them in different cities, like Boulder, Colorado. Eventually, I had 22 home Bible study groups! The secret to our growth as a church was really those home Bible studies. We were going after hurting people to let them know that God loved them and sent His Son, so they could know Him personally.

Over several decades, our church multiplied many times over. It gave us tremendous joy to see and experience all that God was doing in our city, through our ministry. After years of successful pastoring, Wally and I had the wonderful privilege of passing the leadership of the church to the next generation. Our daughter and son-in-law, Sarah and Reece, were called by God to be pastors. To this day, it gives me great joy to see them lead their church with the same passion for the Word of God and desperation for the move of the Holy Spirit that was so important to Wally and me years ago.

Alzheimer's and God's Grace

In 2008, Wally was diagnosed with Alzheimer's and eventually needed to be moved into a residential care facility. Fortunately, we found one that was very close to our church, so we could visit him often. He was there for about two-and-a-half years. Wally's decline in health was hard on our family and me as it signaled the inevitable. It was heartbreaking to see the weakened state of the one I had loved for over 50 years, knowing that he was not coming back home to me. But God gives grace in such circumstances, and I experienced a steady flow of His grace.

The Lord is faithful to prepare us for things to come.

God's grace was upon Wally, too, which made the end much more bearable than it could have been otherwise. Wally was very feeble, but he always knew who we were; and amazingly, even when he was at his lowest and was run down physically, Wally was still his happy self and enjoyed life at the care facility. In contrast, many times with Alzheimer's, the person will become disoriented and sometimes agitated or frustrated with the present. We are so grateful that Wally was peaceful and content throughout the entire time he was there. Reece and Sarah were such a support to Wally and me. Having them lead the church during that time was a big relief.

While Wally was able to recognize and relate to his immediate family, he had diminished capacity overall and could not relate as well to friends or church members. In fact, when they visited, they often confused him. So, we had to create boundaries and not allow many visitors other than family members. That was perhaps one of the toughest things we dealt with during Wally's illness, as it meant that some of the people close to him couldn't visit him at the end. Wally was so loved by the church, and they wanted to share that love with him, but it was not possible. I knew how they felt because I missed him, too. I would visit him as often as I could, but those visits were not the same as when we were caring for him in our home.

The Lord is faithful to prepare us for things to come. Amos 3:7 says, *". . . the LORD does nothing without revealing his plan to his servants the prophets."* Shortly before Wally died, I had a special encounter with the Holy Spirit. I was at my ministry office one afternoon and laid down to take a nap on my couch. I was awakened by the most unusual presence of God. I had never experienced His presence like that before. I looked toward the entrance of my office, and there was light coming through the crack under the door. Then, light filled the door, and I knew it was the Spirit of God. The Lord said to me, "I took you through your father's death victoriously. I took you through your mother's death victoriously. I will take you through Wally's death in the same way." Then the light slowly disappeared. I knew then that Wally's passing was imminent. Though there was sadness, my parents' deaths were not hard on me. I had felt God strengthening me during those times so that I was not weighed down by grief. In that visitation, the Holy Spirit, my Comforter, was promising the same grace during a much harder passing, that of my husband and life partner, Wallace Hickey.

On October 19, 2012, Wally died. He was 87. He had lived a good life, served God well, and it was time for him to be with the Lord. That night, the glory of God came over me, and the next morning I woke up singing in the Spirit. I asked the Lord, "Why am I singing in tongues?" He said, "Because I danced over you last night." And ever since that day, I sing in tongues every day. It's amazing how the presence of God has kept me. I could really feel God sustaining me in that time. It is always a difficult thing to lose a spouse, but the Lord helped me through it, so it wasn't as hard as it might have been.

Wally and I were married for almost 58 years. They were very good, happy, and fruitful years. I know that Wally is in heaven, watching me continue to walk out God's plan for my life and ministry (see Hebrews 12:1). I will see him again; but until then, I will continue to do what God calls me to do until I join Wally and Jesus in heaven.

Chapter 4

THE FIGHT FOR MY FAMILY

ONE OF THE MOST REWARDING experiences I have ever had is that of having a family. It was such a joy for me to hold my baby in my arms within minutes after she was born and see the miracle of God's magnificent creation. I loved counting her ten little fingers and toes and experiencing the joy of cuddling a newborn. That experience was one of the most amazing gifts that God has ever given me. Of all the truly incredible things that God has done in and through my life, I am most proud of being a mother, grandmother, and great-grandmother. My grandchildren call me "Mimi," and it's the most awesome feeling to hear them call me that. I am forever grateful that God blessed me to be able to have a family of my own, even though for years it appeared to be a blessing I would never have.

I got married with the hope and expectation of starting a family as soon as possible. Wally and I looked forward to and planned for the time when we would have our children. However, the journey into parenthood proved to be a long, arduous, and heartbreaking experience. Two years into our marriage we discovered that I could not have children. Two different specialists confirmed that fact. They said that I had a condition that prevented me from having children, and there was no cure for it. The implications were dire; I would be childless for the rest of my life. I was devastated. I was only 25 years old when we heard the news, and it felt as though my future had been ripped from my heart.

If we can see it, it can change. We don't have to settle for
less than God's best in our lives. If it is a problem, challenge,
difficulty, or illness that can be "seen," then we know from
God's Word that it is temporary—which means it can change.

When two specialists give a diagnosis, it can be hard to shake free from it. That negative declaration was a real test of our faith. There were no treatment plans to follow. In the natural, there was no hope. So, in our hearts, it was a question of whether the Most High God had the power to deal with and reverse my condition or not. We needed to put our faith and hope on the line. Personally, I settled in my heart that a childless future would somehow be okay. Wally, on the other hand, was not satisfied with that. He never accepted it as even a remote possibility for us. He always believed that God had the final say in every matter, so he began to pray and claim the promises of God for our family. Second Corinthians 4:18 says, *". . . while we do not look at the things which are seen, but at the things which are not seen. For the things which are seen are temporary, but the things which are not seen are eternal."* Through this challenge in our lives, we were learning a great lesson: If we can see it, it can change. We don't have to settle for less than God's best in our lives. If it is a problem, challenge, difficulty, or illness that can be "seen," then we know from God's Word that it is temporary—which means it can change.

I was blessed to have a praying husband. Having a praying spouse can make a huge difference in tough situations. Throughout our marriage, Wally's faith kept us strong in the face of impossible circumstances. The diagnosis from the doctor was the most devastating trial we had faced in our marriage, but he was unwavering in his faith. When my faith was at an all-time low, or even non-existent, Wally stood firm on the Word of God for us. Wally always believed that God would heal me even when I did not necessarily believe in or pursue that healing. Quite frankly, if it had been left to me, I think I would have settled for the life that the doctors told me I would have. I now know that I would have missed out on so much blessing.

A Wheel Within a Wheel and the Presence of God

In 1957, Wally and I attended a series of meetings called The Voice of Healing in Dallas, Texas. I was 26 and still processing the news from the doctors. One of the speakers was William Branham, who had prophesied over my mother years before. We were not quite prepared for what happened, but we quickly learned that the Lord had a prophetic word waiting for us. During one of the night meetings, Branham called me out to prophesy over me. There was a huge crowd that evening, about 5,000 people. Even though he had never met me, he told me, "You're not from here. You're from a wooded area. You're from Denver, Colorado." While he was prophesying, I had an open vision, which is where the Holy Spirit shows you something that is taking place in the spirit realm that you would not normally be able to see with your natural eyes. Suddenly, I saw something that looked like a wheel at my feet. It was as though there was a wheel within a wheel between Branham and me, just as the prophet

Ezekiel described in Ezekiel, chapter 1. As the wheel turned, I heard a sound like "whoosh, whoosh, whoosh." I thought, *Oh my goodness! This is the presence of God. If I step into it, I will die.* Then, Branham continued, "You haven't been able to have a child. Go home and receive your child." With that, the wheel within a wheel disappeared into my feet. This was not just a prophetic word, it was a divine encounter.

After that experience, I was filled with faith. It was such a powerful encounter that I believed I would get pregnant immediately and have a baby within nine months! But that was not to be. Weeks turned into months and months turned into years, and still, there was no manifestation of that prophetic word. Frankly, after several years had passed, I wasn't sure if I would ever become pregnant. I didn't have the strong faith that Wally had for our miracle baby. Wally's faith never wavered. He always said, "Marilyn, God is going to give us a child." He didn't say it just to comfort me, he believed it. The powerful thing is that God did what He said, but it took 10 long years before we had our miracle.

I am always amazed at how God works out the intricate details of His plans and purposes for our lives.

What do you do when you are waiting for God's promise to come to pass? While we waited for the miracle, we continued to pray, fast, and believe that the Word would become our reality. Wally and I spoke the promises of God over our lives, including Isaiah 54:1, *"'Sing, O barren, you who have not borne! Break forth into singing, and cry aloud, you who have not labored with child! For more are the children of the desolate than the children of the married woman,' says the LORD."* We also continued to serve God and do the work of the ministry as though nothing had changed; God was faithful, with or without children, with or without a miracle. We continued to live and enjoy life; we were not waiting to have children in order to have a good life. We were making every day count. Wally and I went on vacations together, enjoyed our marriage, and thanked God for the blessing of having each other.

I am always amazed at how God works out the intricate details of His plans and purposes for our lives. He sends people across our paths and lines up the circumstances so that His will can be accomplished. We saw this happen again about four years after our experience in Dallas. I still had not been able to get pregnant, but God brought us a child in a completely unexpected way. We were given the opportunity to love and adopt a very special little boy. We were introduced to him through a friend who was a Southern Baptist pastor in our city. This friend was a temporary foster parent to a little boy named Michael. Michael's birth mother was an alcoholic and had deserted him and his birth father, who was older and in poor health, so our friend was taking care of Michael.

Michael Hickey

Michael was three years old when we first met him. He was such a beautiful child, with an olive complexion and long eyelashes. Wally immediately fell in love with him. As time went on, I fell in love with him, too. Our hearts ached for him and his situation, and we wanted to do more than "just pray." Before that time, I had not considered adoption because we were so busy with the church; but as Wally and I talked about Michael and prayed over his situation, my heart warmed up to the idea of adopting a child, and I began to feel a special love for Michael. Wally and I prayed over this for several days, but there was no way to deny the leading we had from the Lord. We said, "Yes" to God and "Yes" to adopting Michael. It was such a joy and a blessing for us to finally welcome a child into our home.

The psychology of understanding dysfunctional family dynamics and adoption has evolved significantly since the 1960s. Back then, there were no books instructing people how to help adopted children who had been abused by their birth families, and no instructions on how to integrate those children into adoptive families. So, Wally and I had little knowledge about Michael's issues, and we weren't prepared for them. Michael was a toddler who felt unloved and abandoned at a very critical stage in his development. Those feelings had ramifications that bled long and deep into our relationship with him.

The difficulties Michael had gone through before he came to our home left him with deep insecurities, anxieties, and fears, which made healthy attachment and normal family interaction almost impossible for him. For instance, he hadn't had enough food to eat when he lived with his biological parents, so with us, he hoarded food and hid it under the bed. Unfortunately, at the time, Wally and I did not understand what was happening. We thought the environment was the key. We assumed that all we needed to do was provide a good, safe environment for Michael and everything else would work out. Sadly, that wasn't true. If you treat an abused child like a child who grew up in a healthy environment, you will expect too much from him and not give him enough support. Michael needed a different approach to parenting, but we didn't know it.

You can't parent with only luck, hope, and faith. Being a successful parent requires much more. You also need wisdom, knowledge, understanding, God's grace, and anointing to parent well. Wally was better with Michael than I was, but neither of us understood how to handle his issues appropriately; and Michael's problems increased as he got older. Looking back, I wish we had known more and done better in parenting him.

When Michael was six years old, he was kidnapped—yes, kidnapped! There are things you never dream will ever happen to you. You only hear about them on the news, and they seem very remote and far away. Kidnapping is one of those things. You don't even wish such a thing on your worst enemies. It's one of the most terrifying things that could happen to anyone, and the feeling for a parent is unimaginable, but it did happen. The devil hit close to home, and we knew that we needed to face the situation and lean totally into God with our faith to get through it.

Crisis reveals the core of who we are. It's when we find ourselves in extremely difficult situations that our faith in God is put to the test.

At that time, we lived in a bad neighborhood, but it was the best we could afford. The park near our house was not the safest place, but we hadn't had any issues before that frightful day. We had a ten-year-old girl temporarily staying with us who had taken Michael to the playground at the park down the street, but when she returned she was by herself. When we asked her about Michael's whereabouts, she said, "A woman came to the park, and Mike went with her." Trembling, we immediately dialed 911 and told the authorities. Then we rushed to the playground to look for him while we waited for the police to arrive. It was the longest wait we had ever faced. As you can imagine, fear tried to overwhelm us with negative possibilities. There were all kinds of gloomy scenarios attacking our minds.

Crisis reveals the core of who we are. It's when we find ourselves in extremely difficult situations that our faith in God is put to the test. As a mother, I was about to fall to pieces. I was quite beside myself as we looked around the park, waited for the police, and wondered what terrible things were happening to Michael, but Wally rose to the occasion. He chose to believe God's Word that promises His protection. Proverbs 3:25–26 says, *"Do not be afraid of sudden terror, nor of trouble from the wicked when it comes; for the LORD will be your confidence, and will keep your foot from being caught."* Isaiah 54:17 says, *"No weapon formed against you shall prosper . . ."* Knowing those verses, Wally grabbed hold of my hands and said to me, "Marilyn, we are going to believe that Mike will be safely returned to us in one hour!"

When the police arrived at the park, we told them what had happened, and they immediately began their search. Thankfully, God was already ahead of us. We had just finished talking to the officers when I looked down the street and saw a woman three blocks away walking with a child. "That's our son!" I shouted. The police quickly caught and arrested her. They brought Michael safely back to us where we were waiting in the park. We hugged and kissed him, thrilled and thankful to have him back unharmed.

I looked at my watch and realized it had only been one hour since we learned Michael was gone. Wally's simple but faith-filled declaration had come to pass. Hallelujah! It was such a remarkable miracle, and it quickly became a front-page story in the local newspaper. The article was titled, "Son of Pastor Kidnapped." Because of that article, a building contractor called us and said, "I feel called to build you a home at cost in a better neighborhood." It was completely unexpected, and we were very overwhelmed by his offer, but we knew that God had redeemed that terrible predicament and provided a home for us in a much safer neighborhood. After the house was finished, we lived there for over 31 years.

Sarah's Miraculous Birth

God has a way of surprising His beloved children when they least expect it. I had reached my mid-30s, and was quite content in ministry, marriage, and my family life. In fact, I was very happy with how things stood. As far as I was concerned, the prophecy from William Branham about me embracing a child was a distant memory and not an active pursuit. We had Michael, and I had totally given up on the dream of having a biological child of my own. Wally, on the other hand, was persistent. Years of delay had not shaken his faith one bit. He would look at me and say, "You will be pregnant with our child." I would smile in acknowledgment without admitting my own unbelief. The truth was, I was more career-minded, and Wally was more spiritually-minded. In the end, it was because of his faith that we saw the miracle come to pass.

When I was 36, I started having some symptoms of pregnancy and wondered, *Could it be?* Naturally, I went to my doctor for a check-up and told him my thoughts. Upon examination, his answer was, "You're not pregnant; you're going through the change of life." Well, I did go through some astonishing changes! My belly kept getting bigger and bigger. So, I went to a different doctor and told him how I was feeling. He confirmed that I was five months pregnant. It was true after all. What I had suspected for months was really happening; I was pregnant! The feeling was wonderful, and Wally was beyond thrilled.

A funny thing happened in the midst of the celebration. After I found out that I was pregnant, I was pleased, shocked, and overjoyed all at once, and decided that I needed to go shopping. I immediately went to a maternity store and bought eight maternity outfits. I usually didn't get the chance to splurge like that, but I was so happy that I didn't even think about the cost. Wally was horrified. "Why did you do that?" he asked, famously careful with money. I replied, "I'm only going to be pregnant once; I want to look good!" He couldn't really argue with that! Nothing mattered at that moment, we were both so elated. Our miracle baby, Sarah, was on her way.

Even though I had finally conceived, the doctors were concerned about my ability to carry the baby full term. At that time, there weren't many 36-year-old women having babies, so mine was considered a high-risk pregnancy. For me, I was determined to do everything right. The doctor was very strict, but I was committed to doing whatever he said. He was very concerned about the possibility of what he considered to be excessive weight gain. He said, "Don't come to my office if you gain more than 15 pounds!" It seems funny now because most contemporary doctors believe

---

Despite what we were told and the impossibilities of our situation, we believed God. Our God is the Creator of the universe and He has power over everything, including physical abnormalities and debilitating conditions.

---

that a healthy weight gain is much higher than 15 pounds, but I took his words to heart. I was very careful with eating and exercise, and by the end, I had only gained 12 pounds. Despite the doctor's concerns, God gave me an easy pregnancy with no complications.

Early the next year, I delivered our baby girl. My heart overflowed with wonder when I first saw our miracle baby. I cuddled Sarah in my arms and thanked God for the gift He had given to us. Wally's smile as he held her for the first time was glorious. The glow on his face could have awakened the entire hospital! Several months after Sarah was born, I went back to my original doctor and told him that I had a baby. "Oh, did you adopt?" he asked. "No, I had a baby," I replied. "That's impossible," he countered. "Well, I did it anyway!" I exclaimed. And that is really how we lived our lives! Despite what we were told about the impossibilities of our situation, we believed God. And in 1968, we had the baby that God had promised us years before. Our God is the Creator of the universe and He has power over everything, including physical abnormalities and debilitating conditions.

After 10 years of praying, believing, and even sometimes doubting, God had shown Himself to be both faithful and merciful. God had been faithful to Wally and merciful to me. It was almost like the story of Abraham and Sarah in the Bible. The joy of carrying life in the womb is one of the most blessed privileges of womanhood, and I am grateful that I had the opportunity to experience it. I can understand Sarah's sentiments when she proclaims, *"After I have grown old, shall I have pleasure?"* This was Sarah's response when God visited Abraham to tell him that she would have a child in her old age. God responded to Sarah's doubt, *"Is anything too hard for the LORD?"* (Genesis 18:12, 14). God had shown us again that nothing was too hard for Him. We named our miracle baby, Sarah, which means "princess" and joyfully took her home from the hospital.

There's nothing like having good news and having those close to you celebrate it with you. My family was so thrilled for me at the news of my pregnancy. My mother encouraged and prayed for me throughout the pregnancy, and she was there at the hospital with Wally and me during the delivery. In my family, there was a history of infertility. In fact, there's a whole line of women with no children on my father's side. When I visited my father's relatives with our baby girl, they were so happy. It felt like a breakthrough for the whole family. Our church family celebrated with us, too. It was a huge testimony of God's faithfulness, and it encouraged the faith of many people in our church.

Since Sarah's miraculous birth, I have had the privilege of praying for thousands of women who desired to have children but had been previously unable to conceive or carry a baby to term. Many times, I have seen God do the miraculous in their lives. For example, several years ago, I preached in a large church in Singapore that had several couples who could not have children. I prayed for them and learned later that within nine to twelve months after I left, there was a mini baby boom in that church; many of the couples even had twins. Since my breakthrough, I have had supernatural faith to believe for babies, even twins, and triplets!

I claimed Joel 2:28 (NIV) over Sarah when she was a newborn, *"And afterward, I will pour out my Spirit on all people. Your sons and daughters will prophesy, your old men will dream dreams, your young men will see visions."* I believed that she would be saved and filled with the Holy Spirit at a young age. When Sarah turned four years old, there was a manifestation of that Word in her life. One day, out of the blue, she told me, "Mom, after I wake up from my nap, God is going to fill me with the Holy Spirit. I am going to pray in tongues." It was a bit unusual, and I wondered if that were just something she was saying because she thought it would make me happy. With a smile, I replied, "That sounds wonderful, Sarah." Later, I checked on her, and she was sitting up in bed, smiling, and praying in tongues!

The Bible says, *". . . 'According to your faith let it be to you'"* (Matthew 9:29). We saw this come to pass over and over again in our lives and our family. Michael's remarkable recovery after being kidnapped, my ability to conceive and deliver a baby, and Sarah being filled with the Holy Spirit as a young child are but a few examples. We found that as our faith stretched, the miracles in our lives increased. God always wants to touch our lives with His supernatural power and provision, but we need to allow Him to increase our faith. We need to trust God and trust that His Word is true in every situation and circumstance.

From the time Michael met Sarah, he loved her. He was very good to her, and she loved him. It was wonderful to see our young family grow and develop. However, once again we were naïve and slow to learn. The family dynamic had changed quite a bit, and we did not realize the full impact of that change. Wally got totally absorbed with Sarah and didn't quite give Michael the fatherly attention he needed. We didn't understand how to make Michael feel included in the family configuration. It was all too easy to become absorbed in a new baby.

If I could go back, I would do things differently. I would have paid closer attention to Michael's needs. There were little things we could have done that would have made a big difference. We could have gotten him involved with Sarah's care. Just saying, "I need you to help me, Michael," would have made a big difference with him. Michael never told us that he felt left out, but when we look back, some of the mistakes we made became obvious. Thankfully, God is a Redeemer, and He helps us even when we make mistakes.

We were far from perfect parents, but Wally and I were always supportive of our children in academics and athletics, attending their sports activities and other events whenever we could. It was something we enjoyed doing as a family. We also prayed with and for them every day. I also shared with them my love for memorizing scriptures. One summer, I had started memorizing the book of Proverbs, and I wanted Michael and Sarah to memorize Proverbs, too. Michael and Sarah were about 11 and 4 when I hatched a plan. I told them that they had to memorize scriptures to watch television. Six verses of Proverbs would equal one hour of television. Michael set about memorizing as much of Proverbs as he could, so he could watch television. Sarah had a different reaction. She decided it wasn't worth the effort and gave up watching television. Even now, when I talk with Michael, he encourages me with some of the scriptures he memorized as a child.

One particular event in Sarah's childhood really speaks to the power of faith and the importance of parental role models in shaping a child's life and future. When Sarah was in third grade, I went to her room one night to pray with her before she fell asleep. She was in tears. "Sarah, what's wrong?" I asked. She replied, crying her words out, "Mom, every year on field day, I get the lowest number of ribbons out of all my classmates. I'm just not good at sports." It took only a second for me to quip back an answer. I felt like I knew exactly what to say to Sarah. It was a page right out of my mom's parenting book. I told her something Mom had told me, "You are so good in academics; you're a wonderful Christian; you are beautiful inside and out; you can't be good at everything." I had said it to encourage her and it was exactly the "truth" that had been given to me years earlier, but I didn't realize that those were not the right words to say.

Naturally, my goal was to help her manage her expectations. My approach was well-intentioned and seemed wise, but the supernatural life is different than the natural life. Instantly, I felt the Holy Spirit speak to my heart, "You are teaching your daughter unbelief. Why can't she be good at everything?" Wow! God looks at things differently, doesn't He? So, I repented. I told Sarah, "Forgive me. You can be good at everything. You can be good at athletic events; so, let's start confessing the Word of God about your field day." Her eyes lit up with hope and the pursuit of excellence was on.

How Many First-Place Ribbons do you Want?

When we pray, we need to be specific with God. If we believe for "nothing in particular," guess what? We will get "nothing in particular." Because of this truth, I wanted to give Sarah something specific for which to aim and believe God. So, I asked her how many first-place ribbons she wanted to win on field day. Her response was rather pathetic, "Mom, I don't know. I've never even gotten a second-place ribbon, let alone a first-place one." I was undaunted, and I wanted to stretch our faith. I told Sarah, "We are going to believe big! I want two first-place ribbons." Then, for the next three weeks, I helped Sarah confess positive scriptures such as, *"I can do all things through*

Christ . . ." (Philippians 4:13), and *". . . I am more than a conqueror in Christ Jesus"* (Romans 8:37). It really was a walk of faith because with our natural eyes it didn't look like our goal was at all within reach.

When we pray, we need to be specific with God.
If we believe for "nothing in particular," guess what?
We will get "nothing in particular."

Field day arrived, and I went to support Sarah and watch her events. When I asked how she felt, she replied with a scripture, *"I can do all things through Christ"* (see Philippians 4:13). It was very exciting to hear her say that. But I wondered, *Would God come through?* The answer is, "Absolutely!" That day, the strength Sarah received from God's Word enabled her to win two first-place ribbons! She was so excited; and because of that day, her attitude toward athletics completely changed. From that day on she was an excellent athlete, even competing on her high school varsity basketball team for years. The ability the Word of God has to change our mind, and even our life, is amazing! We were learning that in raising children, there were many situations that would challenge our faith, but nothing was beyond the grace and power of Jesus in our lives.

Grace and Tough Love

One of the most difficult memories to share involves the struggle that Michael went through growing up. We faced behavioral issues with him that only grew worse as he got older. When he entered his teens, Michael's deep-seated issues began to surface in different ways. The trouble really escalated in middle school when he started smoking marijuana. By the time he was 16, he was slipping out of the house through his bedroom window at night to meet a group of kids to get harder drugs. He promised over and over again that he would stop. We prayed with him and gave him incentives to keep off drugs, and at other times punishments for using drugs, but the situation got worse.

Tough love is easy to preach but hard to practice.

Michael was actively in the drug scene for nine years. What had started as a little experiment with marijuana had culminated into a full-blown cocaine addiction and the situation had come to a boiling point. We dealt with Michael the best way we could. Repeatedly, we would confront him and tell him, "You can't live here and do drugs." He would act remorseful and say, "Well, I won't keep doing drugs," but he never really stopped. It was heartbreaking. Finally, we went to counseling, and the counselor told us, "Put him out on his own because you've tried and tried and tried." Those words were like a knife through my heart.

The idea of our sweet Michael alone and living on the streets was hard to contemplate. We struggled with the decision for days, but it was our only recourse. Michael was almost 19 when we told him that he had to leave our home. That was one of the hardest things I have ever had to do. I thought, *I can't do that.* Wally said, "We're doing it, and I don't want you giving him money or helping him." Tough love is easy to preach but hard to practice. A couple of times, I helped Michael without telling Wally. Of course, I couldn't get away with that. God spoke to me, reminding me that I should submit to my husband. So, I confessed to Wally, "I've been giving Michael some money." Wally replied, "I knew you were." I should have known that I couldn't fool a spiritual man!

As scary as those drastic measures were, they did bear some fruit. Today, Michael tells us that being forced to go on his own was the one thing that woke him up. He started sleeping in a very unsafe park in Denver where people were being murdered. With no roof over his head, Michael began to realize that he had to change his life, though it took a period of years for him to surrender fully. It was a very frightening time. I would wake up in the night imagining the worst; *My son is sleeping in a park. Will someone kill him?* The only way to get back to sleep was to confess the scripture, *". . . an evil person shall not go unpunished; but the offspring of the righteous shall be delivered"* (Proverbs 11:21, ESV). I prayed for angels to surround, watch over, and keep him (see Psalm 91:11).

I seesawed between faith and fear; but each time, the Word of God was my salvation. As I confessed the Word over Michael and believed the promise that my seed, my son, would be delivered, I was able to trust God for him once again. In one of those dark times, I had a dream in which I saw Michael standing and holding a Bible. God showed me things like that to help me believe that He would deliver my son and that He had a good future planned for Michael.

He replied, "When you are about My business, I will be about your business." I accepted that truth by faith, and quickly discovered that God had been actively engaged in our battle.

As Michael battled himself, the elements, and addiction, we battled anxiety, shame, and guilt. There were many times over the years that I felt guilty over the mistakes Wally and I made as parents. I repented to God over and over. God spoke to my heart each time and said, "I have forgiven you," but I still struggled with the guilt. I was about to preach at our church on a Sunday night when the devil came at my mind with the thoughts, *Who are you to preach? Your own son is not saved and is into drugs. Who are you?* So, I asked the Lord, "Who am I?" He replied, "When you are about My business, I will be about your business." I accepted that truth by faith, and quickly discovered that God had been actively engaged in our battle.

Two weeks later, I saw Michael, and he asked, "Mom, what were you doing two weeks ago on Sunday night?" I said, "I was preaching." He said, "Well, I was hitchhiking, and some guy picked me up. He asked me, 'What's your name?' I said, 'Michael Hickey.' He said, 'Really? Are you related to Marilyn Hickey?' I replied, 'Yeah, that's my mother.'" Michael said that for the rest of the drive home the driver preached the Gospel to him! That incident was another way that God reassured me He was working with Michael. Those things helped me get through the harder seasons when things seemed to get even worse.

During that season, The Happy Church had been growing tremendously. God had blessed our efforts, and we were pastoring a church of over 3,000 people. My personal ministry was booming as well, including my teaching on radio and television. But at home, we faced what appeared to be an absolute parenting failure. Just when we thought things could not get any worse, they did. One night, Michael and a friend broke into our church building and stole some very valuable artifacts that Wally had collected. When the police caught them, the headline on the front page of the newspaper read, "Son of Happy Church's Pastor Breaks in and Steals." It was a new low that crushed us and sent us to our knees in prayer.

The years of pain and pent-up emotions erupted. Wally and I were hurt, angry, and frustrated, and blamed ourselves for the situation. We thought, *Why did we take him? What should we do?* It was an ugly response from a very low place. We were definitely not at our finest as Christians. It was as though the devil had won. Thankfully, by the grace of God, we pulled ourselves together. We took what we had been dealing with privately and admitted it publicly, and went before our church and truthfully told them about our situation. We told them, "Our son Michael has been hard to handle. He's into drugs, and we need your prayers." We didn't hide it from the church. We told the truth and our church gathered around us, supporting and praying with us.

What the devil meant for evil, God turned around for our good. That devastating event eventually led Michael to freedom from drugs. He was 21 at the time and was only in jail for a few days. During his time in jail, a man associated with the justice system had compassion on him and began to work with him. He helped Michael deal with the situation and get into a rehab center. That was the turning point for Michael. It took time, but he was delivered from the cocaine addiction. Over a period of years, we were fully reconciled, and the wounds we had from the relationship with Michael began to heal. It is incredibly difficult to face the failings we have as parents, but I am so grateful to God that He is a gracious God Who redeems every situation.

One amazing quality that was always evident in Michael, even in his darkest times, was his compassion. He was truly like Wally in that way. If he saw someone on the street asking for money, he would give it to them. Michael always wanted to help people who were hurting. When he was forced to leave our house in the depths of his cocaine addiction, he found out about a mattress factory that had extra mattresses they couldn't sell and needed to give away. So, he asked Wally to help him find people who needed them. God gave Michael a soft heart that was always moved to help others, even when he needed help himself.

After he left the drugs behind, Michael met a beautiful woman and her daughter. She had gone through horrific trauma as a child. Michael's soft heart wanted to help her, so he married her and adopted her daughter. Later, they had a daughter together. We all thought the marriage would last. Unfortunately, the trauma she had been through was too much and she couldn't handle being a wife and mother; so, she left Michael and both girls. At a young age, he became a single parent to two small children.

Michael is a fighter, and in spite of all that he has been through, he loves deeply. He was naturally angry at his ex-wife, but he was determined to be a good father to the two girls. He loved them both so much! Because he had been adopted and knew that an adopted child could feel left out, he always treated his first daughter as if she were his own biological daughter. Wally and I loved the girls, too. They were our first grandchildren, and we wanted to do as much as possible to support Michael through that tumultuous season of his life. We loved spending time with our granddaughters and seeing their distinct personalities. Michael did very well raising them. The strong bond between the girls continued into their adulthood and blossomed into a strong, sisterly friendship that is very refreshing to see. They have since moved to another state, and Michael moved with them. He wanted to be close to his daughters who are now married and have children of their own; the oldest has three children, and the second daughter has two. They are both outstanding women who are loving, kind, and successful in business.

Michael is now in his mid-50s. Our relationship is good, and I still visit his whole family whenever I can. I have prayed for them for years, and it is such a blessing to see them all happy and successful, despite the difficult start to their family. Recently, I spent some time with them and told them I was so proud of how well they were doing. The youngest, now in her mid-30s, told me how proud they were of me! That touched my heart and brought tears to my eyes.

As I reflect on Michael's family, I am encouraged to see the hand of God in the lives of my children and grandchildren. One specific testimony in their family is of my great-granddaughter. When Michael's oldest was very young, she had a baby girl. Her daughter is a true success story. She has her bachelor's degree and is working on a master's degree in social work. Moreover, she loves Jesus and has a very strong walk with God. I believe this is a miracle that has come from years of prayer.

We Win With Our Families

One day, I started to cry as I was thanking God for the miracles He did in Michael and his family. God told me, "You prayed for them every day. What did you expect?" Their story is proof that it is not over until you win! I stood for Michael, prayed in faith for his family, and believed that God would turn things around for them. Now I have seen it happen. There really is power in prayer!

One of the blessings of having a son and a daughter is that I was able to enjoy and appreciate the differences in their temperaments and experiences as they grew up. They loved each other very much even though they were very different from each other. Sarah is a phenomenal Bible teacher, pastor, writer, humanitarian, wife, and mother. It gave Wally and me great pleasure to see her called into ministry; however, we never planned or sought that path for her. In fact, we were surprised by it. When Sarah was growing up, we never anticipated that she would be called into ministry and we didn't try to steer her in that direction. As parents, our priorities were to ground her in the faith and enable her to pursue whatever God laid on her heart.

Sarah had many aspirations throughout the years. When she was seven or eight, she said, "I want to be an astronaut." We said, "Wonderful; we will help you." Then, when she was about 11, she said that she wanted to be an architect. We said, "Wonderful; we will help you." Then she wanted to be an engineer. Our response was the same, "Wonderful; we will help you." But when she was 17, she felt that God wanted her to go to Oral Roberts University to major in German and Education. She liked languages, just like I did. We said, "Wonderful; we will help you." We were very supportive of her in her choice of careers, and it was quite interesting to watch how God eventually directed her path to ministry. God is a master at those things.

Some of the most formative experiences of Sarah's life were at our church prayer meetings. When she was little, we had all-night Friday prayer meetings in our church, and we always took Sarah with us. Those services went from 9 p.m. until 3 a.m. Sarah would fall asleep under the pew, and I would take her home around midnight while several people, including Wally, stayed until 3 a.m. Even as an adult, Sarah remembers people praying in tongues all around her and how she felt so much peace in those times. The impact is remarkable in her life. Today, she lives, eats, drinks, and breathes the Holy Spirit, so to speak. I believe that her intense passion for His presence in her life was birthed from those early experiences. Sometimes it takes years for us to see the fruit from the good seeds we sow into the lives of our children; but if we are patient and continue to trust God, those seeds will bear good fruit.

While Sarah was never a difficult child, I had my share of surprises with her, too. There's one incident that was a wake-up call for me. I had offered to help clean out her car but when I opened her car door, a beer can rolled out. I was astonished. Heartbroken, I started to cry. Sarah stood there fidgeting nervously and said, "Mom, you never listen to me when I talk to you. You always preach at me." Her outburst was even more shocking to me. I thought that Sarah and I had a pretty good relationship. I had no idea she felt that way about me. It was a come-to-Jesus moment for me. In other words, it was time for me to allow God to change me. It was a difficult circumstance, but I decided to change. I started listening instead of preaching. God helped me become a better parent and made my relationship with Sarah much stronger.

Sometimes it takes years for us to see the fruit from the good seeds we sow into the lives of our children; but if we are patient and continue to trust God, those seeds will bear good fruit.

The darkest struggle over Sarah's destiny happened when she was in college. It was a joy for us to see her pursue her passion at ORU, an amazing Christian university in Tulsa, Oklahoma. But, in the midst of her university studies, the enemy struck. Between her junior and senior years, she spent a summer in Germany taking some summer courses. When she returned, she said, "I don't believe in Jesus anymore, and I don't know if you will still love me." That is a parent's worst nightmare. Sarah had been raised in a Christian home, had been taught the Word of God, and had even been filled with the Holy Spirit at a very young age. Suddenly, she was "falling away" from the faith. In that moment, the Holy Spirit spoke to me and said, "Don't fall apart!"

There are very critical moments in our lives when we absolutely must have the wisdom of God, and that was one of those moments. Staying calm and not panicking in that situation was the first victory, but the next victory was receiving timely wisdom from God. Thanks to the inspiration of the Holy Spirit, I responded, "Sarah, when you were born you didn't believe in Jesus and we loved you. We don't love you because of what you believe. We love you because you are ours." I continued, "The enemy is trying to steal your faith, but Jesus will make Himself real to you." Sometimes, all our prayers boil down to being able to stand in that one moment. We had prevailed in the battle of acceptance and trust, and we were well-positioned in her life, not just for damage control but for complete recovery.

Having won the battle for her affections as parents, it was time to wage war in the spirit realm for her destiny. Over the next few months, Wally and I prayed constantly for her; and as a mother, I shed many tears over her in my prayer closet. We continued to engage with her as if nothing had changed, making her feel welcomed and loved like never before. It was another hard experience, but we did not give up and we did not back down. She returned to ORU where she had already committed to be a Resident Advisor in one of the dorms. Her job was to encourage and support the young women on her floor in their spiritual and academic growth. That is not something she should have been allowed to do when she wasn't walking with the Lord, but the Dean of Women worked very closely with her and gave her a lot of grace in that season.

One night in November, she called us to say that she had rededicated her life to Christ. She had been studying with a young man when he had shared his story with her. He had begun to doubt and then eventually walked away from his faith when he was a student at Harvard. After that, his father had forced him to attend ORU where he experienced the love of God in new ways and recognized that he needed to accept that love and embrace God's plan for his life. She said, "He got into the Gospel of John, and we've been studying it together." His story was the perfect one to reach her heart and lead her back to the Lord! It was a huge breakthrough for her, but what made it even more personal for me was when I found out that the young man's father had received salvation in one of my meetings 15 years earlier! God is faithful, and He was teaching me that sowing and reaping is a very powerful principle. As I taught the Word of God and shared His love with others, I was "sowing into spiritual things." I did not know that 15 years before that time, the young man's dad would be in one of my meetings, get saved, and eventually send his son to ORU where that son would lead my daughter back to Christ. But God had been working to bring good into Sarah's life and my life, and by His grace, caused me to "reap spiritual things." He was taking care of Sarah in wonderful ways.

Reece Bowling

After Sarah graduated from ORU, she came home and taught in the K-12 Christian school at our church. She was a great teacher and loved teaching! When she was 25, Sarah met a young man at a singles conference we were hosting. The story is very interesting. Years before, when Sarah was only 15, I was a speaker at a conference in Kansas City. During that conference, a young man helped to host me and drove me around while I was there. His name was Reece Bowling. He was 21 years old at the time and had just graduated from college. He had a real heart for God and was very gracious. He wasn't a minister; he just loved God. I commented to the pastor's wife, "That's the kind of guy I would like Sarah to marry." It didn't feel spiritual at the time; it was just a comment.

Ten years later, when Sarah was 25, he was the young man that she met at our church's singles conference. After dating for months, they got engaged to be married. Then, just two days before the wedding, Sarah attended a special meeting at a local church with Rodney Howard-Browne. Rodney was used mightily by God in a revival of signs, wonders, and miracles that swept across the United States. At the meeting Sarah attended that night in Denver, the Holy Spirit was moving in powerful and unusual ways, and she had an incredibly spiritual experience. She felt Jesus calling her into full-time ministry. We didn't call her into ministry; we were as shocked as anyone! However, it was extremely satisfying to see her mightily touched by God and called into the ministry.

As amazing as Sarah's encounter was, it rocked Reece's world. He was very upset. He said, "I didn't get engaged to some world evangelist." This troubled Sarah quite a bit and she asked me, "Mom, what should I do?" I said, "Do you feel that he is the one God has for you?" "Yes," she replied. I said, "We do, too. If I were you, I would marry him and let God take care of your call." It is important to have wise, mature counsel in times of critical life choices. When in doubt, always follow the Word. If God called Sarah, He would make a way for her to walk out that calling and He would work with Reece to bring him around.

Sarah married Reece and moved to Kansas City, Missouri. After two years of marriage, Reece felt called to move back to Colorado. He worked for the ministry as an administrator for a while and then he came to me and said, "I would like to preach some." That surprised me. I said to him, "Is this an ambition or a call? I am not putting ambition in the pulpit." He replied, "I don't know." I said, "Until you know, don't come back to me about this." So, Reece prayed, and he felt God calling him into ministry. We began to allow him to preach in the church occasionally as he grew in his giftings. Over time, he became a very strong voice, not just in our church but in the body of Christ.

It is important to have wise, mature counsel in times of critical life choices. When in doubt, always follow the Word.

Sarah and Reece are now the lead pastors of Encounter Church in Centennial, CO. It is a thriving church that was birthed out of The Happy Church. Sarah has her own ministry, as well. She is a gifted writer and Bible teacher with deep insights and revelations that God enables her to share with people around the world. She has an unshakable conviction that unconditional love transforms everything, which permeates every message and connects individuals to the heart of God. Additionally, Sarah leads an international, humanitarian organization called *Saving Moses*, which saves babies in nations where the needs are the most urgent and the care is least available. Sarah's story should inspire every parent who has ever struggled because of their child's relationship with the Lord. Not only did she recover the most precious thing of all, her faith in Christ, but she married, and then stepped into her calling as a minister of the Gospel. Sarah and Reece have three children. I am so pleased to be in ministry with them and to know that the work of the Lord through them will continue.

Chapter 5

BREAKING BARRIERS

THE POWER OF THE HOLY Spirit is not partial to men. In fact, it is gender neutral, equally accessible to all without regard to culture, tradition, or social norms. Empowered by the Spirit, we can rise to amazing heights of success and accomplishment. The Bible emphasizes this in Galatians when it says that in Christ Jesus, *"There is neither Jew nor Gentile, there is neither slave nor free, there is neither male nor female . . ."* (Galatians 3:28). All are free to dream and believe for a life beyond their current conditions, regardless of their history or status in life. When I was growing up, I was inspired to believe that I could do anything. I was told that nothing could stop me. My gender was never factored in; being a woman wasn't a stumbling block or a hindrance. In my mind and upbringing, there was nothing negative about being female; it was something God created, and that made it good. As a woman, I felt like I was beautiful and powerful because that is how God made me. I knew that some people would set their own limitations, but God doesn't limit us.

A Different Kind of Pastor's Wife

It is fashionable now to be a woman speaker. Some of the most popular speakers worldwide are women. It has become so commonplace to see women preachers that it is hard to envision a time when women were confined to the back room. But, when I started in ministry, women were not allowed in the pulpit. Our role was intended to be supportive at best. People felt that my job was to be Wally's wife, a "pastor's wife." There were very specific expectations for any woman in that position. These included the ability to sing, knit, and cook for crowds. I was an acceptable cook but singing and knitting were not my strengths.

When we started Full Gospel Chapel, everyone expected me to lead worship. The problem was that if I had led worship, no one would have been worshipping! My singing was terrible. Additionally, every pastor's wife was expected to sew blankets for those in need. I wasn't good at that either. The things I was "supposed" to do did not interest me. I was a different kind of pastor's wife than the expectation would have dictated. I had a passion for the Word of God, and I desperately wanted people to understand that God loves them and sent His Son, Jesus, to die on a cross for their sins so they could be saved from eternal destruction. That type of focus and passion was not what you saw in the "normal" pastor's wife; so without intending to be, I became a trailblazer.

Pioneers, by nature, break ground and make it easier for those who come behind. As a pioneering woman speaker, I went through many roadblocks. When I started to speak at churches, many of them wouldn't give me more than five minutes to speak, simply because I was a woman. It was incredibly frustrating at the time; but eventually, I realized that it was still an opportunity. I became proficient at maximizing the use of whatever time they allowed. I didn't know it then, but that skill and discipline of conveying my point in five minutes would be invaluable once

I started to teach the Bible on the radio. When that first happened, I was only allowed five-minute time slots, but my previous experience enabled me to communicate effectively, even in five minutes. I discovered that you could change someone's life in five minutes. This taught me to maximize every opportunity that was given to me. God can use anything, even if it is only five minutes.

I made up my mind that what God said was more important than what anyone else thought.

Whenever you attempt something new or atypical, you become a subject of criticism. I had to remain strong and positive in the face of ever-increasing condemnation and misunderstandings, especially knowing that I was not meeting expectations as a pastor's wife in my own church. I remember facing great contempt from a well-known Welsh evangelist whom our church loved. He remarked, "Of all the pastors' wives I know, you are the biggest failure of all. You are only doing those silly little home Bible studies." His comments were devastating to me at the time. At first, I felt unspiritual because I couldn't fit the mold everyone had for me; but eventually, I realized that I had to follow God's plan for me, not everyone else's plan for me. I made up my mind that what God said was more important than what anyone else thought.

Some of the strongest disapproval came from my extended family, which was very hurtful to me. My favorite aunt had always believed in me and had declared many times that I could do anything I put my mind to; but when she found out that Wally and I were pursuing a life of ministry, she was not pleased. She protested quite adamantly, "Why are you throwing your life away? You are smart. You could have gotten your doctorate, but now look at what you do—these silly little religious things." That specific type of discouraging comment was much harder to overcome because it came from people I loved who were close to me. Fortunately, my mom and dad were not a part of the criticism. They were very supportive and encouraging. Yet, I had to fight hard against the impact of the negative voices. It was a struggle to have ongoing relationships with people who could not see the value in what I was doing.

Faith, Not Gender, is the Focus

Throughout my journey, and whenever things seemed more difficult, I stood in faith on one specific revelation. At the beginning of my ministry, when God first called me, I said to Him, "I am a woman." He said, "I am aware of that. That will never be your problem; it is My problem." But then He added, "Your problem will be your faith." That's the truth! I could only move forward as far as my faith would let me. People would always tell me that I couldn't do ministry because I was a woman, but the question was, "Did God call me?" That settled the issue. It doesn't matter whether you are a man or a woman, if you are looking for excuses and reasons why you can't respond to God's calling on your life, you will find plenty. But if you will believe and step out in faith, you will realize that *". . . with God all things are possible"* (Matthew 19:26).

I also had questions about where I belonged. Having grown up in a time when there were already so many Christian expressions and traditions, especially regarding the position of women in ministry, I wanted to know where I would fit as a female minister. I asked God, "Whose camp am I going to be in? The Pentecostals are not going to accept me, surely the Baptists aren't either." Neither group at that time believed women should speak in church. So, I asked the Lord, "Whose camp am I in?" He answered, "You will never be in a camp. You will be a bridge, and you will go to all of them." That word from God has definitely come true in my life. I have always been a bridge between different factions, denominations, and groups in the body of Christ. It wasn't always the easiest road, but I was on it with God, and the road was supernatural.

To reach their full potential, a person needs to learn to respect and receive from the ministry and giftings of others. One of the things that helped me mature as a preacher was the willingness and humility God gave me to learn from others. Along the way, I was blessed to have various ministers of different capacities and revelations whose lives and teachings were instrumental in developing my faith and helping me foster a better understanding of the Word of God.

Kenneth Hagin, Sr. was one such person who impacted me immensely. As I mentioned earlier, Wally and I attended a meeting Brother Hagin held at a Foursquare church the first year we were married. I was so encouraged by his teaching on how the Word of God can work in your life. It made me think, *If the Word of God can work like that for him, it can also work that way for me.* I followed his teachings for years, in books, tapes, and meetings, and learned so much about the power of the Holy Spirit and how the Word and Spirit work together. I know there are some negative reactions to "faith preachers," but I have always considered myself a woman of faith. I always teach faith because it gets better results than doubt!

Bill Gothard is another person who had a significant impact on my life. He was a Christian teacher whose seminar, *Basic Youth Conflicts*, shed so much light on how to deal with life issues and problems that arise with our children. However, the real lifelong impact that he had on me was in the final session, when he taught about the power of meditating on and memorizing scriptures. I was inspired by the testimony he shared. When he was in elementary school, he was failing academically. However, at the same time, his Sunday school teacher had the class start memorizing scriptures, which in a short time, changed the trajectory of his education and his life. His class started by memorizing short books of the Bible. As Gothard continued to memorize the Bible, he saw his grades get better and better. He was so encouraged by this success that he pursued a life of memorizing and meditating on the Word of God.

Putting Feet to Faith

One simple thing that has been critical to my effectiveness over the years is that when I learned something new, I implemented it into my life. Gothard's discipline was so inspiring that I challenged myself to do it, too. I started with Proverbs, determined to memorize the whole book. It has 31 chapters, but I was not daunted. I also enlisted my children in the process, practicing memorization by reciting verses to them. Over the years, I

As we read, meditate on, and memorize the Word of God, the supernatural kicks in and we are no longer just reading it, it is reading us.

---

have enjoyed memorizing scripture. At this point, I have memorized a total of 27 books of the Bible and 100 psalms. I am currently working on the book of Ephesians. Memorizing scripture became one of the daily, lifelong disciplines that drastically changed my life. I discovered that as we read, meditate on, and memorize the Word of God, the supernatural kicks in and we are no longer just reading it, it is reading us. It reveals to us the things in our hearts that need to be strengthened, changed, or totally eradicated.

Another person who made a difference in my life was not a minister. His name was John Helms, a consultant who helped leaders communicate more effectively. Being an effective communicator is not just about your knowledge base; how you deliver the content is also very important. Early in my career as a teacher, I developed a very distinctive teaching style. I felt that my students needed to learn everything I knew about a subject and I didn't want them to leave my classroom without hearing all of it. I used that same approach when I started in ministry. When I taught a subject, I was very detailed and thorough. The downside to that approach is that I overloaded my audience with too much information. It wasn't the most effective approach. I needed coaching, and God sent me John Helms. Starting in 1975, he mentored me for several years and helped me become a much more effective communicator.

I met John Helms through the CEO of a major company in Colorado, who I had been asked to pray for. When I prayed with him, he was filled with the Holy Spirit. John was in Denver to mentor that company's executives on how to speak effectively. Some of the executives attending my Bible studies knew John Helms and asked me to pray with him. He became Spirit-filled at one of my meetings. Afterward, he said to me, "I could help you if your ego can take it." I was shocked at first, but I wasn't too proud. I was just happy someone wanted to help me. I really wanted people to understand what I was teaching. If they weren't getting it, then I was missing it.

John was a very in-demand communication consultant and helping me required a huge time commitment from him. Amazingly, he was willing to do it *for free*. He came to Denver twice a month for two years to give me intensive training. He was a great friend and very special, but he was so hard on me! He came to one of my meetings and said, "Marilyn, you are so boring!" I was shocked. "Why would you say that?" I asked. "Well, it's as if you take a cup, cram it full of knowledge, then dump it on the people you teach. You need to watch your audience and be more responsive to their reactions." As soon as he said that, I knew he was right. Wally had been telling me the same thing for years. Wally would ask me, "Do you have to tell them everything you know? Can't you save something for next week?"

As he began to coach me, John asked, "What is your goal?" I answered, "My goal is to be really prepared." He replied, "That's not a godly goal." He said, "What you do, Marilyn, is you study and study and study, and then you get up and dump what you have learned on them. They are informed, but they are not inspired. What you want is for people to remember what you are saying. You should never go over four or five points!" I understood what he was saying and slowly started changing my speaking style. It wasn't easy, but I was determined!

Two closely related skills that must be carefully cultivated in our lives are flexibility and the willingness to change. If we are inflexible, we will miss God's best and run the risk of being broken and ineffective.

One time, I went to Boulder to raise money for the ministry. John went with me, and after we returned home, he told me all the things that I had done wrong. Then he said, "If you get anything from that meeting, I will be surprised." Well, the next day they counted the offering, and it was the largest offering I had ever received for the ministry! So, I called John, and said, "Oh John, you were wrong," and told him about the offering. He said, "No, I am not! Think about what you would have received if you were good." He never let me off the hook, and it forced me to learn and grow. I miss him, as he has since passed away, but I still try to put his lessons into practice.

Two closely related skills that must be carefully cultivated in our lives are flexibility and the willingness to change. If we are inflexible, we will miss God's best and run the risk of being broken and ineffective. If you think about it, you will realize that dry, brittle things break easily. We don't want to be that way. We must always be open to new ways to serve the Lord and His people. Even if we are using models and delivery systems that have been successful for years, they may have become unsustainable and ineffective. Change can be difficult; but if we break out of our traditions and submit to the necessary changes, we will be productive and effective in ministry and life.

Five Minutes at a Time

My early ministry started with small home Bible studies that grew and multiplied in number to the point that I was holding 22 Bible studies a week. The home Bible studies were held in multiple cities throughout Colorado: including, Denver, Boulder, Fort Collins, and Greeley. I even had a home Bible study for a while in Cheyenne, Wyoming. Even though they were wonderful, I began to realize that there was a limit to the number of people I could reach with small group Bible studies. People began to talk to me about expanding my reach. They asked, "What if you produced a five-minute radio program that aired once a week? You could reach so many more people with the Gospel." Sometimes God uses other people to speak to us, but we need to pay attention. I heard what they were saying, but it took me months to move forward.

If you want to be successful at anything, you have to be persistent. You must not take "no" for an answer. You must stand your ground.

In the late 1960s, when I first contacted a Christian radio station, they were not willing to even consider allowing me to air on their station. I asked, "Could I purchase five minutes of airtime per week?" I may have imagined it, but I thought I could hear just a little snicker in the reply when they said, "Well, we don't really sell to women." The anti-woman-preacher bias was not just in the church, it had infected almost every aspect of the Christian culture. And it was trying to stop me from getting on the radio. But, I didn't give up easily. In fact, I didn't give up at all. I kept asking, and asking, and asking. At one point I asked, "I know you don't sell to women, but would you let *me*?" Finally, after weeks of persistent asking, they agreed. That was one of my first encounters with the truth that it's not over until you win! I learned that if you want to be successful at anything, you have to be persistent. This is even more true if God is calling you to do things that no one has ever done before. You must not take "no" for an answer. You must stand your ground.

To move forward with new strategies to expand the kingdom of God, there must be faith for financial provision as well as a solid plan to raise money to pay for the work needed to be done. After the radio station finally said, "Yes," my next thought was, *How are we going to meet that budget?* While it had not been the most efficient way to reach multitudes of people, the home Bible studies were very inexpensive; radio airtime was not! First, I went to Wally to see if the church would help pay for it. He said, "No, it's your baby. I am for you, but you have to pay for it." Even though it would have been easier if the church had financed it, I wasn't upset by his response. I knew that he supported me even though it would have been too much of a financial burden for the church to pay for my radio airtime. It was time for me to allow God to stretch my faith again.

Relational Equity

The key to funding the new endeavor lay with my relationship base. I reached out to my home Bible study groups. They really believed in me and were determined to fund the radio program. When I had first started the studies, I did not know that I was developing support for broader outreaches through radio, but that was exactly what happened. The people in the home Bible studies said, "Of course we'll pay for it." It cost $60 per month, a huge sum at that time, but they were faithful to pay that bill every month. Over time, the program grew more and more popular; and eventually, the broadcast increased to 15 minutes every day rather than five minutes per week. God was causing my ministry to grow, and He was challenging me to increase in faith to support that growth. As I think back over the process, I see that there is no way to overemphasize the value of the "little" opportunities God brought to me. I had to step into those opportunities and faithfully pursue them because they would be used by God to take me to the next level on the path He had for me to walk.

I had a very peculiar ministry opportunity in the early 1970s. I had been on radio but had not yet ventured into television. A woman wrote a letter to me and said that she listened to me regularly. Her letter said that she was a Mormon and had received salvation by faith in Jesus Christ. She went on to say, "We have a women's conference coming up in Nauvoo, Illinois. Would you be willing to speak at it?" I was a little perplexed. I had never heard a Mormon say they were saved, so I called her to talk more about the conference. I asked, "If I speak at the conference, what should I teach since I don't know much about *The Pearl of Great Price* or the *Book of Mormon* (the two Mormon holy books)? I only know the Bible." She said it would be fine for me to teach what I knew. So, with a small amount of trepidation, I agreed to be a speaker at the conference.

I arrived in Nauvoo, and quickly discovered that the 200 women at the conference were not very friendly, at least not to me. They wouldn't even sit next to me at the dinner table. They wouldn't pass me food or water unless I directly asked them to do so and even that seemed to make them very uncomfortable. It was like I had some horrible illness they were afraid to catch. Most of the time, they ignored me as much as possible. Obviously, they were not fans of mine! Such cold treatment could have been discouraging, but I was learning that ministry is not always rosy. Not all great doors of ministry will be accompanied with open arms or sweet smiles. I needed to bite the bullet, stay the course, and do what God had called me to do—which was to share the love of Jesus Christ with that group of Mormon women.

When we decide to obey God, we never know where He will take us, and we cannot begin to imagine the wonderful things He will do.

When it was my turn to speak, I greeted them warmly and told them about a free Bible reading plan that we had created and were giving away. That was well-received, and everyone signed up to receive the Bible reading plan. After that, the women became a little friendlier to me. Of course, the Word had changed the atmosphere. I called Wally every night during the conference, because frankly, I didn't know for sure what I was doing there! He encouraged me and helped me stay focused on the mission to preach the Word. Just before the last session of the conference, I asked Wally what topic he thought I should teach. He answered, "Well, it's your last night. They can't throw you out, so have an altar call." He was telling me to give an opportunity, after I taught, for the entire group of Mormon women to receive the love and salvation of Jesus. Wally's counsel was risky, but it was right on. So, I went for it.

Before that night, I had held back some because I had not wanted to overstep any boundaries or offend anyone. However, on the last night, I braced myself and did not hold back. I shared the plan of salvation and told the women how Jesus is the living Word of God. It was one of the most daring things I had ever done at that point in my ministry. I may have been shaking on the inside, but when I boldly asked everyone who wanted to receive Jesus in their heart as their personal Lord and Savior to come forward, all 200 women came to the front of the room. I was so thrilled that God had touched them and that they were responding to His love for them. It was a very fulfilling experience. And Wally had been right; they couldn't throw me out for saying something they didn't believe because I left right after the service. It is true that they never invited me back, but that was okay. After the conference, I heard from several of the women there that night who shared with me about their life-giving relationship with Jesus and the encouragement they were getting from reading the Bible. It was a completely atypical mission field, but I learned that when we decide to obey God, we never know where He will take us, and we cannot begin to imagine the wonderful things He will do.

You are not Television Material

In 1971, I felt like God was pushing me to stretch my faith and expand my media outreach. He had blessed the radio program, which had been very successful, was fully syndicated, and aired each weekday across the entire United States. But in my heart, God was saying that radio was not enough. The logical next step to reach more people with the knowledge of God's love was to go on television. At that time, while it was unheard of for a woman to preach, it was totally inconceivable for a woman to preach on television. The thought of me trying to teach the Bible on television was very shocking to many people; however, I felt strongly about it and made up my mind to explore the possibility.

After a person overcomes the naysayers, they must then overcome their own nerves. Fear is one thing that will cripple you if you let it. I contemplated the idea of being on television for quite a while before I did anything specific. I knew I was the one who had to do something. I needed to trust God and knock on the door of television, but I was afraid. Finally, even though I was apprehensive, I mustered my courage and set up a meeting with the television executives of Channel 9 in Denver, Colorado. When I met with them, I was the only woman in the room, but I pushed forward and proposed a Sunday morning television program called, *Life for Laymen.* I had hoped that by calling it that, I would appeal to a broader audience and the decision-makers at Channel 9 would give me a chance. Their response was rather predictable and consistent with what I had experienced in the past. They were unanimous; unanimously against me! All nine of those men totally agreed that I would fail. They said, "You will never make it. Stick with radio. You are radio material. You are not television material." I appeared unimpressive to them, but God's hand was on me, and that was all that mattered.

That day, even though the meeting had started with a seemingly impossible roadblock, before it was over, God had the last word. He always does. What I did not know was that God had an advocate for me in the meeting who had not spoken up. The events at the end of the meeting became an unforgettable experience for me, one that would again change the path of my life. In the midst of all the back and forth and negativity, one man on the board spoke up and said, "Well, let's try her." The room went silent, but that man must have had a lot of pull with the other men. When he said, "I think she'll pay her bills," the rest of the men reconsidered their previous decisions. They voted in my favor and decided to give me a chance. Because of one man and because God wanted me to do it, I went on Channel 9 and stayed there for eight years. I always paid my bills; and now almost 50 years later, I am still sharing the love of Christ on television!

Within a couple of years, another media opportunity presented itself. It was even more unconventional, but then, there was nothing traditional about me or what God had been doing with me up to that point. Without any positive preconceived ideas, I ventured into the world of educational television. The female director of educational television in Denver had started attending one of my home Bible studies. At the Bible study, she was saved, Spirit-filled, and delivered from an addiction to cigarettes. A few months later, she asked, "Have you ever thought about teaching the Bible on educational television?" I had thought about it, but I had no idea how such a thing could be possible. But with God, nothing is impossible. With her help, the possibility became more of a probability, and then it got exciting!

. . . I knew that it's not over until I win! If God is for me, no one and nothing can be against me; so, I refused to give up.

Together, we went to the president of the Denver Educational Station. He agreed to let us tape two pilot programs to see how such an unorthodox educational format would look. After we submitted the pilot programs, the president called. Full of doubt, he hesitantly said, "I don't think this will work. We won't be moving forward with it." I pushed back by saying, "I think it will work, and I think you should give it a try." I was determined to see this through. We had put time and effort into it, and we knew that the program was well-planned and well-produced. I thought desperately, *We at least deserve a shot.* But, the president of the network was determined to deny us the opportunity. He ended the call with a flat denial that was void of any hope.

I felt totally rejected, but I refused to give up. I believed in myself and in what God had called me to do. At times, the negative attacks or rejections that came against me were personal; they attacked my identity. But at other times, they came against what I did or produced, my product, so to speak. I had to have the courage to stand against both of those types of attacks. After the conversation that day, I realized that the attack wasn't against me personally, it was against what I could do. But by then, I knew that it's not over until I win. If God is for me, no one and nothing can be against me (see Romans 8:31); so, I refused to give up.

Three weeks later, the president of the Denver station called back to say, "Let's try your program for six weeks in the summer." I was thrilled with that answer to prayer! We moved quickly and produced six 30-minute segments about special Bible characters, how God was involved in their lives, and how He could be involved in the lives of the viewers as well. After those aired, the president called me and said, "We have had a better response to your programs than any others we have ever produced." I was overjoyed and shouted, "Hallelujah!" The president of the station gave me a regular Monday evening slot for an ongoing broadcast on educational television. Another amazing thing was that I was paid for those programs. Normally, people must pay the station to have their program aired, but instead, they were paying me. Who could have imagined that God would take the "no" and turn it into such a resounding "yes?"

The broadcast was successful for the station, even popular with the viewers, but not everyone was pleased with it. In fact, to force the network to cancel my program, a group of atheists picketed the station. My first thought was, *God, this is so embarrassing! Why are you allowing it?* God responded by reminding me that my work had to be *"revealed by fire"* (see 1 Corinthians 3:13). Anything that survives the fire will come out as gold. The station refused to cancel us. We had won the first major battle! But the opposition wasn't finished. They took their case to the school board that provided the oversight for the television station.

The board meeting took place on the same night as our midweek service, so our church took the opportunity to spend that time in prayer for a breakthrough, that *"No weapon formed against you* [us] *shall prosper"* (Isaiah 54:17). It was a David and Goliath scenario. The atheists sent their best and most knowledgeable speaker to the meeting, but when the superintendent of schools brought him to the microphone, his speech was so confused that he couldn't even pronounce his own name correctly. The superintendent gave him one more chance, but his speech was still unintelligible. Finally, the superintendent said, "Sir, please sit down, and don't bother us with this case again!" That was a true miracle which enabled us to be on that station for many more years. In all your pursuits, make sure to have the prayers of other believers behind you. Their prayer support will be imperative when you hit roadblocks and opposition.

In 1973, I had another huge media break that only happened because of God. I was 42, and at that time I had been blessed by God with success in several areas. I was about to find out that God had even bigger plans than I could have ever imagined. In those years, Trinity Broadcasting Network (TBN) had what they called "TBN teachers," who were individuals TBN selected to teach on their network. They asked me to be one of their TBN teachers. Once a month, I flew to California to tape my weekly programs. They filmed and aired the program for free, but all the donations that were given because of the program went directly to TBN. I did that for years, and it was a supernatural time of seeing the Word of God work in people's lives to bring salvation, healing, and breakthrough. While the audience response was great, all the benefits were going to TBN. So, I decided to take a big leap of faith. After serving as a TBN teacher for years, I went to TBN's founder, Paul Crouch, and told him that I felt it was time for me to produce my own daily television program and air it on TBN. He said, "That's a lot of work. Are you sure you want to do that?" I had never shied away from hard work. I knew in my heart that God wanted me to move forward with the daily program. I also knew it would be very expensive. When I discussed the situation with Wally, he felt very strongly that he needed to focus on the church and that the church should not take on the financial burden of television airtime. Once again, he told me, "The church isn't going to pay for it." I understood his response. He was 100 percent behind me going on television. He had always supported and pushed me to move forward in my ministry, but he didn't want the church to be responsible for the bills. It was hard at first, but it was Wally's principle. My faith simply had to stretch again, and it did. We began producing and airing a daily Bible teaching program that quickly became a success across the United States.

God's Word has repeatedly proven true in my life. I have seen that His faithfulness never fails. I know I can rely on Him in every situation and every endeavor because He is a faithful, loving, heavenly Father. Throughout the next few years, my television ministry grew exponentially and aired on many other channels in the United States and multiple foreign nations. Now, more than 45 years later, the daily Bible teaching program that I produce with my daughter, Sarah, *Today with Marilyn and Sarah*, has the potential to reach over 2.5 billion people every weekday and is available on Dish Network, DirectTV, Comcast, Daystar, The Word Network, Love World USA Network, GEB America, YouTube, ROKU, Apple TV, Amazon Fire TV, Android TV, and other media outlets. From the very beginning, when I was told to stay on radio because I would never make it on television, until now, my program is available for people to view in almost one-third of the world. The growth that God has caused and the lives He has changed by His Word being taught, is truly mind-boggling.

God is Always a Step Ahead of the Need

Throughout my years in ministry, finances were never easy, and the provision was never automatic. Each time God called me to do new things, I had to stand in faith for open doors and for the money to pay for the outreaches. As I look back, I know that He increased my faith incrementally with each new opportunity to stand in faith and believe for more. It has been a process of allowing God's faithfulness to increase my faith. As He answered one set of prayers, that victory enabled me to believe for the next, greater need to be met. Then, when He met that need, it encouraged me to believe for the next, seemingly more impossible, need to be met. God was gracious to work through a process that increased my faith over a period of time.

As the television program grew in popularity and we expanded into other networks, the airtime costs also grew. At one point, we were $5,000 behind in our payments, and I didn't know where we would get the money to pay our bills. I went to Wally to look for help, hoping the church would be able to support me. He responded, "No, the church can't help. But I will pray with you that God will give you a miracle." Frankly, at that moment I wasn't as interested in his prayers as I was in the financial help I needed, and I wondered, *How is God going to do this?* It was a challenge of my faith. It didn't seem like God was working in my situation or that His help was in any way imminent.

That same day, I was teaching a Bible study at an Episcopal church in Fort Collins, Colorado. At lunchtime, a married couple asked me to eat with them. I was sure that they needed some kind of marriage counseling, but I was so wrong. The woman asked, "Marilyn, how much does it cost to be on the radio?" I thought that she might want to go on radio herself, so I gave her the daily rate. "It costs $15.50 per day." "No, that's not what I want to know. What does it cost to air for one year?" she asked. I said,

"Well, it is $15.50 per day for five days a week, 52 weeks per year." She said, "Well, figure it out, and then let me know."

God is never late, but He can be very last minute!

I was in the process of the miracle and still did not have a clue. I calculated the total and told her that it was over $4,000 per year. She turned to her husband and said, "Honey, write Marilyn a check for $6,000." Oh, my goodness was I slow, but at that point, I got it. They were about ready to help in a big way. I was so grateful and fairly overwhelmed. We had already paid the radio bill, so I asked if I could put it toward the television bills. She agreed, and we were able to catch up on that bill as well! God always met the need, but it wasn't always an easy journey. We had to stretch our faith constantly as God caused the outreach of the ministry to grow.

My first huge budget shortfall came a couple of years later, after the radio ministry had grown into syndication on 488 stations across the United States and we were airing our daily program on television. My faith was still stretching to meet that growth and we were way behind on our bills. The situation looked so bad that my team wondered if we should pull off all the radio stations. I couldn't imagine doing that, but we still needed $70,000. In my mind, it might as well have been $70 million, because both seemed totally impossible to me.

While I was trying to figure out how to resolve my financial woes, I was asked to preach at a church in New York. The pastor asked me to help him raise money for the Teen Challenge ministry they were about to launch. I asked, "How much do you need?" He replied, "$70,000." I thought, *$70,000?! That is exactly what I need! God, how can you ask me to raise that for someone else when I am in desperate need myself?* What seemed like a sour experience at that moment of need, turned into a very sweet memory of God's provision that impacted my philosophy of giving for the rest of my life.

In answer to my whiny question, God immediately reminded me of Daniel 6:16. That scripture describes how Daniel served God faithfully, right up to the point where he was thrown into the lions' den. God asked a question in my heart, "Even when it doesn't make sense, will you obey Me? Will you be faithful in the dark times?" What else could I say? I chose obedience and trusted God to do whatever He wanted to do. That night,

Needs that we have are simply opportunities to sow seeds into other people and their needs. We should never miss those opportunities.

God gave me such tremendous faith and a special anointing to receive that offering for Teen Challenge that the total amount raised surpassed their biggest offering ever! They met their goal. Several days later, after I returned home, $70,000 came in for *Marilyn Hickey Ministries*. To this day, I don't know exactly how or where it came from, but it was a miracle provision from God, and it came right on time. God is never late, but He can be very last minute!

When we have a need, there is the tendency to get caught up in it and lose sight of the needs of people around us, as well as the amazing power of the God we serve. We must learn to see that God is the Lord over every need we have, and we must step up to help meet the needs of others in any way we can. Sometimes God will have us pray for, encourage, or even give money to someone else. We need to obey Him and trust that as we obey Him, he will take care of us. Needs that we have are simply opportunities to sow seeds into other people and their needs. We should never miss those opportunities. When we sow those seeds, we will be amazed at what God does.

Throughout the years, I have discovered that God is always ahead of our need. One summer, our ministry had a serious financial crisis. Our local post office had experienced mail theft that victimized us as well. Over $200,000 had been stolen from us over the course of several months, and we were facing the reality of closing our doors if we didn't have an immediate breakthrough. That was a huge test of our faith. The natural circumstances caused me to tremble, but my faith said that God had an answer. Before I ever shared about the crisis with anyone, a man felt the Holy Spirit impress on him to give us a gift of $50,000! When he called me to tell me about his gift, I was overwhelmed by the goodness of God and could hardly speak. That was the largest one-time gift we had received up to that point in the ministry, and it was the first big chunk of the miracle provision that God brought to us to overcome the shortfall.

Sometimes our faith can be stretched thin, but we must remain persistent, especially in those moments. I remember in 1980 when our young church, Full Gospel Chapel, had a serious financial need. That was probably one of the worst situations we had ever faced as a church. We had moved into a new building but hadn't yet been able to sell the previous building. Since we had to pay for both buildings, we faced a severe financial shortfall. For our new building, if we didn't make the outstanding payment, our cost would increase $120,000! Unfortunately, we couldn't pay it, and the Denver banks weren't lending at that time. Thank God, He doesn't send you into ministry alone. One of our deacons was determined to find an answer. So, he went to 51 banks and was turned down each time. He didn't give up, and at the 52nd bank, he received the loan. You never know how God is going to do things, but if you continue in faith, you will see miracles.

Meeting Oral Roberts

One of the most impactful and formative relationships for me since the early days of my ministry has been my relationship with Oral Roberts and his university, Oral Roberts University (ORU). It has been a very important, long-term relationship. It started years before when my mother received healing from a tumor while watching Oral Roberts on television. After that experience, she became a faithful partner to Oral Roberts. She prayed for him and his ministry and supported him financially. When we do something like that, when we give to others, it is like planting seeds in the ground. Seeds grow up and produce a harvest. If we plant good seeds, we get a good harvest. If we plant negative seeds, we get a negative harvest (see Galatians 6:7). I have reaped a harvest of blessing in my life and ministry because of all the good seeds that my mom sowed into Oral Roberts and his ministry over those years. It matters what parents do and how they invest their time and resources. My mother's giving became a memorial that took me into a deep connection with that institution and its founders, gave me an opportunity to be impacted by them, and allowed me to help them in the process.

When I was first in ministry, I was an admirer of Oral Roberts and his ministry, but I had no personal relationship with him or his family. Interestingly, the relationship began through an ORU student. Sarah's close friend from high school, who was a little older than Sarah and went to ORU, asked me, "Why don't you come to ORU and teach on Sunday night at Campus Church?" I thought that would be a wonderful thing to do because I loved Oral Roberts. Somehow that first speaking engagement at Campus Church came together. I was excited to speak to the students and encourage them in the Word of God. My message was well-received, and they invited me to return later that week to speak at a weekday chapel service, attended by all the students. That time of speaking to the entire ORU student body was wonderful. It opened the door for me to speak regularly at the ORU weekly chapel services. I loved the opportunity to speak to the students, and my messages were always well-received.

Over the next decade, I developed a wonderful relationship with Oral and his wife, Evelyn. Many times, when Evelyn was in Denver, she would come to our church to hear me preach. Oral asked me to speak to the ORU student body multiple times each year. One year, I received a very unexpected letter from ORU. It said that the university wanted to award me an honorary Doctor of Divinity degree. I was amazed! I had earned my bachelor's degree but had never gone back to get my master's degree, let alone work on a doctorate. It was a tremendous honor for me, and I was deeply humbled by the experience. Oral Roberts said that the honorary doctorate had come through a more demanding learning process than an earned doctorate, because the learning experiences had all taken place in "real life." When I went to ORU to receive the honorary doctorate in 1986, Oral gave me a specific word about my ministry. Even though we were in the infant stages, Oral said that God would bless the ministry and use me in international ways. After that specific word, the international call upon my life slowly became more evident.

Oral Roberts was a man with a renewed mind and fresh ideas. That was evident in his philosophy and in the fruit of his ministry. He also pushed beyond conventional practices and norms in the church. Not too long after receiving my honorary doctorate, Oral asked me to be a member of his Board of Regents. Having a woman on the board was uncommon, and I appreciated the honor. By then, Sarah was a student at ORU so being on the board and attending bi-annual board meetings was also a blessing to me. It gave me an opportunity to see Sarah more often. As a woman serving on a predominately male board, I felt I was making progress, not just for myself, but for all women in ministry. But Oral was not done stretching past the traditional limits to challenge the status quo.

After I had been on the board for only one year, Oral came to me with an even more shocking proposal to consider. The chairman of the Board of Regents was resigning, and Oral asked me to take his place. Being part of the board for a year had been a big enough deal, but the idea of leading the board was absolutely unthinkable. All my insecurities were stirred up in my thoughts, *I am a woman with little experience in ministry. How am I going to lead that group of men who are much further along in ministry than I am?* You can guess what my initial response was, "No, I don't think I can do it." My response to Oral sounded like the time when Jeremiah told God all the reasons he would not be able to serve as a prophet (see Jeremiah 1:6).

Oral didn't withdraw his offer; in fact, he pushed even harder, and was very persuasive. Finally, he asked me, "If you were voted in unanimously, would you be willing to lead the board? If that happened, would you think it was God's will?" Knowing that my family's thoughts on this could be a game changer, I pulled the family card out. "First of all, I need to talk to my husband about it. Then, I need to ask Sarah to see if she is comfortable with me becoming Chairman of the Board. But, yes, if my family agrees and I receive unanimous approval, I would serve as the leader of the board." So, I did my homework: Wally agreed that this was God's will. Sarah said, "Yes, go for it, Mom." That took care of the family question. Then it became a proposition for the members of the board to consider. I am sure Oral also did his homework because they voted unanimously for me to lead the board. I honestly had not expected that to happen, but with the overwhelmingly positive acceptance, I knew it had to be God.

With their support, I accepted the chairmanship and eventually served as ORU's Chairman of the Board for over 18 years, the longest term ever served by an ORU Chairman.

I learned a very important lesson on co-leadership as I served ORU. There were many instances, especially in the beginning, when I became frustrated by the decisions that were made because I felt there was a better path. After one meeting, I was sharing my frustration with God, and He spoke to me, "Who is the head of Oral Roberts University?" A little sheepishly, I said, "Oral Roberts." God then asked, "Which part of the body has vision and sight?" "The head," I replied. "Yes," He said. "He is the one with the eyes and ears, and your job is to support his vision. You are the hand not the head, and you are supposed to serve ORU." It seemed so clear and simple when He said it! My frustration melted away as I realized that I didn't have the whole picture.

Partnering with someone to lead can be hard if you don't appreciate the unique roles that everyone plays within the context of leadership. Even though I was leading the board, which was a very important responsibility in the organization, my job was to support Oral, the visionary head of the institution. After this revelation, I was able to serve many years with peace, trusting the vision that was given to the head. Although I am no longer on the board, I am still serving ORU today in other ways. I firmly believe that my friendship with, and mentoring by, Oral Roberts birthed a faith in me to believe for healing and the supernatural. The time I spent on his board changed me, and I am grateful for that change.

Meeting Dr. David Yonggi Cho

In addition to serving on the board of ORU, I had the honor of serving on the board of Dr. David Yonggi Cho's ministry, based in South Korea. Dr. Cho, who is now retired, started the world's largest church in South

Korea, which now has over 800,000 members! Interestingly, in the 1980s, Dr. Cho considered his church small, as he "only" had 200,000 members. His faith and passion for God inspired me to dream and believe for bigger things from God.

I first met Dr. Cho when I had the privilege of being part of a large charismatic conference in Buffalo, New York with my good friend, Tommy Reid. At that time, there was a great charismatic renewal all over the world. Believers from all denominations, including Catholics, Presbyterians, Lutherans, Baptists, and Nazarenes were experiencing the reality of a Spirit-filled life. Thousands of people attended the conference, were saved, Spirit-filled, healed, and transformed. Approximately 5,000 people attended the meetings at night, and over 1,500 came to participate in the

> I have always been very careful to refrain from pursuing opportunities or open doors just for my own sake. I have seriously only wanted doors to open if God was the One opening them. If God opened a door, I was assured of His protection and provision.

daytime sessions. Tommy had invited Dr. Yonggi Cho to that conference because Tommy and his father had previously ministered with Dr. Cho in South Korea.

Dr. Cho was powerful on stage but even more impressive off stage. At the speakers' luncheon, Dr. Cho shared his passion for ministering to the world and taught us how to walk and live in God's vision for our lives. He had such an anointing on his life. He was very gentle but oh, so powerful. I thought, *God, I want to be around this man. He exudes faith.* At that time, Dr. Cho had started an American board for his ministry, and I felt that if I served on his American board, I would have a good opportunity to get to know and learn from him. Tommy Reid was already on the board, so I asked, "Don't you think Dr. Cho needs a woman on the board?" Tommy replied, "Are you thinking about yourself?" I said, "Absolutely!" He said, "I'll ask the men on the board." Unfortunately, all 21 of the other board members said, "No, we don't want a woman."

That is the key—don't give up!

I know that I am very motivated, even pushy at times; however, in all my striving to achieve, I have always been very careful to refrain from pursuing opportunities or open doors just for my own sake. I have seriously only wanted doors to open if God was the One opening them for His purpose. To push a door open by myself, or for my own advancement, would have been foolish. If God opened a door, I was assured of His protection and provision as I walked through that door. If I pushed the door open, I was not guaranteed either of those; I was on my own. But I felt strongly in my heart that I was to push for a strategic relationship with Dr. Cho. Despite that definitively negative answer that Tommy had received from the male-dominated American board, I didn't give up. That is the key—don't give up!

I took the matter before the Lord over and over again. I prayed, "Lord, if Dr. Cho invited me to be on his board, nobody could say, 'No.'" It took six months of consistent prayer, but I finally received a letter from Dr. Cho, inviting me to be on his American board. Praise God! It was a huge opportunity. I felt honored to serve Dr. Cho in that way.

Just being on Dr. Cho's board was fulfilling for me. I attended meetings faithfully but did not say much. I felt that just being around radical people of faith would cause my faith to grow, and it did. I was blessed to be with people who stretched their faith to believe God for amazing things, and I was content to serve Dr. Cho with them; but, after a while, I started to have a desire to speak in Dr. Cho's church in South Korea. Even though I was on his board, it was not one of those situations that I could just push my way into. I had to trust the Lord. As I prayed, hoped, and waited to be asked, the devil whispered in my mind, *"Why would he ask you to speak? He can have anyone in the world speak."* But I didn't give up; I believed that I had favor.

One day, I walked into his board meeting in Florida and Dr. Cho, with a big smile on his face, spoke up, "Oh, Marilyn, I am so glad you are here. I want you to come and speak at my cell leaders' conference." What? I was amazed! It had finally happened. I smiled back, and said, "Of course, I would be delighted," not letting it show that I was really over the moon with joy. Each of his cell conferences had over 20,000 attendees! I was honored, thrilled, excited, and full of joy to have the opportunity to speak at his conference. But that was just the beginning. After I spoke that time, Dr. Cho asked me to be on his international board. Since then, I have spoken at his church many times. I was grateful for the opportunity to teach God's Word to so many people, and I was thrilled and humbled by the opportunities he gave me. But the impact Dr. Cho had on my life far outweighed any influence I had on his church and any blessing I was to them. I was so grateful to be with Dr. Cho multiple times. He inspired me to pray. He lived such a life of prayer that it naturally rubbed off on me. I was privileged to serve him and his church! He was an incredible mentor to me. He will always be one of the greatest men of faith that I have ever known.

My Box of Unbelief

Planning events will test your character and stretch your faith like almost nothing else. No matter how well you plan, there are always circumstances and surprises that arise. When we were planning our first women's conference, I thought that preparing for 2,000 attendees was reasonable. I knew that having that number of women allowed us to have the event in our own church building. I actually thought that our target of 2,000 attendees was high. After all, I reasoned, it was our first women's conference. That was the maximum amount my level of faith could

---

I lived in that box of unbelief, preoccupied with littleness. Great things were knocking on my door, but I wouldn't let them in.

---

envision. As registrations started streaming in, my staff began to talk to me about the possible size of the crowd; they were concerned that the church building couldn't hold all the women who were interested in attending. I thought they were overreacting because I was totally convinced that we wouldn't have more than 2,000 women. I couldn't stretch my faith to anything beyond that number. My faith was maxed out!

For months before the event, I lived in that box of unbelief, preoccupied with littleness. Great things were knocking on my door, but I wouldn't let them in. The day before the conference, my staff explained how serious the situation was. "We have 2,500 women registered, and that doesn't count the people who will register on the first day! Most of those who registered are coming from out-of-town. What are we going to do with the local people who just show up?" At first, I thought, *They registered, but they won't all come.* I was still in denial; but with God's help, patience, and grace, and a great deal of help from my amazing staff,

I slowly began to realize we really might have many more people than we could accommodate.

When reality hit, it was almost too late. I realized how foolish I had been. I also fully understood that we needed divine intervention. I went to God in prayer and humbly asked, "What are You going to do?" He replied, "I know how to take care of crowds. Look at what I did in the wilderness. I fed over one million people with manna, and then blew in quail to feed them with meat. Now, I am going to send the wind of the Holy Spirit and blow in provision for you." Despite my unbelief and in spite of how slow I had been to believe that God could truly bring in more people than I could even imagine, God brought a miracle. In less than 24 hours, He provided a coliseum for us that more than accommodated all the people who attended. When I saw all the people at the conference, God spoke to me again, "I could have brought in 10,000 people, but you were too busy with 2,000!" I repented. I told God I was sorry for not believing He could do more than I could even think or imagine. It was time for my faith to stretch even further.

Our God is not a genie. He does not operate out of a container. He is not limited to the three wishes or ideas we have in our heads. He is the God of the universe, transcending time and eternity, and He is "*. . . immeasurably more than all we ask or imagine*" (Ephesians 3:20, NIV). As you walk with God, exploring the life He has for you, make sure to examine not just your heart but your mindset. Your heart may be truthful like Nathaniel's (see John 1:47), but your mindset may be limiting you. If you can think from a divine perspective rather than a human framework, you will be amazed at the impact your life will have and the legacy you will leave behind.

Chapter 6

PASSION AND PURPOSE

C HILDHOOD PASSIONS ARE OFTEN HONED and sharpened until they become an integral part of one's calling as an adult. My childhood passion was the Word of God, but I had no clue about any calling in my life. When I was 11 years old, I discovered the Bible and became devoted to reading it. I had an insatiable appetite for the truths it held. I often thought, *This is just too good to be true.* It was so exciting to me! Several years later, when I invited Jesus into my heart, the Bible took on a totally new dimension. The words were more personal and relatable because I knew the Author. I was no longer reading limited anecdotes and facts about history; I was consuming a living Book that had the power to change and transform my life.

As passionate as I was about reading and sharing the Word, I did not realize that teaching the Word of God was a personal calling for me.

As I grew in my relationship with the Lord, my hunger for His Word accelerated into a lifelong pursuit. Every morning, I looked forward to reading my Bible and enjoying its content. It invigorated me because it drew me into a closer relationship with God and gave me a deeper understanding of His love for me. When I was filled with the Holy Spirit, my passion for the Word of God went to a whole new dimension. My eyes were opened to the Spirit of the text and a greater understanding of the Truth. The more I read the Bible, the more I became "hooked on the Book." I was also thrilled by the privilege I was given as a pastor's wife to share the Word with others, to get them engaged at a much deeper level. From my earliest days in ministry, I had a great desire to get people into "The Book." My love affair with the Word continues to this day: loving it, reading it, memorizing it, obeying it, teaching it, and spreading it.

As passionate as I was about reading and sharing the Word, I did not realize that teaching the Word of God was a personal calling for me. It had not even occurred to me that I had a calling from God. I often reminded Wally that he was the one "called into ministry," not me. I maintained that position even when my home Bible studies grew into a radio ministry and then expanded into television; but in 1973, everything changed.

True maturity demands that we set aside our fears and ask God and ourselves the hard questions. I was at a point where I needed to ask those questions. I was 42 and incredibly busy with ministry. God had used me to teach His Word to hundreds of people in a variety of places, reaching thousands of people through radio and television, but in my heart, I knew that something was missing.

Desperate for clarity and direction, I took some time off to fast and pray. I cried out to the Lord in prayer, "Lord, I can do a lot of good things and miss Your best. I don't want to miss Your best. I think I have lived under Wally's call. I am a pastor's wife, and I love it, but what is my calling? What do You want me to do?" As I bared my heart to God, I prepared for an extended time of seeking Him, but it only took one day. Within 24 hours, God spoke so clearly to me and said, "I want you to cover the earth with the Word." My heart was totally thrilled. His words to me brought peace and direction. For years I had been fulfilling my purpose, and I did not even know it; that day, I knew the assignment He had for me. I knew my purpose. God gave me two scriptures that confirmed His direction for me. The first was Isaiah 11:9, "*. . . for the earth will be filled with the knowledge of the LORD as the waters cover the sea.*" The second was Proverbs 4:18 (NKJV), "*The path of the righteous is like the morning sun, shining ever brighter till the full light of day.*"

I was overwhelmed, in a good way. That day, over 45 years ago, I knew that I had a personal calling. There was a purpose and plan for my life. It was such a powerful time, and I should have savored the moment, but almost immediately, I thought, *Thanks God, but how do I do that?* I didn't know how to go about "covering the earth" with God's Word! It seemed like a totally overwhelming and completely daunting assignment. In answer to my panicked question, God put peace in my heart that He had a plan. He also showed me that I had already been walking in my calling; I just needed to stay the course and allow Him to expand my vision. Thankfully, God doesn't leave us in confusion. Not only did He give me peace and allow me to see that I had already been walking in my calling, but He also spoke three important keys to my heart. That day, He talked to me about vision, networking, and the "how to" (plan), for accomplishing the call.

The vision comes from God and gives us direction and purpose. In my case, the vision came from the verse that God gave me and His voice inside of me telling me to "cover the earth with His Word."

Building Kingdom Connections

Knowing how to network well has been a huge key in all our domestic and international outreaches. The key is to build and maintain relationships, then work with stakeholders, gatekeepers, and influencers that God causes you to meet. We recognized meetings and appointments that God had set up for us and allowed Him to use those meetings to accomplish His purposes through us. At the same time, we need to make sure that we never see people as a means to an end. We cannot be transactional in our relationships. We must genuinely love, care for, and pray for each person God puts in our path, and then allow God to make what He wants of the relationship. God brings some people into our lives for "reasons," for us to bless them and for them to bless us. He brings other people into our lives for "seasons," where we walk alongside each other for a period of time and help one another fulfill God's calls upon our lives. He also brings a few people into our lives for "lifetimes." These people are the ones that God calls to walk alongside us, pray, and speak wisdom into our lives, for our entire lives. God has blessed me over my years of ministry with "reason," "season," and "lifetime" people for whom I am extremely grateful.

Having confidence in what God has called you to do is often half the battle.

The plan, or the "how to," speaks to the steps needed in executing the vision. The truth is, I don't think people can ever really know exactly how to do everything God calls them to do; it is always a process. It is a dynamic step-by-step learning process that must be walked through with the Holy Spirit. My process started with our church, grew into home Bible studies and evangelism, then went into radio, television, and international healing meetings.

After that special time of hearing from God about His call upon my life, I started moving more intentionally into television. I also started focusing on writing more books and producing more media to get the message of the Gospel out to more people.

In 1973, when God called me to cover the earth with His Word, I did not imagine that He would open such amazing doors and send me to over 137 countries to share His love, healing, and plan of salvation. I knew that there was nothing impossible with God, but to walk out the call He had for me, I needed to grow in my confidence in that calling. Having confidence in what God has called you to do is often half the battle. That is why God introduced me to T.L. and Daisy Osborn.

A couple of months later, while I was still processing the word God gave me about my calling, I was invited to speak at a church in Tulsa, Oklahoma where T.L. and Daisy lived. I had followed the Osborn's ministry for years, but I had never met them, so I decided to be bold. I called their ministry and invited T.L. and Daisy to lunch. I was pleasantly surprised that they graciously agreed to meet me for lunch.

When I walked into the restaurant to meet them, Daisy stood up, and the first thing she said to me was, "Marilyn, God is going to use you to be a world evangelist. You are going to affect leaders of nations." I was overwhelmed, and thought, *That's your call, not mine.* The next thought that came to me was, *Daisy and "crazy" rhyme!* My faith was definitely not as strong as Daisy's. I felt like I was daydreaming. Even though God had spoken to me privately about world outreach, to have the call confirmed by someone I had never met before had a profound effect on me.

The Osborns made a tremendous impact on my ministry. Their anointing absolutely directed my life. As I said earlier, the call of God on our lives is the assignment He has given us. The anointing on our lives is the supernatural gifting or skill set God has given us to accomplish that assignment. Even though I didn't know it at that time, their anointing for healing and evangelism fell on me that day, specifically for reaching the nations of the world. It was T.L. and Daisy who taught me that healing is the "dinner bell" God uses to get to the hearts of people and draw them to you and to God. They shared with me that everyone, including Buddhists, Muslims, Hindus, and even atheists, had health issues; meeting those needs with the power and Word of God enables you to reach their hearts. They taught me that healing is what Jesus did, and therefore, healing is what we must believe God will do through us. The Osborns kept it simple, and I've learned to do the same.

You must find your God-given passion and pursue it.

When a prophetic word from God is spoken, it goes to work to open doors that were once closed. It was after Daisy's prophetic word to me that the door opened for me to become a part of TBN and teach the Word of God across America. I didn't teach internationally right away—that part of Daisy's prophetic word took a little longer to manifest. I was doing a little international travel, but it wasn't to teach or hold meetings; I was simply taking vacations. But they proved to be early reconnaissance missions because they were a part of the process God used to prepare me to reach the world. If we let Him, God uses everything in our lives to serve His purpose and none of our life experiences are wasted.

You must have a passion for the things you pursue, because it is critical for your success. The quest for fame, fortune, or great speaking platforms can carry you for a while, but it is not sustainable over time. You must find your God-given passion and pursue it. No matter how honorable a cause, or how compatible it is with your skills and talents, if you don't have the passion for it, you will burn out quickly, especially in the face of opposition or criticism. Passion will give you discipline and fortitude that will sidestep burnout. Sadly, there is plenty of burn out in world missions. I didn't want to start strong and then burn out without accomplishing God's purpose for my life. Having a passion for the Word was a wonderful thing, but I needed to cultivate a passion for the nations if I was going to minister to the world for the rest of my life.

Passion and Prayer for International Ministry

God has a wonderful way of stirring our hearts and developing our passions to fulfill His calling on our lives. My process began with the very first countries I visited on family vacations. Those trips were just opportunities to refresh and have fun. We went to several countries: including, Mexico, Greece, Italy, and Israel. I especially loved visiting Europe, using my proficiency in various languages, figuring out how to stretch our dollars in foreign currency, and enjoying new and different types of food. Those trips may have been vacations in my mind, but they allowed me to see the needs in different countries. After a few trips, I thought, *You know, there are too many needs over here. I cannot go to countries just to visit.* Seeing the needs of the people was part of what sparked my desire to take the Gospel to other countries.

Passion is stirred by prayer. If you want to develop a passion for something, start praying about it. That process in my life was amplified by Freda Lindsay, co-founder of Christ For the Nations Bible School. I met Freda when I was 47. Freda and her husband, Gordon, had touched millions of lives around the world through their ministry and their school. Before I met her, I had heard that she prayed for every country in the world by name every day. I couldn't imagine how she was able to do that. The idea itself was overwhelming, but it was also exciting. Freda had a passion for the nations, and I wanted that passion.

Shortly after I learned about her prayers over the nations, God gave me the opportunity to meet Freda in person. We both spoke at a convention where we were able to eat breakfast together one morning. It was a defining moment in my life, a time for me to be mentored by an amazing woman of God, and I was not going to waste that opportunity. I asked, "Freda, how can you pray over every nation *every day*?" She replied, "Marilyn, I took a map and memorized the countries by continent. It isn't too hard if you memorize them by continent." She was very serious as she said, "If you don't do this, you won't have an international ministry." Well, I thought that if she could do it, then I could do it, too. I got a map and started memorizing. Africa was the hardest because it had so many countries, and it seemed that the names were always changing.

I accepted the challenge and began to develop the necessary discipline. It took me an hour every day to pray over all the countries; as I prayed, my heart was drawn toward certain countries: Egypt, Morocco, Sudan, Kenya, Pakistan, and other countries in East Africa. I didn't realize it at the time, but all those countries were Islamic, with significant Muslim populations. I also didn't know that God would give me an unquenchable love for the people in the Muslim world which would later blossom into a thriving ministry to Muslims. I was simply being obedient to God in His leading me to pray over the nations of the world; but God was doing something even greater—He was fostering in me a love for the world.

God used Freda to mentor and birth in me a prayer life for the nations, but it was the Holy Spirit Who led me into a particular direction of prayer, which later defined my specific calling. Initially, for about 12 months, I prayed for every nation on every continent. After that, I felt like the Holy Spirit had me target about 40 countries. Those were the nations that God put on my heart. Even now, I always travel with a little map of the world. Sometimes, a country will stand out to me that I haven't prayed for in a while, so I will direct my attention and prayers toward that country. Prayer has caused me to carry the nations of the world inside my heart and has been foundational for my international ministry.

Even though I was called to international ministry in 1973, God has always reminded me that despite the size of any organization, the real ministry is about "the one." It is not about the masses; it is about the individuals. Large crowds are good, but the individual response is what matters. You don't have to be at a big healing meeting to have that. God wants us to focus on sharing His love with the people around us, regardless of where we are. I personally like to talk to people about God's love when I am on airplanes because the people seated next to me are a captive audience! I also like to share His love here at home because every person is important to God.

I have enjoyed some very fruitful ministry in unusual places. For example, God used me to share His love with the people at the salon where I get my nails done. It is owned by a Vietnamese family, and most of the nail technicians are Vietnamese. They are such beautiful people and years ago I asked the Lord, "How can I win these people to You?" He gave me one word, "chocolate." So, I took chocolate. I didn't know it earlier, but the women at that salon loved chocolate. When the three sisters who owned the salon saw me walk in, they would always say, "Oh, here's Marilyn again. She brought us chocolate!"

God wants to use each of us to share His love, truth, hope, healing, and salvation. Don't limit God and don't limit yourself.

After a while, when I felt like the relationship was strong enough, I asked, "I am going to a small group Bible study, would you like to go?" They said, "Yes, we will go with you." They attended the small group, which I thought was a big stretch for them, but then they said, "We have never been in a church. Can we go to church with you?" That surprised and delighted my heart. So, they went to church with me for several weeks in a row. Then God gave me another idea. I started a breakfast Bible club in my home, just for them. Over a period of months, they all ended up getting saved! As it turned out, getting my nails done and taking chocolate to them was just one example of the totally unorthodox but wonderfully successful ways God gave me to share His love. God wants to use each of us to share His love, truth, hope, healing, and salvation. Don't limit God and don't limit yourself.

With God's help, evangelism has become my lifestyle. I don't hesitate to claim people, places, businesses, restaurants, cities, and even nations for God, believing that the people there will know Him and His love. Deuteronomy 11:24 (NIV) says, *"Every place where you set your foot will be yours . . ."* When I walk into a new place, I claim it in prayer for Jesus. Why not? That promise in Deuteronomy was made to us. It is ours!

You may be thinking, evangelism is so easy for Marilyn, but it isn't always that easy for me. It's just like everything else in life. There are ups and downs, wins and losses. Unfortunately, I am not received with open arms every time I share the Gospel. Many times, people want to debate intricacies and argue points of contention, but I choose not to do either of those things. I know that the Gospel brings hope and salvation to those who hear it. Romans 1:16 says that the Gospel is *". . . the power of God that brings salvation to everyone who believes . . ."* (NASB). I prioritize the Gospel of Jesus Christ and push through the resistance and challenges I face when I share it, whether I am in a salon chair or on a platform.

Many years ago, God gave me an answer to give to people who want to know if people of other religions will go to heaven. I was flying home, sitting next to a Colorado rancher, when he asked me what I did. I said, "I teach the Bible all over the world, including Muslim, Hindu, and Buddhist countries." He said, "Well, I was taught growing up that there is only one way to heaven, through Jesus, but now I don't believe that." I thought, *Here we go again—another person who just wants to argue!* But God is so kind and loving. He never takes offense at people's questions. God spoke to my heart at that moment and said, "Don't try to teach the Bible to him, just share your experience." So, I shared my story: as a child I knew God, but didn't have Him in my heart; then, when I received Jesus in my heart, He changed my life.

Apparently, I had touched a very important nerve. This rancher broke down in tears and told me that he had just been diagnosed with cancer. Somehow, he knew that he was supposed to sit next to me. Amazing! Even with all his doubts and questions, God ordered and directed his steps to sit by me on the plane. God is always finding ways to show us how much He loves and cares for us. That rancher received Jesus as his Savior because my testimony touched him. You see, if you tell people your experience, how you received Jesus or were healed, they will listen to you. If you try to tell them the truth from the Bible, they may or may not argue with you, but they cannot argue against your personal experience. Sometimes after I share my experiences with someone, I give them a small business card that I carry with me. I tell them, "The prayer on this card changed my life. May I leave it with you?" The front of the card says, "Heaven is for you." The back of my card has a short prayer which says:

Dear heavenly Father,
I know that You have a plan for my life, because You created me,
and You love me. You created heaven to be my eternal home with

You. Forgive me of all my sins, failures, and my past. I believe the blood of Your Son, Jesus, cleanses me from all my sin. I repent of my sins and invite You, Jesus, to come into my heart and be my personal Savior.

I am always looking for opportunities to share His love because I know that the souls of people are important to God. He doesn't want anyone to die and go to hell, where they would be eternally separated from His love. He wants every single person to know Jesus Christ as their personal Lord and Savior and spend eternity with Him.

An Ambassador for Christ

What if every 11-year-old fell in love with the Bible as I did? And suppose every 16-year-old became passionate about the Scriptures? Imagine a world in which every pastor's wife gets excited about the Word and shares it with her church and neighborhood. How would the world look then? To cover the earth with the Word of God, we must get His Word into every heart. That means getting a Bible into every hand.

If you give people candy, it will make them fat. If you give people flowers, the flowers will wilt. But, if you give people the Word of God, it will change their lives.

I am a firm believer in the power of the written Word. So first and foremost, our priority as a ministry is to give people Bibles. When I began my international outreach, a team of people joined me who believed in the vision to give away Bibles in native languages. Additionally, our goal was to always disciple and develop people to be mature believers in Christ. Therefore, we also took teachings and books in the people's native language, so they would be inspired and changed by the power of the Word of God. I have produced over 1,500 audio messages and have published more than 110 books in over 25 languages. Those resources are missionaries that work 24 hours per day, seven days per week. Those resources minister even when we sleep! If you give people candy, it will make them fat. If you give people flowers, the flowers will wilt. But, if you give people the Word of God, it will change their lives.

World Outreach Begins

Ethiopia was the actual birthplace of our world outreach. In the early 1980s, there was a severe famine in that country. Caused by drought and exacerbated by political instability, the famine was estimated to have claimed the lives of over a million people. I desperately wanted to help, and God challenged me by saying, "Do something major." Then He told me to take 10,000 Bibles, in their native Amharic, and $10,000 worth of food for the children to Ethiopia. That was a huge step of faith for me. I had never done anything like that before, but I was determined to "do something major."

I began to plan the trip and started working on my travel documents. I called the Ministry of Affairs at the Ethiopian embassy in Washington, D.C. to see if I could get visas for myself, a staff assistant, and a videographer to record the trip. He was very positive. "Yes, you will be able to get visas. You can bring Bibles in, and of course, the food will be *very* welcome." However, three days before we were scheduled to fly out, my assistant and videographer had received their visas, but I had not. My staff was in quite a panic, "We have 10,000 Amharic Bibles that can only be used in Ethiopia!" There was a strong temptation to be anxious about it, but God helped me choose peace rather than anxiety and trust Him for the victory.

I sat there amazed, as I realized that God had a solution long before I even knew there was a problem.

I did not know that God had already made the provision, but I was about to see it for myself. As I prayed about the situation, it occurred to me to call an Ethiopian woman who had accepted Christ in our church and served faithfully there. She agreed to meet me in my office. When she arrived, I explained the situation. While we were meeting, she called the Minister of Affairs in D.C., speaking to him in Amharic, laughing and talking for over 15 minutes. When she got off the phone, she said, "You will have your visa tomorrow." Shocked, I said, "How did you get them to issue the visa so quickly?" She replied, "He's an old boyfriend." I sat there amazed, as I realized that God had a solution long before I even knew there was a problem.

The trouble with the visa was just the beginning. When I arrived in Ethiopia, my adventure through customs was a nightmare. Fortunately, God was with me through that, too. As I was trying to clear customs, I was singled out and asked to step into a separate room for questioning. It was an unbelievably nerve-racking situation. The officials were convinced that I was a spy and they set out to prove it, interrogating me for hours. Questions like, "Why are you really here? Who sent you here?" were asked over and over again. When I told them what I was doing, they didn't believe me, and they became louder and more forceful with their questions. The men asking the questions were like bullies trying to get me to go along with something I didn't want to do. They were rude and menacing, and it was easy for me to see how someone could say anything to be released. They confiscated all our video equipment and insisted that there were things I wasn't telling them. I wasn't sure if they were mad about the Amharic Bibles, the video equipment, or the fact that I was a woman! I knew that God had told me to "do something major," but at that point, it seemed like I wouldn't even make it through customs. There was one bright spot in the day. The interpreter the men were using was a female. She was very nice to me. I could tell that she wasn't comfortable with their accusations or approach and that helped me get through those very uncomfortable hours. Later, I found out that she was a Christian.

After several hours of trying to explain my mission and clear my name, there was an abrupt interruption. Suddenly, another man barged into the room, whispered to my interrogator, and called the interpreter to the side. After several minutes of heated discussion between the three of them, they turned to me and told me that they were going to let me into the country with our video equipment as well. It was a miracle. They said, "We are going to send you as our guest with a large group of American congressmen who want to see the drought area." God had done it again. My trip somehow coincided with the trip of a large group of high-ranking U.S. government officials, and that became my ticket into the country.

I was relieved and excited, but I was also shocked at the turn of events and very curious about what had caused the change, so I asked my interpreter what had happened. She responded, "He called you an evil woman and said you were a spy. I said that you were not evil; you just want to feed babies and help our country." He said, "She is probably just some dumb woman. Let her go ahead." Dumb woman! He meant the label as a slap in my face, but I didn't take it as an insult because it gave me access to a closed nation! I don't mind if people think I am stupid or if they underestimate what I might do, as long as I can go into places and do what I am called to do.

The large congressional delegation, my team, and I were flown to the devastated region and then transported by helicopter to one of the villages to see some of the people who were hit the hardest by the disaster. However, the helicopter couldn't hold all of us at once, so we needed to split into groups. At that time, Ethiopia was a communist country and antagonistic toward Christianity, but God gave me amazing favor. The communist officer told my team and me to take the first helicopter trip. "We know you need to video the area. It is about 4:30 in the afternoon, and it looks like rain. If you don't get on this first helicopter, you might not be able to film." He made that decision even though there were other groups waiting and some of those groups included U.S. congressmen who would determine the amount of U.S. aid that would be sent to Ethiopia. It was unexpected and extraordinary favor.

When we boarded the helicopter, the head of the congressional delegation who was already on the helicopter looked at us, extremely irritated. "Why are you on the helicopter?" he asked. I replied, "They told us to board now." He said, "You need to get off. My aides need to come with me. You can take the next flight." We were torn. It would be almost an hour before the helicopter could return for us, but what could we do? So, we stepped off the helicopter. But the Ethiopian official shouted, "What are you doing? Why did you get off after we told you to go?" A little embarrassed, I said, "The head of the U.S. congressional delegation told us to get off." The officials replied, "It's our helicopter. Get back on!"

Boarding yet again, I met the anger of the head of the congressional delegation. "How dare you get back on this helicopter! I told you to get off!" Smiling through gritted teeth, I replied, "The Ethiopian officer told me that it was their helicopter and I should get back on." He exploded, "I don't care whose helicopter it is! I need my aides, so get off!"

It was an example of being between a rock and a hard place, but I had to trust the Lord with it. We stepped off the helicopter once again, and my videographer was near tears, "Marilyn, we will never be able to get the videos we need!" I took hold of his shoulder and said, "Listen, even if we have to tell the sun to stand still, we will get the film we need!"

An hour later, we made it to our destination, but the congressmen and their aides who had gone earlier were visibly upset as they were getting on the helicopter that had just transported us to the site. "What's wrong?" I asked. "It's been raining, and we haven't been able to see anything," one aide complained. Yet, even as he said those words, the clouds dissipated, and the sun started shining! Did God orchestrate the rejection and delay earlier in the day so that we would miss the rain? I didn't know the answer to that question, but I did know that the weather was perfect for us to document and share the plight of the Ethiopian people.

The conditions were dire, that was no exaggeration. I saw the most emaciated, pitiful-looking people, whose skin and hair had both turned gray. They were literally starving. When I saw the devastation for myself, I was moved with great compassion and so grateful that I had been able to take food and Bibles to those suffering people. I was thrilled that we had the Bibles for them because they so desperately needed hope. We quickly distributed the food, but I didn't know how we were going to distribute the Bibles because we had no connections to help with that. We were sitting on 10,000 Bibles and had no way to give them out.

As I wondered about how to distribute the Bibles, we were recommended to an Ethiopian Orthodox priest. He had previously been imprisoned by the communists for 10 years, but upon his release, was determined to gather together the church of Addis Ababa that had been scattered by the communists. When we talked with him and told him our dilemma, he was thrilled to help us. He became our connection for distributing the Bibles; he also became my friend. He encouraged me that God was about to move in a powerful way in Ethiopia. I believed it. Before I left Ethiopia, God spoke to me about having a healing meeting, so I asked the communist officials for permission to hold a meeting. They said, "We don't even believe in God, so why would we allow you to have a healing meeting?" They denied my request, so I had no other option but to leave the country without holding a meeting. But the story wasn't over.

Though they would not approve a healing meeting, the officials approved my request to return with food and Bibles. In 1984, we returned to Ethiopia with another shipment of $10,000 worth of food and 10,000 Amharic Bibles. We distributed the food by helicopter and handed out the Bibles through the same Ethiopian Orthodox priest. We went again in 1985 and in 1987 with more food and Bibles, but the officials still would not let us hold a healing meeting. Ministry is a faith walk that requires persistence and obedience—there's always opposition, even when you are in the perfect will of God. We were not able to hold meetings, but we were still touching lives through the power of the Word and the food we were giving to the people.

In 1994, we began to see a turnaround. Communism was no longer the rule of the land and democracy began to flourish in Ethiopia. Almost a decade after my first trip, I made yet another request to hold a healing meeting. That time, I received a favorable response, but there was a catch. The government told me that if a denomination would sponsor me, I could have a healing meeting. That was more difficult than it seemed, as God had told me to be an independent ministry. As a bridge to different ministry streams and denominations, I had never officially affiliated with any of them.

Even though I didn't have official affiliations, I thought that I could get either the Pentecostals, Charismatics, or Lutherans to sponsor me. On one of my earlier trips, I had befriended a Spirit-filled Lutheran pastor. When I asked him for his help, he said, "We have never had a woman speak in a stadium; it will just never happen. We are not going to sponsor you." By way of encouraging me, he continued, "We like you. We think you are

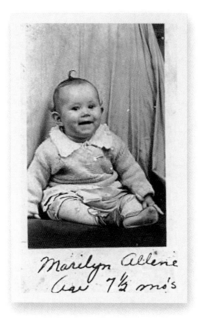

I was born Marilyn Allene Sweitzer
in Dalhart, TX on July 1, 1931.
Here I am at 7 ½ months.

With my mother, father, and brother, David, in 1949.

Wallace Hickey and I were married on December 26, 1954. We were married for over 57 years.

Wally, Michael, and me along with church leaders in front of Full Gospel Chapel in 1967.

Wally, Michael, Sarah, and me in 1968.

Wally and I began our ministry in 1957. Together, we pastored Full Gospel Chapel, Happy Church, and Orchard Road Christian Center.

Recording at a studio for my weekly radio spot, which began in the late 1960s.

Leading the women's Bible studies around the city in 1977.

My mother, Mary Sweitzer, and me in 1976.

Marilyn Hickey Ministries had humble beginnings with much of the behind-the-scenes work done by a small, faithful group that met at our dining room table.

Prayer and the Word are the foundations Wally and I built our marriage and the ministry on.

In 1983, signs advertising the Happy Church could be seen on yellow cabs driving around the city.

Wally, Sarah, and I traveling to the Great Wall of China in 1989.

In 2004, Wally and I stepped down as pastors of Orchard Road Christian Center, appointing our daughter and son-in-law, Sarah and Reece Bowling, as the lead pastors.

Michael Hickey (2009).

The Bowling family:
Reece, Sarah, Isabell,
David, and Benji (2013).

Sarah and I ministering
together on a group tour
in Ethiopia in 2014.

In 1986, I was awarded an honorary Doctor of Divinity from Oral Roberts University.

In my 1987 trip to the Philippines, we provided medical supplies, food, and Bibles, and helped dig wells to supply clean water.

In October of 2000, on a group tour to Bolivia, one of the travelers had a dream of three rainbows in the sky presenting as perfect circles. During the first day of the pastors' and leaders' training, three rainbows forming perfect circles appeared in the sky. The publicity from the rainbows drew many people to the scheduled healing meetings, and thousands were saved and healed.

In 2002, I met with the President of Ethiopia, Girma Wolde-Giorgis.

In 2003, I held one of the largest healing meetings of my ministry in Lahore, Pakistan. Many people were healed and prayed the prayer of salvation. During the healing service, this little girl was healed of diabetes.

In December 2004, I was with survivors of the tsunami in Indonesia. I traveled there to work with Jimmy Oentoro of World Harvest to provide food and personal supplies to the victims of the storm.

Rain could not stop us from bringing the anointed Word of God to those in attendance at a healing meeting in Panama in 2004.

I've always had great favor with international leaders, and in 2005 I sat down with King Abdullah II of Jordan.

In 2005, I met with the future Israeli Prime Minister, Ehud Olmert. He served as Prime Minister of Israel from 2006-2009.

Sarah and I met with the First Lady of Cambodia, Bun Rany, in 2006. During this meeting I was able to present several tons of rice to the First Lady's charitable organizations.

In 2007, I sat down with long-time friend, Oral Roberts, to share great memories and have a time of sweet anointed prayer.

With one of the children in Sderot, Israel, near the Gaza Strip in 2007, who benefited from our ministry of building bomb shelters that children could use on their way home from school.

In 2008, I traveled to Egypt, where I ministered to and prayed with the people living in an area called Garbage City. These people make a living by rummaging through the garbage, looking for items of value that they can sell.

Over the years, I have prayed prayers of healing for millions of people around the world. In a 2008 healing meeting in India, a woman came on stage to testify of her miracle.

It was definitely a memorable trip to Cairo, Egypt in 2008, where I ministered to over 5,000 spiritually hungry leaders. We went to the meeting with the number of lunches we thought we would need (3,500), however many more leaders attended the event. God did a supernatural multiplication of boxed lunches and we gave out over 6,200 boxed lunches. We shared the leftovers with the security guards and police officers at the event, and the children and homeless nearby. Everyone near us benefited from that miracle.

While hosting a group tour to India in 2008, I was given an opportunity to ride an elephant. This was in the town of "Amer," part of Jaipur; one of the many cities that we toured while ministering in the city of Chennai.

At 77 years old, I walked through the barricade and then down the dusty mile-long demilitarized zone to get to Gaza.

Looking at the Dome of the Rock from the Mount of Olives, on my trip to Jerusalem in 2009. Jerusalem has a special place in my heart.

In 2009, I was honored to speak at an inter-faith prayer meeting at the Islamic House of Wisdom in Dearborn, MI. I also had private meetings with the founder, Imam Mohammad Ali Elahi, using the opportunity to build bridges with the Muslim community.

I traveled to Bethlehem at Christmas in 2010 and had some very sweet meetings during this sacred time of the year. While there, I met with the Mayor of Bethlehem, Victor Batarseh.

At the 2012 healing meeting in Karachi, Pakistan, I met a little boy who was blind from birth. After we prayed for his healing, he was able to see for the first time ever.

I was so excited for my first visit to Iran in 2013. I met many wonderful women on the streets. I love these women and their style.

During a group tour to Tibet in 2015, I gave Bibles to the head lama of the region. He was grateful for the opportunity to read the Word in his own language.

On my latest trip to Ethiopia in 2014, I stopped at a small village and spent some precious time with this family.

While prayer walking with my team on a trip to Tibet in 2015, we met this family and spent time visiting with them.

During a trip to Pakistan in 2016, I met with local pastor Anwar Fazal and Grand Imam Azad.

Here I am with J.B. Brown, American Sportscaster and CBS Special Correspondent, and body guards provided by the government on my 2017 trip to Lahore, Pakistan. CBS filmed segments of the trip for the *CBSN On Assignment* program.

I loved being on the set of *Heart for the World* with Marcus and Joni Lamb and others at Daystar in 2017.

In 2016, I spoke at Faith Church in Budapest, Hungary. I had the congregation stand and lay hands on themselves and pray for their own healing. Many people received amazing miracles.

I have a very special relationship with Joseph Prince. I have been invited to speak at his New Creation Church in Singapore many times. Here I am in 2017, speaking to an excited congregation.

After I ministered at a Leadership School and Healing Meeting in Ulaanbaatar, Mongolia, I ventured out into the country and came across some locals who had this camel. We became fast friends.

Sarah and I are privileged to tape our program, *Today with Marilyn and Sarah*, which is a daily television program reaching over 2 billion households. All the programs are taped in our studio at the *Marilyn Hickey Ministries'* headquarters in Colorado.

a real Christian, and we appreciate the Bibles and food you have given to our people, but we are not going to help you." I had expected to hear "no" from the communists, but the continuous negative responses from my brothers in Christ were truly discouraging.

It was rather ironic and sad that for a full three years after I had the approval of the government in Ethiopia to hold a healing meeting, I still did not have a sponsor from the body of Christ in Ethiopia. In 1997, I sent a staff member to Ethiopia to speak with the government and religious leaders yet again. The response was resolute, "Tell her to stop asking! No woman will ever speak in a stadium in Ethiopia. It will never happen." This was the last straw that broke through my persistence. I was convinced that the door was firmly closed.

A few years later, after I had put Ethiopia behind me and had set my eyes on other pursuits, my daughter, Sarah, reawakened in me the dream of having a meeting in Ethiopia. She asked me, "Mom, have you really given up on Ethiopia? Don't you live what you teach?" Ouch! Kids will challenge you to practice what you preach! Her words caused me to realize that I had given up. In the natural, it was understandable and almost excusable. After all, it had been almost 15 years since God had first spoken to me about having a healing meeting in Ethiopia. Who would have blamed me, really? I had given up, but God had not, and He was rebuking me through my daughter. After Sarah spoke to me that day, I repented and told God that I was ready to start again. I began to believe and confess the Word about the situation: I would have a healing meeting in Ethiopia!

It took five more years of standing in faith and confessing the promises of God, but in 2002, we were granted permission to have a healing meeting in Nazret, Ethiopia, which had a population of 150,000 people. God blessed us with outstanding results. More than one-quarter of the people in Nazret attended the healing meetings. A large percentage of the people were Muslims. Many of them were healed and received Jesus. We also held daytime meetings to train and encourage the national pastors and leaders. Many of them were healed and filled with the Holy Spirit during those training meetings. Because the meetings were so well received, and the media coverage was so positive, I was invited to meet with the president of Ethiopia. It was an exciting and humbling experience. We had tea together in his palace. He was an orthodox believer who graciously and sincerely welcomed me to pray for him.

It had taken 19 years from my first trip to Ethiopia until I had been able to hold the healing meeting that God had spoken to my heart. Despite the years, the opposition, and the lack of national sponsorship by a Christian denomination in Ethiopia, God was glorified. In the process, the support of my home Bible studies and ministry partners was invaluable. They provided the funds and the prayer support that made my trips possible. Since that first meeting, I have been back to Ethiopia several times, and Sarah has been there, too. In fact, her vision for the humanitarian organization she leads, *Saving Moses*, was birthed during one of her trips to Ethiopia. If I had given up on the vision God had given me, Sarah's connection to Ethiopia might never have happened. The miracle healing meeting did not come quickly or easily, but it was worth the time, prayers, and faith we invested to make it happen.

I find it interesting that one of the first countries where I ministered was a Muslim country. In the natural, it would have made sense to visit the "easy" countries first, but I didn't ever follow the easy path. In the early 1980s, I was on both radio and television, so I had seen God do "the impossible." After all, during that time, women didn't preach publicly, and they definitely didn't preach on radio and television! So, when I was contacted to film a television program in Egypt that would air live via satellite in 29 cities to raise money for Arabic Bibles for the Egyptians, I didn't stop to consider how a female Christian minister might not be received well in a Muslim country. I saw the need, felt peace in my heart about it, and agreed to do it.

We reached out to the Egyptian government and received approval to air the program out of Cairo via satellite. We were instructed to bring $5,000 in cash to cover the costs of taping and airing the program. That was still very early in my international ministry, and I was very naïve about how to deal with international governments; so, when we arrived in Egypt, I visited the government headquarters, signed their paperwork, and gave them the $5,000.

"... God loves stupid people!" That's a real key for us. Even in our stupid decisions and actions, God's redemptive power is always at work, and we can trust Him to make things right.

My next stop was our hotel to meet with my team. We had flown a technician in from New York to handle the technical side of the television program. The first thing he said when he saw me was, "Don't give the money to the government until after we film the show, otherwise, it will never happen." I said, "But, I have already given it to them." He said, "How could you be so stupid?" I replied, "I don't know." He said, "It won't happen now." I said, "It will happen because God loves stupid people!" That's a real key for us. Even in our stupid decisions and actions, God's redemptive power is always at work, and we can trust Him to make things right.

Naturally, I was half disappointed, half embarrassed, and very worried, but there was no time to beat myself down. I was determined to see the project through, and God reminded me that we had a Christian friend who was serving in the Egyptian parliament. I had just taken him a gift from a mutual friend in the States, so I felt confident enough to call him and ask for his help. His initial response was the same, "How foolish could you be? You will never be able to air your program now!" I explained, "I know that now, but is there anything you can do to help me salvage the situation?" In circumstances like that, you must swallow your pride. I didn't want to tell anyone about my mistake, but if I wanted to fix it, I had no choice.

When the Gospel is on the line, nail your shame to the
Cross, swallow your pride, and reach out for help.

It is a huge blessing when people can see your flaws and still help you recover. This friend knew the widow of the late President Anwar Sadat (who had been assassinated just the previous year). With our friend's help, Mrs. Sadat agreed to meet me at her beautiful mansion on the Nile River. She was a charming and gracious woman who spoke fluent English, as her mother was British. She served me tea but then got right to the point and asked, "Marilyn, why are you here?" I told her about the television program, and she immediately said, "Whatever you do, don't give the money to the government before you film." Sheepishly, I said, "Mrs. Sadat, I've already done that." She gasped in dismay, "Oh no, how could you be so foolish?" I was not surprised by her remark. I said, "Mrs. Sadat, I believe it will happen anyway."

Fortunately, Mrs. Sadat was down but not out. Even though her husband had been a victim of religious fundamentalists, she still wielded great political clout. With one phone call, she cleared the way for us to film our television program, air it via satellite in 29 cities, and raise money for many more Arabic Bibles. I was so relieved and had learned many valuable lessons. Most importantly, I had learned to keep hold of faith even in the face of grievous mistakes, even if those mistakes were terribly embarrassing. There are people who can help you recover. Learn to reach out. Don't try to resolve the situation all by yourself or be afraid that you will be rejected or shamed. When the Gospel is on the line, nail your shame to the Cross, swallow your pride, and reach out for help.

Ministry to Egypt

God used that humiliating experience to plant seeds in my heart for future ministry to Muslim nations. Several years later, another seed was planted. In 1998, Wally and I had planned a vacation to enjoy the history and beauty of Egypt. We had just finished an extremely busy season of ministry, and I was looking forward to a good time of rest and relaxation. As we stretched

---

Preaching the Gospel is important but doing the Gospel is vital.

---

out in our business class seats on the plane, a woman walked by me in a burka, sobbing as she limped down the aisle to first class. My heart reached out to her, and I felt God tell me to go pray for her. *I can't go into first class,* I argued. But the prompting in my heart wouldn't go away.

Finally, I unbuckled my seatbelt and made my way to first class. I tapped the woman on the shoulder and said, "I can see you are in pain. Would you mind if I prayed for you?" She was visibly surprised, but she still replied, "Yes, you can pray for me." I laid my hand on her shoulder, said a quick and quiet prayer, and then made my way back to my seat. I didn't realize it at the time, but small encounters like that were used by God to plant more seeds in my heart for future ministry in the Muslim world. The secret again was to care about people. God continued to teach me that it was always because of and through individuals that ministry was propelled forward. He has helped me to never forget that lesson.

Preaching the Gospel is important but doing the Gospel is vital; this includes loving our neighbors, feeding the hungry, clothing the poor, and visiting those in prison (see Matthew 25:35–40). As a minister, I have always held a holistic approach to missions. From our earliest days in ministry, we provided help for the physical and spiritual needs of the people. Part of our outreach in each country included taking the people food, books, clothing, or whatever else they needed. The specific help we gave them depended upon our local connection in the country and what we were allowed to distribute. We also tried to help pastors and leaders whenever possible. Sometimes we helped them build churches, but every place was different. We tailored our outreach to the specific needs in each country.

Over the years, our healing meetings have often been accompanied by humanitarian aid. God has enabled us to give money, food, and other physical necessities to people in countries across Latin America, Eastern Europe, Asia, and Africa. At one point, we had a ministry called *Fill the Ship*, which took medical supplies, food, and Bibles to developing countries such as Haiti, the Philippines, Ethiopia, Honduras, and El Salvador. We also had the privilege of distributing food in Manila and helping dig wells to supply clean drinking water for families in that area. We helped victims of earthquakes in Mexico; orphans in Romania, Rwanda, and India; leprosy victims in Africa; and street children in Brazil, just to name a few.

The Jungle of Honduras

An interesting opportunity for humanitarian outreach came to us in the early 1990s, when I spoke at a conference in Honduras. I helped a woman who was supplying food to the Contra army, which was fighting against the communist-oriented Sandinista government in Nicaragua. There were battles waging between those two groups in both Honduras and

Nicaragua. The Honduran woman said, "I sell food to the Contra army back in the Honduran jungle. They live in the jungle with their wives and children. The women don't have anything to wear, and the children don't even have diapers. They don't let anyone back there, but you could go in with me as my assistant, give away clothes and diapers, and then share the Gospel."

When I heard that I could share the Word, I was on board. We flew to Tegucigalpa, Honduras and then drove deep into the jungle. I was naïve and had no idea how dangerous it really was to be there. As we drove, I saw one army on one side of the road and another army on the other side. When I asked who they were, my contact said, "On one side are the Contras, and on the other side are the Sandinistas." I replied, "So, we are in the middle? Could they attack us?" She said, "Yes, a van like this was attacked about three weeks ago, and everyone in it was killed." That's when I began to realize just how much danger was all around us. I thought, *And here I am, right in the middle. God help me!*

We must meet people at their point of need. When we do, it
gives God room to move and do His miracle work.

After hours of bumping along dusty roads between two hostile armies, we finally arrived at the camp. We gave away the clothes and diapers and handed out Bibles. Then, I preached and invited people to receive Jesus in their hearts. The response was amazing. Before our time with them, those precious people had nothing to read; but as we left, I saw several people reading their new Bibles. As we drove back to Tegucigalpa, I had great joy in my heart. At that time, a large, Spirit-filled church in Honduras might have had 75-100 people in attendance. However, 12-14 years later, I was invited to be a speaker at a women's conference in San Pedro Sula, Honduras. When I arrived, I asked them, "How many women do you expect?" They replied, "We will probably have 5,000 tonight and about 10,000 tomorrow night when you speak. For the meeting in the stadium, we expect between 15,000 and 20,000 people." You may ask, "What had changed to cause those numbers to be so high?" I believe that the seeds of love and the Word of God that God had allowed me to sow years earlier, had contributed to the revival that Honduras was seeing. We must meet people at their point of need. When we do, it gives God room to move and do His miracle work.

The Open Door to Indonesia

Some of my most memorable times of being used by God to meet immediate needs took place after major natural disasters. One of those was the 2004 tsunami in Indonesia. It was a horrendous disaster that killed over 230,000 people. It was devastating. The loss of life was so high that people had to be buried in common graves with seven layers of bodies in each grave; there just wasn't enough space to give them separate burial plots.

Before that tragedy, Indonesia, the largest Muslim country in the world, would not allow Christians in to minister. After that tragedy, they were desperate. The scale of the need meant that they were ready to accept aid from anyone and everyone. In fact, the first people on the scene to help the Indonesians were Christians. I traveled to that area quickly and worked with Jimmy Oentoro and World Harvest to provide humanitarian aid and medical help.

Experiencing the devastation of the tsunami in Indonesia was heartbreaking. It's hard to even explain. Everything was just gone. It was very surreal and eerie. I remember seeing a huge ship stranded in the middle of a road, like a child's toy that had been tossed out of place. The huge passenger ship had been carried by the water and plopped down in the middle of the road. There was no way to get around it, so it caused an entire road to close. My heart broke as I saw the extreme needs of the people because so many were without food, water, and clothing. Everyone had lost loved ones. Before the disaster, I had prayed for Indonesia for years, but being there at that time put that country closer to my heart than ever before.

I was there to serve. I had no agenda except to help in any way I could. Thankfully, we were able to provide food, personal supplies, and love to people who had been crushed under an unimaginable wave of devastation. God, in His redemptive way, used our acts of kindness and outreach to open that country up to the Gospel in ways we never expected. I believe that because God allowed me to travel to Indonesia and enabled our ministry to give substantially to the people in need, seeds were planted that contributed to a powerful harvest years later. Since the time of the tsunami, I have been allowed to go back to that country many times. I have held healing meetings where people were saved, healed, and delivered. I have been so grateful to be part of God's purpose and plan for Indonesia.

Demonstrating the Love of Christ in Pakistan and the Gaza Strip

In 2005, Pakistan experienced a horrible earthquake. When I heard that more than 80,000 people were killed in that one event, my heart broke for the Pakistani people. We contacted our friends in Karachi and strategized how we could best help. For weeks, entire villages were trapped in rubble, waiting desperately to be rescued. God enabled us to send money for food, water, and bedding supplies, and to support a school that served earthquake victims in a Hindu community.

Pakistan faced another major disaster in 2010 with flooding that impacted more than 20 million people. Many were left homeless and hungry as homes, crops, and infrastructure were destroyed. We sent money to help support those who were suffering. We were also able to translate some of my teaching resources into Urdu to give to the Pakistani people.

Our ministry is unique, and we don't shy away from atypical ways to demonstrate the love of Christ. Several years ago, we were made aware of a serious situation in the Gaza Strip. Missiles were being strategically fired into nearby Israeli communities where they could cause the most devastation. This was done by targeting the time in the afternoon right after school ended. To help with this situation, God enabled us to fund the building of bomb shelters that were placed where the school children could use them on their way home from school. It may seem strange that a ministry would fund bomb shelters, but that is what the people in the area surrounding the Gaza Strip needed. One of our goals has always been to meet people at their point of need, and over the years, God has helped us do that in many different ways.

A critical element in prioritizing the physical needs of the people we reach is to make a tangible difference in their lives. The goal is to solve problems and make their lives better. In doing so, you are revealing the love of Christ. The people were able to feel His love, not just in their hearts, but also in their stomachs, now full of food, and in their bodies, warmed by clothing and healed by the Lord. The love God has for them is experienced in real, personal, and practical ways. Meeting physical, practical needs builds credibility and trust with the people, making them more receptive to the Gospel.

God Gets all the Glory

None of this could have been done without God. I am deeply humbled by the way God has used my team and me to help people around the world. I am also extremely grateful for the ongoing relationships He has given me with people inside those countries. I have been privileged to have friendships with people all over the world, and those people have become very special to me. I am so grateful that God has used the work we do as a powerful bridge for people of all cultures and religious backgrounds.

Being recognized for your work is a good thing if it brings glory to God and not to you. I don't ever seek recognition for my ministry for its own sake. However, I also know that as people see Christians giving to meet physical needs, they will be more open to receiving what we say about their spiritual needs. For that reason alone, I am open to recognition.

Recognition happens in a variety of ways. One time the First Lady of Cambodia expressed her gratitude for my ministry. We had given six tons of rice to Cambodia's poorest people. She considered it to be such an unprecedented act that she felt she had to acknowledge it. In Ethiopia, I was granted a private audience with President Girma Wolde-Giorgis, and Sarah met with the governor of Gondar for them to thank us for our humanitarian efforts in their country. In 2008, Egypt gave me a gift of recognition that typically only presidents and dignitaries receive. In 2015, Oral Roberts University gave me an unexpected award, the prestigious Lifetime Global Achievement award. I was surprised when ORU contacted me in 2015 to tell me they were giving me the award, which goes to individuals or organizations that have made a significant positive impact in the history of ORU and the world.

I am privileged to receive these honors on behalf of my ministry, but ultimately, they all go to the feet of Jesus. Every effort we make must not be for our personal exaltation, but to make Him famous throughout

157

the world. As long as I am able to do so, I will continue to use every breath in my lungs to proclaim His name, and every action in my body to show others His love. My goal is to love people with the same love I have received from my Lord and Savior, Jesus Christ.

Chapter 7

MIRACLES AND THE UNDERGROUND

WHEN I SURRENDERED TO GOD, I had no idea of the marvelous plans He had for my life. I have been blessed beyond my wildest imagination with family, relationships, opportunities, excitement, and adventure that totally surpassed every expectation. I am grateful beyond words that He allowed me to serve Him and that He enabled me to obey that call. I am thankful that He graciously helped me overcome fears, failures, obstacles, and disappointments that could have crippled and stopped me from walking in a full and rewarding life.

When God calls you to do something, it is always crucial that you look to Him and His resources rather than focusing on your limited abilities and glaring deficiencies. If you take your eyes off your inadequacies and focus on God's unconditional love, abundant resources, and vast provisions, you will begin to see the amazing plans He has for your life, and where needed, the team of people He has waiting to help you walk out that plan. He can put together a team of people to help you fulfill the vision while you teach, inspire, and encourage each member of that team. I could have never covered the earth with the Word, operating in my own strength and using my personal resources. However, God blessed me with an outstanding team of people who walked with me, stood in faith, and worked diligently to increase the knowledge of His love throughout the earth and glorify His name. He also knit the hearts of partners and friends to my ministry who loved, supported, and consistently prayed for me. I do not take my team or my partners for granted. I love them, and pray for them every day, asking God to help, encourage, and pour out His blessings upon them.

My Love for China

Of all the countries where I have traveled, one of my favorite nations, without a doubt, is China. I love China and the Chinese people. I became passionate about China early in my ministry, which is why I have traveled there more than any other country.

My passion for China started early in my life. In 1971, when Mao Zedong was ruling China, we were having our normal Sunday night service at The Happy Church when a church intercessor approached me as I stood on the platform (An intercessor is a person with a special gift of praying for other people). Many times, intercessors will be burdened or weighed down in their hearts for particular nations or individuals who specifically need prayer. When she came up to me, she whispered, "I have such a burden for China right now. There are evil people who are killing Christians and persecuting them." Wally was leading worship, so I went quietly up to him and repeated what she had told me. He replied, "Tell her that I want her to share this with the church." I invited her to the pulpit, and she said, "We need to pray for China; people there are killing Christians." We immediately started to pray. While we were praying, two of the gifts of the Holy Spirit described in 1 Corinthians 12 were given to us. First, someone in the congregation had a message in tongues that sounded like Mandarin. Shortly after that, a woman was given the interpretation, and boldly declared, "There is an angel in our midst that will mark those who will sigh and cry over China." As she spoke those words, each of us could literally feel an angel marking us. It was a powerful and life-changing experience.

You may have a skill or a talent that you don't think amounts to much, but in God's hands, it can become the key to the healing and restoration of the nations.

For the next 30 days, we held prayer meetings for China every day. At the end of the 30 days, we knew that China was experiencing a miracle. President Richard Nixon was given an invitation for the U.S. National Table Tennis Team to participate in a tournament in China. It was an unprecedented invitation that marked the beginning of better relations between China and the U.S. and paved the way for President Nixon's official visit in 1972.

We should never underestimate the powerful prayers of God's people. Who would have thought that as people prayed, God would use a sporting event as His weapon of peace and deliverance? Then, of all the possible games, God used ping-pong for diplomacy! He is not only all-powerful, He has a great sense of humor! You may have a skill or a talent that you don't think amounts to much, but in God's hands, it can become the key to the healing and restoration of the nations.

From then on, I could not forget about China. I wanted to find ways to help the underground church there, a seemingly impossible task. For decades the Chinese people did not have access to the Word of God.

Because the Chinese people were not allowed to have Bibles, they were impossible to buy in China. Often, Chinese believers would handwrite a chapter or a book of the Bible and then share those pages with others in their group.

The destitute state of the Chinese church broke my heart; but, in spite of the oppression and persecution, an amazing underground revival had begun in China and literally millions of people were getting saved. Still, there were no Bibles for them to read. The believers were hungry for the Word and lacked the most basic tool to know about God, the Bible. God put a passion in me to help solve that problem. I decided to do something, but my soul was bombarded with questions: *What should we do? How could we help? Where should we start?* Then we had to ask, "If we actually get into China with Bibles, what happens next?" I struggled with those questions for years as I prayed over the situation and sought an opportunity to enter China.

An Open Door to China

In the mid-1980s, God gave me a great breakthrough utilizing a man He sent across my path. By that time, the international relationship between the U.S. and China had improved to some degree, and China was open for business, just not church business. Even though China's constitution allowed limited religious activities in state-sanctioned Protestant and Catholic churches, evangelism was still very tightly controlled and often prohibited. Underground churches mushroomed as Christians searched for freedom of worship, the teaching of the Word, and opportunities to talk with and encourage other believers. At that time, I hosted a meeting in Chicago where I met a man who told me that he was going into China to deliver road equipment. I immediately asked if he knew any way that I could get into China to minister. His response was like music to my ears.

He said, "I can get you in. You will be able to get there and minister in the underground churches." I was so excited! God had begun an amazing work through a supernatural, divine appointment, which is something I have seen Him do over and over again.

That open door to China was an answer to prayers that my staff and I had consistently prayed for more than 10 years. As we discussed the specifics of the mission to China, my Executive Vice President at that time, Mary Smith, said to me, "Why not lead a group tour into China? That way you could take a team of people with you and multiply your effectiveness." It sounded innovative and interesting. We had never tried anything like that before, so I was committed to praying over this possibility. Traveling with a group of people would be very different than going alone or with a small team of my employees. As I prayed, I felt God tell me to move forward with the idea. We continued to pray and began to offer the opportunity for our first "group tour" to our friends and partners on radio, television, and through our mailing list. We called it a "tour," but from the beginning, it was more of an opportunity for our friends and partners to travel with us and minister in other nations.

Launching new programs can be daunting. You have to wonder if people will respond, if all the details will come together, and if the concept of taking people with you will work. But, the response of that first group tour was startling: 150 people signed up to go with us to China! They were willing, able, and fearless enough to smuggle Bibles into China! On our way to China, we stopped in the Philippines to deliver financial support to dig wells in areas that were without clean water. It was with great joy that the group of travelers prayed for and dedicated the wells that were dug for the Philippine people. After we finished with the wells, we continued our journey to China. The plan was for every person to carry one suitcase filled with Bibles along with their personal suitcase. If one person went into China, they could only smuggle in a handful of Bibles, but with our group of 150 people, we were planning on taking in 10,000 Bibles to bless the underground Chinese Christians. We knew it would be risky but none of us fully grasped the extent of the danger we were about to encounter.

We discovered that prayer is more powerful than we could ever imagine, and miracles can become a normal part of our lives.

When we arrived in China, we were shocked and deeply troubled to see that scanners had recently been installed at the airport. That was an unexpected and dangerous development. The customs officials were directing all the passengers to go through a scanner with their luggage. That was a problem because the scanners would reveal the fact that we were taking in thousands of Bibles. If our plan was exposed, there could have been dire consequences. At the very least, the customs officials would have confiscated the Mandarin Bibles and denied us entry into the country. Even as we stood in line, we desperately prayed for God to make a way where there seemed to be no way. As we waited our turn to go through the scanners, everyone tried to stay calm and not show how nervous we were. We prayed under our breath, with as much faith as we could muster.

When it was our group's turn to have our luggage scanned, we approached the scanner with more than a little trepidation. As we did so, an amazing thing happened. The scanner broke just before our first suitcase was put through. There was some confusion, and a small delay before one of the officials decided that we couldn't be allowed to delay the line and that all our suitcases could go through without being scanned. We made it through customs without any issues! Since that time, we have discovered that prayer is more powerful than we could ever imagine, and miracles can become a normal part of our lives. We have now made over 38 trips to China, and God has always protected us. One trip coordinator told me that our ministry had smuggled more Bibles into China than any other group! I am so grateful to God for His faithfulness and His grace in allowing us to bless the Chinese people. I love the people in China. I may be American on the outside, but at times, I think I am more Chinese on the inside. It's always a joy to be reassured that God is faithful to His faithful ones, and He rescues them.

As we encountered various difficulties and challenges on mission trips, we also experienced God's hand at work in miraculous ways. When God shows up and shows off, our faith is strengthened, and we are forever changed. We are ruined for any type of "normal" Christian life because we have seen God move in miraculous ways. That first trip to China gave back to us more than we had given to it. It also had a tremendous impact on the group that traveled with us. Some of the people from that first trip have now traveled with us for years. Others on that trip have since been called into full-time ministry. Leonard Dawkins is one of the people who were greatly impacted by that first trip to China. That trip "hooked him." Since then, he has traveled on every one of our group trips. Each time he signs up to go with us, he orders Bibles and tracts in the native languages so that he can take them into the country and give them away. He has become an integral part of these trips, leading our early morning prayer sessions, and is a great encouragement to my staff and me.

We developed a routine for our group trips to make them very rich and powerful. Every morning our group spends 30 minutes in prayer and then Sarah or I teach for 30 minutes. This is a special training time for the travelers where they learn how to pray for the sick and with people for salvation. The training enables each member of the group to confidently pray for the sick people who come to our evening meetings in each country. The love and passion for the lost that the members of our group took on mission trips literally changed those nations. I have led 59 group trips to more than 75 different countries, and have seen the participants lives changed, too.

After the success of our first trip to China, group tours became an important part of our international mission strategy. We continued to lead group tours to China and smuggled in thousands of Bibles. I also started going into China to speak to underground churches. The person who enabled me to reach the underground church was Dennis Balcombe. Dennis had been a missionary in China for many years. They call him "Mr. China" because he speaks both Mandarin and Cantonese fluently. He truly has the Chinese people and the nation of China at the center of his heart. He lived with the underground church and faced many dangers because of that commitment. One time, he was facing arrest and had to be smuggled out of the area in a casket. His commitment to China is extreme and contagious! During my first meeting at Dennis's church, a man was saved who ended up becoming his son-in-law. In so many ways, Dennis has been like family to me.

God had given me such a heart for the Chinese people, and I was so grateful to Dennis for connecting me to the underground churches, so I could minister to the people there. On one of those trips, I traveled to a city in the Qinghai Province, the largest province geographically. It lies in the central, northwest part of China, bordering Tibet. One team member and I met with an underground Christian in that city and then we drove almost three hours to an isolated farm for a meeting with 150 Chinese church leaders. Each of those leaders had as many as 10,000 people that they ministered to through home cell groups. That meant that God was allowing me to impact over 1 million people through those meetings. I was humbled by that opportunity. I was also impressed and amazed at their dedication. They prayed and testified with a passion I had never seen before. They woke at 4:30 a.m. to pray, listened intensely to my teaching all day, and then prayed again in the evening. Their love for God was overwhelming and infectious.

The opportunity to teach the underground church was thrilling, adventurous, and challenging all at the same time. There were never any Hilton Hotels. I slept where they slept. In the case of that meeting in the Qinghai province, it was at a farm with no heat during a bitterly cold winter. I almost always traveled to China in the winter, as it was easier to bundle up and hide the fact that I wasn't Chinese. That particular time was especially cold, and there were rats in the walls and ceilings of the building where we stayed, but the people were warm and gracious. Every night before we slept, our hosts would come into our rooms to bathe our feet in hot water and give us something with which to brush our teeth. Then they literally rolled us up in a blanket, almost like a hot dog, and put a hot water bottle at our feet to keep us warm all night.

On the Run

The unbelievable cold was not the greatest danger we faced. If one of the Chinese believers had been caught with us, they could have gone to prison, suffered intense beatings, or been killed. So even though we were with them all day, we always stayed separate from them at night, so there was less chance of them being seen with us. On the second day of the meetings, as I was teaching from the book of James, suddenly, the pastor who was traveling with me said, "Get on the floor." I said, "What do you mean, 'Get on the floor?'" He said, "Someone is here! Get on the floor." While I dropped to the floor and made myself as flat and small as possible, the Chinese believers suddenly stood up and sang loudly. They were trying to create a diversion and block anyone from seeing me. After what seemed like an immeasurable amount of time where every minute dragged on forever, the pastor told us that the person was gone. They were gone, but the danger wasn't! We were told that someone had come to the farm suddenly to read the electric meter. That was unusual, and our hosts were very concerned about what had happened. They said, "At midnight we have to move you. We think they know you are here."

It was official—I was on the run. At midnight, our hosts brought a van, snuck us into the back of it, and covered us up with blankets. They drove us almost three miles before we were able to get out of the van. Then we walked almost two miles in the bitter cold to get to a different farm. It was a frightening experience, but God helped me use the time to pray not only for our safety but also for the amazing Chinese leaders who had risked their lives to hear the Word of God. When we arrived at the new farm, our hosts went through the "bedtime ritual" again, bathing our feet, letting us brush our teeth, and wrapping us up like hot dogs. By the next day, all the leaders had walked the distance to the new meeting place to continue our sessions. Although they had walked most of the night, they were fresh and alive with anticipation at being taught the Word of God.

I have so many stories from China, but my favorite ones involve the underground church and the supernatural intervention of the Holy Spirit to keep us from being caught. The danger for us was that we could be detained, questioned, and then deported without any hope of ever being able to minister there again, but my real concern was for the Chinese people who could be jailed or killed. One example of God's supernatural protection was during a trip to the Anhui province on the eastern side of the country. We were meeting with 150 Chinese leaders of the underground church, but to get there, we had to drive six hours to a remote farmhouse. The meeting lasted three days and three nights, and then we had to travel six hours back to the airport. The meetings were amazing as God encouraged and inspired that incredible group of dedicated leaders of the underground church.

During the six-hour return trip, the situation became perilous. We were in a van with three rows of seats. There were several Chinese believers in the van, and I had one staff member with me, Mike, who was the youth pastor at our church. Mike and I were in the very back of the van, wrapped in blankets for the trip. We were exhausted and cold, and trying to sleep. Suddenly, after only a few minutes of traveling, we screeched to a halt. Our driver rolled down his window and talked rapidly to someone for a minute and then that person climbed into the van. As he climbed into his seat, the only one open in the first row of the van, I realized with bubbling panic that the man was a Chinese soldier who was hitchhiking to his next post. During that time period, everyone was required to give rides to soldiers, but the timing was precarious because it would have been extremely dangerous if the Chinese soldier realized that we were from the West. In the next instant he looked directly at Mike, and each of us held our breath. We were only able to breathe when we realized

---

Our "cloak of invisibility," provided by the Holy Spirit, was an absolute miracle that saved us from being deported and saved our hosts from prison.

---

that the man seemed to be looking at Mike but not really seeing him. It was unbelievable. It should have been completely obvious to the soldier that Mike was Caucasian. He was obviously not Chinese, but the soldier seemed completely blinded to us as he settled in to ride in our van.

For the next five hours, we huddled tightly in the blankets and prayed under our breath that the man would remain oblivious to us and that the precious believers in the van would not be caught. About an hour from our destination, the soldier asked the driver to stop the van. Again, we held our breath, but the man got out and started walking down a different road without ever realizing that we were there. Our "cloak of invisibility," provided by the Holy Spirit, was an absolute miracle that saved us from being deported and saved our hosts from prison. As I boarded the plane to go back home, I was exhausted. It had been three long days since I had showered and I looked terrible, but that didn't stop me from rejoicing. Nothing could diminish my gratefulness to God or my passion for China. The 150 leaders who had been taught the Word and encouraged by the Spirit, were individually responsible for thousands of people in each of their churches. Their fire for the things of God, even under the very real threat of prison or death, was inspiring to me. I couldn't wait to return.

As I ministered to the underground churches in China, I heard some of the most unforgettable testimonies of divine intervention, especially from the Christians who had been thrown into prison. A woman who attended one of our leaders' meetings testified about her time in jail. Even though she had just been released after years in prison, her face was glowing. It literally looked like someone was shining a bright flashlight through the back of her head, making her face glow. She described her time in prison with a deep awe of God's power and protection, "My captors tried to use electric rods on me, but they wouldn't work. Somehow the electricity didn't function when they tried to shock me. They then tried to starve me, but I gained weight instead of losing it! They tried to break my bones, but they wouldn't break. Then, I began preaching in the prison, to both the prisoners and the guards. So many prisoners and guards got saved and Spirit-filled. I was originally supposed to be there for two years, but they kept me for an extra six months. They didn't want me to leave because I helped improve the attitudes of the other prisoners." Can you imagine? I met that woman two days after she had been released from prison. What an honor. She also shared that while she was in prison, her husband had received a raise, and her children had flourished. That was unheard of because the normal experience for the family of a prisoner was shame, censure, and loss. What a testimony! Most of the leaders of the underground church ended up in prison for at least two-and-a-half years.

Despite the great persecution, I heard countless stories of people who faced prison, torture, and even death, yet experienced the faithfulness of God in those horrific circumstances. Their willingness to face such hardships to serve God makes our comfortable Christianity a little more uncomfortable to me!

Hearing about the needs of the underground churches fueled our passion for smuggling in more Bibles. We experienced amazing miracles as we took thousands and thousands of Bibles into China over several decades. Even now, although we no longer have to smuggle in Bibles because Chinese believers can get them in China, I look back at those "smuggling trips" as some of the most rewarding and exciting trips I ever experienced. Our lives were truly changed as we visited the underground churches in China and took them the Word of God. I am deeply honored to have been a part of the revival in the underground churches and to have had the opportunity to encourage believers in that nation who were passionately pursuing God.

One time, we had an extremely rare opportunity to hold a healing meeting in the Three-Self Church in Kunming, China. The church was sponsored by the communist government, but the pastor was a Christian. It was almost unbelievable that after years of only being able to speak at underground churches, I was being allowed to speak openly about the saving love and healing power of Jesus Christ. We had taken a group of about 125 travelers with us. For three days we were tourists during the day, sightseeing and taking pictures, then we held healing meetings in the evening. Everything, including our sightseeing tours, was watched closely by members of the communist party. The woman in charge of our group was named Li. She was a beautiful woman in her early 40s who spoke fluent English.

I wanted so badly to reach out to her, so I said, "Li, I would like to have breakfast with you sometime." Curtly, she replied, "I don't want to have breakfast with you." Undeterred, I asked, "How about lunch?" She turned me down again, "I am busy at lunchtime." I asked, "Well, could you come to the service tonight?" She said, "No. I am a communist; I would never go to your service." Everything I tried received a solid "No" from Li. I knew I had hit a brick wall of resistance and I was totally out of ideas of how to bridge that wall. However, the Holy Spirit was still at work.

If you are going to be effective for God, you must believe
in the absolute power of the Gospel to transform lives
and hearts.

The next day, Li completely shocked me when she said to me, "I was at the service last night, and you showed the video from Pakistan." The video she referred to was of a meeting we had held in Pakistan with more than 100,000 people in attendance. She continued, "I just couldn't believe that." And I, on the other hand, was beyond surprised that she had come to the service! Wanting to seize the moment, I responded, "Come back tonight." But, just like the day before, she replied, "No, I am not coming tonight." My courage had been strengthened by her evident interest in our services, so I persisted. "Have breakfast with me in the morning." But she was adamant and almost rude as she said, "No, I don't want to spend time with you." Still hoping, I made another suggestion, "Lunch?" "No, I don't want to be with you," she replied curtly. Her tone gave no indication of her being even the least bit open to me or the Gospel, but I knew God was working on her heart. After all, she had attended one service, and I believed she could attend more.

If you are going to be effective for God, you must believe in the absolute power of the Gospel to transform lives and hearts. On the last night in Kunming, we heard amazing testimonies from people who were saved and healed during the service. Afterward, we were so happy for all that God had done, but we were weary from the intense heat and the hours of ministry. I had just climbed into the van and begun to settle into the cool air conditioning with a chance to rest for a few minutes during the ride to the hotel, when I looked up and saw Li running toward the van. Apparently, she had attended that service after all. The Lord spoke to me at that moment and said, "Get out, and get her now." Instantly, despite my exhaustion, I got out of the van and I said, "Li, would you like to be saved?" She said, "Yes." I said, "Li, let's pray right now; let's do it." Right there beside the van, she prayed with me and asked Jesus to be her Lord and Savior. Eventually, Li became a key leader in that church and saw her family members saved, too. Over the years since that meeting, I have heard from her multiple times, and it always brings joy to my heart to know she is doing so well in her walk with God. He loves everyone. He isn't bothered by their ethnicity, social status, political persuasion, or moral deficiencies. There's no one beyond the reach of His saving grace. Our job is to be persistent in love and prayer as we wait for God to bring them to the knowledge of His love.

Ministering in China changed me. Those trips showed me God's love for people and put His love for them deep in my heart. Additionally, I discovered that God could get His Word into China, which convinced me that He could get it into any country in the world. I am very grateful to the many brave men and women who responded to the need, partnered with us, and even traveled with us on our trips. It was encouraging and powerful to have groups of people going with us. Their help, along with the assistance and support of my family, was imperative. Wally was a huge part of those early trips, and Sarah was involved, too. I loved being able to share my passion for China with Sarah. She helped us smuggle Bibles, and she loved it. She developed a deep love for that country and even learned to speak enough Mandarin to get by without an interpreter when traveling there. Mandarin is a tough language because of all the tonal and picture aspects. But Sarah inherited my love for foreign languages and has a gift for learning them, which helped her in China.

As long as I live, I will keep returning to China. It's been almost 50 years since that first encounter at our Full Gospel Chapel, where God had us pray for people in China. I know that God truly changed my life as a result of the events He started that night in prayer.

The Iron Curtain and Ministry in Hungary

In the years of the Cold War between the Eastern Bloc nations led by the USSR and the Western Nations led by the USA (1947-1991), Christianity was seen by the socialist and communist governments of the East as the source of Western ideology. Therefore, the Bible was considered a threat and was banned in those countries, and Christians were persecuted to varying degrees. However, during that time, there was also a group of brave individuals who kept the flames of the Gospel burning in underground churches. Suppressed and denied the opportunity to freely express their faith, those persecuted Christians were starved for the Word of God. They were forced to survive on minimal fellowship, sparse teaching, and limited access to the Bible or Christian literature. At times, a whole group of believers would pass around a few tattered pages of a Bible or a Christian book for months or years.

The term "Iron Curtain" was used to refer to the ideological and political wall between the East and the West. The Iron Curtain was also an actual physical barrier that made it virtually impossible for people to cross the great divide between the East and West. I've never been one to shy away from a challenge, and as a matter of fact, I have often run straight into very dangerous situations. During the era when the USSR exerted a dangerous influence throughout Eastern Europe, God began to place in my heart the desire to minister behind the Iron Curtain. I was very passionate to obey God, but I knew it wasn't going to be an easy thing to accomplish.

Timing is a key element in obeying God. It is always important to respect His timing and wait patiently for what He has promised and what He has told you to do. In 1989, a man from Florida wrote to ask me, "Would you be willing to do a Jesus Encounter in Hungary, if I could get you in?" The Jesus Encounter is a multi-day teaching where I share the presence of Jesus, and how He can be seen in every book of the Bible. I was thrilled even to contemplate the idea of teaching the Jesus Encounter in Hungary. Of course, at that time, Hungary was still a communist country under the power of the USSR, so I knew it would be very difficult to travel there and teach. I prayed about the opportunity because I didn't want to do something that seemed good but wasn't God's plan. At that time, I hadn't done much traveling and it was extremely important for me to hear God concerning every trip. After praying about it, I felt that God said that I should accept the invitation, so I replied to the man in Florida and told him I was willing to go.

Don't just accept a closed door! If God tells you to do
something, keep knocking until the door opens.

He replied quickly and said that he would need to confirm the plans with a Hungarian pastor who would host the meeting for me. That pastor, of course, was living under communism, and he knew that inviting a Westerner to have a Jesus meeting was a very bold and potentially dangerous proposition. When the pastor prayed about it, he didn't think it would work, and he told my contact, "No, I don't want her." Now that could have been devastating to my heart because it was an outright and complete rejection, but I couldn't ignore the burden God had placed within me. Hungary was resonating in my spirit, so I told my contact, "Tell the pastor to pray again!" My contact in Florida replied, "Well, I'm a little embarrassed to ask him to pray again." I said, "Do it anyway." I was determined not to quit until I got a "Yes!" He asked again, and the pastor prayed again. That time, the pastor had a different response. He said, "Tell her to come." Praise God! I was headed to Hungary.

On my first trip to Budapest, Hungary, we had more than 700 people attend our healing meetings. That was unheard of during that era of communist rule. Budapest was a very cosmopolitan city, with many nationalities living there, so the services were translated into three languages: Hungarian, German, and Romanian. It was a powerful time where we saw people healed and delivered every day. Today, that church has more than 125,000 members, and it is one of the biggest churches in the world. I return to Hungary about every two years, and I always tell people, "Don't just accept a closed door! If God tells you to do something, keep knocking until the door opens."

On that same trip, I found out that their church had been secretly smuggling food across the border to the underground church in Romania. It was very dangerous as they could have been arrested, but it was also exciting because it was meeting the very tangible needs of the people. I practically begged the church leaders to let me go with them. I told them, "I want to be a part of what you are doing." They finally said, "Yes." I could not have been more thrilled.

To reach our destination with the food, we had to drive across Hungary and then into Romania. Because gasoline was drastically limited and rationed, there were very few gas stations along our route. We couldn't refuel on demand. After several hours of driving, we had crossed the border into Romania and driven almost to the town of Arad, when we ran out of gas. The driver wanted to walk into town and try to find gas, but I was scheduled to speak at an underground church. I knew that if he walked away, there would be no way for him to get back in time to get me to that meeting. I asked him if I could try to get someone to stop and help us. Shaking his head, the driver said, "That is not a good idea. It is dark and dangerous. Besides that, the only people that would have gas in their cars are treacherous people involved in the black market. It's not safe!" I desperately persisted, "Please, let me try!" After several minutes of listening to me practically beg for the opportunity, he reluctantly agreed to let me try; so I boldly stepped out of the car. It was dark and quiet. No cars had been on the road with us when we were driving, and not one car had passed us since we ran out of gas, but I had to try. Suddenly a car appeared on the horizon, coming toward us. As the car got closer, I stood in the middle of the road frantically waving my arms and signaling for them to pull over. It felt a little bit like the game of "chicken," and I wasn't sure which one of us would flinch first. Everyone in my car was surprised when the other car began to slow down as it approached me. Then it stopped. The moment was full of tension because we didn't know who the people were, if we were safe or in grave danger. None of the people in that car spoke any English or Hungarian, but they indicated that they were willing to help. Whew, was that a relief! Fortunately, they had a big container of gas in their trunk. With lots of hand signals to make ourselves understood, we paid them $5 in exchange for enough gas to make it to the meeting. With the gas in our tank, we took off down the road. We even made it to the meeting on time. It may have been an oppressive and intimidating time, but I was lit up on the inside of my heart. I saw yet again that God takes care of us even in dark and scary times!

As we drove in the country of Romania, I saw signs everywhere about their head of state, Nicolae Ceausescu. The signs said: "We love Ceausescu," and, "Ceausescu our Hero." In my heart, I knew that the signs did not represent the heart of the Romanian people. I knew that Ceausescu was a very wicked man and a brutal dictator. He often turned off the heat in hospitals to kill the sick, and in orphanages to kill the orphans. He had no respect for life. He was extremely cruel to Christians under his regime. It was April 1989, and as we traveled, God led me to pray. I started praying that God would break the power of Ceausescu off that country. Later that night, when we met with the underground church, prayed, and ministered to them, I felt God drop a word for them into my heart. I prophesied, "Ceausescu is going to die before the end of the year." As soon as I said it, I thought, *What did you just do?* I was horrified. The Bible says that if the words of a prophecy do not come to pass, that person who spoke those words was a false prophet. My words had certainly put me on the hook. If Ceausescu didn't die before the end of the year, I would be labeled a false prophet! But the word had felt so strong in my spirit, I had actually said it before I even thought about it.

God moved in a very sweet way at the meeting that night, and several Romanians received the love and salvation of Jesus. The next day, before we left Romania, we had the privilege of baptizing several of the new Romanian believers. There wasn't any place "normal" to baptize them in water, so we used the bathtub in our hotel room. It was a little unorthodox, but it worked!

When I went back home, I prayed more over the word God had given me about Ceausescu, and I watched the news expectantly as the year progressed. In October, Ceausescu was still in power, and I was getting nervous. However, I knew the situation was in God's hands, so I continued to pray. It wasn't until December that the word came to pass. On December 17, 1989, a political demonstration against the government led to a serious miscalculation by Ceausescu. He had his soldiers open fire on the protesters and the deaths and injuries he caused turned the country openly against him. A coup led to his arrest and execution on Christmas Day of that year. The misery Ceausescu caused his country had risen to heaven, and God had determined that his time in leadership had ended. That was a phenomenal turn of events for the people of Romania and a wonderful example of how the Lord can use a prophetic word to break the chains of bondage that a political leader held over his people.

In my healing meetings, I am often led to pray for the healing of specific illnesses and issues. In one Hungarian church, before I even taught the message, I felt led to pray for people with lung problems. After I prayed, I asked everyone in the group who felt a dramatic difference to come forward. Eight or nine people came up to the front to say that they could breathe much better. It was magnificent to see the Holy Spirit at work. One of the people who received healing that night was the mayor of the town. Earlier in the week, he had been diagnosed with pneumonia, and before prayer, he had been in a great deal of pain. He testified with great excitement, "I have no more pain in my lungs!" Later that night, after the message, he prayed and asked Jesus to be his Lord and Savior. The fact that a high-profile person had been healed and then committed his life to Jesus made a huge impact in that town.

During the next night's service, I felt led to pray for people with growths, tumors, or warts. After I prayed, we heard great testimonies of healing. The next day, when I was at the Budapest airport preparing to leave, something highly unusual took place. A Hungarian couple walked up to me and said that they had been at the meeting the previous night. Then they surprised me. The husband said, "I knew you were going to be at the airport getting ready to leave, so I brought you the growth that fell off of me last night." Then he took out a cloth and unwrapped an ugly mass that had fallen off his body when I prayed the night before. Sometimes it is hard to believe until you see it, but God's miraculous power had defeated that growth and they wanted me to see it. That healing power is available to each of us every day, regardless of where we live or who we are. We must take God at His word and step out in faith to receive all that He has provided for us.

In 1991, the Iron Curtain finally came down. The wall between the East and the West had been broken into pieces, and Germany had united. While many rejoiced at the sweeping changes that spread across those once dark and isolated areas, for us, it was more than that. It was a signal to respond to the urgent cry of God's people. Over the preceding decades, many people had starved for physical food, but there was an equally deep unmet hunger for spiritual food. When the wall came down, we rushed in with Bibles to meet the needs of the spiritually starving people. We knew that the Word of God would change people's lives. For years, the underground church had worked passionately and sacrificially to get people saved, but the church needed Bibles to feed them.

In the early 1990s, we focused our international mission efforts in the former Soviet Union. God gave us creative ideas to enable the Russian Christians to minister with us. We partnered with Pastor Rick Renner, a missionary to Eastern Europe, and took a group tour of 100 people in a boat on the Volga River. Then, we invited 50 Russian pastors and their wives to join us on the boat. We traveled all along the river and stopped twice each day to hold street meetings where we sang worship songs, preached the Word of God, and prayed for the people in the streets. We gave away clothes, glasses, and even seeds to plant. Giving the seeds was illegal, but we were too naïve to realize the mistake we were making. Those were amazing times of ministry with great results and long-term fruit.

Ministering Deliverance in Ukraine

I also had Ukraine on my radar. Right after the Berlin Wall fell, I traveled to Ukraine to see if I could set up a healing meeting in that country. I was hosted by a group of students from ORU who were doing missionary work there. They were scheduled to pick me up at the airport and drive me to the hotel. As we started to drive, they were not very optimistic. They told me that no one would want me at their churches because they didn't believe in women ministers and that after 70 years of communist party rule it was going to be very difficult to put meetings together in that country. That bit of total discouragement, delivered shortly after I finished traveling for over 24 hours, didn't do anything to give me energy. I desperately wanted to get to my hotel, sleep, and recover from the trip.

But, a quick drive to the hotel wasn't on their agenda. As we left the airport, the leader of the group asked me, "Would you mind stopping on the way to the hotel and praying for a demon-possessed girl? We've been doing some street witnessing, and we met this girl and her grandmother. We finally convinced them to watch the *Jesus* film in Russian, which they are just finishing now." I thought, *Demon possessed? I am not feeling spiritual enough for that!* I said, "Could we do it tomorrow?" They replied, "No! We just got her off the streets." I said, "Well, how do you know she is really demon possessed?" "Oh, she is," they replied. Then they shared her story.

Natasha was 16 years old, and had been tormented for years. When she was younger, Natasha's mother had invited Gypsy fortune tellers to tell their fortune, and a curse had been placed on Natasha. From that time on, evil spirits spoke to her and told her repeatedly, "We are going to kill you!" Invisible hands cut obscenities and blasphemies into her arms and caused her to bleed. Natasha had been completely at their mercy and had no idea how to stop their continual torment.

When I heard Natasha's story, I was both moved with compassion and overcome by my inadequacy. I prayed under my breath, "Oh, God, I'm so tired." His response was as fast as it was emphatic, "I'm not." It was one more reminder that the work God had for me was not dependent on my strength, He needed my obedience. So, I told the students that I would go with them to meet with Natasha and her grandmother. When I met Natasha, she was disheveled and unkempt in her appearance. There was torment and fear in her eyes. Neither Natasha nor her grandmother spoke any English, so we used an interpreter. I began to read scriptures about Jesus and His delivering power. After several minutes of reading the Word, we prayed and commanded the demons to leave her in the name of Jesus. Natasha fell on the floor and lay there completely quiet for almost 10 minutes. It was unusual, but it wasn't scary. She no longer looked tormented. Finally, she stood up. The first thing I noticed was her eyes. They looked totally different and her face was relaxed. She no longer looked like she was about to jump out of her skin. As we talked to her through the interpreter, we knew that she was free. Before we left that day, Natasha and her grandmother both gave their hearts to Jesus. We all rejoiced at the change that had begun in their lives.

I had felt about as spiritual as a fly and I was physically and mentally exhausted, but that didn't stop God.

The next day, we worked out the arrangements for the healing meetings, which we were able to host six months later. For those meetings, we traveled to Ukraine with almost 100 friends and partners that were part of our ministry team. When we arrived at the airport, a beautiful girl with a huge bouquet of flowers walked up to me. It was Natasha! Not only had she remained free, but she had also learned one sentence in English:

"I love Jesus." One of the most powerful parts of her testimony could be seen when she showed me her arms; there were no scars from the demonic writings that had been cut into her flesh! God had completely and miraculously taken away those physical scars, just as He had healed the emotional and spiritual scars that were created by the years of torment. I have seen her several times over the years. She is married, has children of her own, and her entire family has given their lives to Jesus. That is one of the most amazing experiences of my entire life. I had felt about as spiritual as a fly and I was physically and mentally exhausted, but that didn't stop God. Natasha's story always reminds me that it is truly not about me; the miraculous is completely dependent on God and His strength.

Smuggling Bibles Into Vietnam

In the early 1990s, we took a group of people with us to smuggle Bibles into Vietnam. Even though it was illegal to take Bibles into that country, our travel agency helped us, and we were able to take in thousands of Bibles. The agency was owned by Freda Lindsay's friend who had an underground Bible school that was actively reaching the people in Vietnam. We couldn't do much overt ministry while we were there, so we focused on prayer walks, where we walked through different areas and prayed for the people and the nation. We were able to meet some underground Christians, and through them, found out that there was a revival going on at the rubber factories.

Rubber is a big industry in Vietnam because there are so many rubber trees in that country. I was asked, "Would you like to go out there and talk to the factory workers?" It would have to be in secret, of course. They had an elaborate plan. "We can take you to a rubber plantation at night. We will travel about three hours outside of Saigon, and then we will get on motorcycles and ride for 30 more minutes into the interior of the plantation." The strategy was for me to do an evening meeting and then sneak away afterward. I thought, *While I am here, I'm going to do it all. When will I have another opportunity like this?*

That night, my adventure into the plantation began. It was about 10:30 p.m. when we started out. It was pitch dark as we drove through the countryside in a van. Three hours later, it was time to get on the motorcycles. You have to remember, I was in my 60s and the plan was for me to ride behind someone else on a motorcycle for 30 minutes over bumpy and dusty paths. I wasn't sure that was the smartest thing I had ever done, but it was too late to back out. I climbed on the back of the motorcycle, wrapped my arms around my driver, and held on for dear life. I prayed fervently as the loud motorcycle revved up and took off. In complete darkness, except for the dim light of our motorcycle headlamps, we rode through a large rubber tree grove, hitting multiple bumps and weaving wildly around the trees on our way to the factory. Thirty minutes later, we finally made it to the plantation.

We arrived at almost 2 a.m., and to the biggest surprise of my life, there were almost 1,000 people sitting on the ground, waiting for us! It was embarrassing and exciting at the same time. Their hunger made all my complaints look puny and the small sacrifices I had made well worth it. Those desperate and hungry people had no pastors; they only had what I could give them. It was pitch dark, and there was only one light and one microphone, both of which were for the interpreter. So, I did what I always did, I gave them everything I could. I shared the Gospel, led them in the prayer of salvation, prayed that they would be healed, and prayed for them to be filled with the Holy Spirit.

We wrapped up the meeting about two-and-a-half hours later. It was close to 4:30 a.m. and my body was exhausted, but my spirit was exhilarated. I climbed on the back of the motorcycle and found the strength to wrap my arms around my driver once again. After 30 minutes, we arrived at our van. Somewhat panicked, our driver said, "We have to get out of here now!" We quickly loaded into the van, and as we drove away, our driver said, "The police showed up looking for a van with an American Christian in it right after you left to go to the factory." He said that the police had asked him where the Christian woman was and he had responded, "She is in the rubber plantation." The police had waited and waited for me to return because they couldn't follow me into the plantation in their car since the terrain was too rough. Minutes before we arrived back at the van, the police had decided to leave briefly to get something to eat. We reached our van while they were gone, which is why the van driver had been so insistent that we move quickly. I loved hearing that the terrain was too difficult for them. I rejoiced that God had allowed me, at over 60 years of age, to make a trip that the police couldn't make! God had definitely worked overtime to ordain our steps and protect us from the plans of the enemy.

After returning to Saigon, we continued our prayer walks and one of our partners ministered to two Buddhists. They got saved, and then he baptized them in a bathtub! The trip's testimonies continued as I sponsored a breakfast meeting with a group of Baptists. Even though they weren't traditionally open to the working of the Holy Spirit, I had the freedom to teach about being filled with the Holy Spirit at that meeting. We had such a huge response! Many of them were filled with the Spirit and spoke in tongues. We were so grateful that God had opened the door, taken us into Vietnam, and used us to share His love, hope, healing, and salvation with those precious people.

Three Rainbows in Bolivia

In October 2000, I took a group of 125 people to Bolivia. Before we left, one of them told me of a very unique dream she had: "I saw three rainbows in perfect circles in the sky. I don't know what it means, but I wanted you to know." I didn't share this conversation with anyone, but I kept it in my heart, wondering what God was saying. I didn't realize it at the time, but that trip would hold many unique experiences. Not only did it bring me into public view, but it also brought me into an open confrontation with a coven of witches.

Our strategy in Bolivia was to do healing meetings and training sessions, as well as distribute literature. We held three nights of healing meetings for everyone, two days of training for the Bolivian ministers, and gave away books and training materials translated into Spanish. While we were there, the president of Bolivia invited me to join a breakfast meeting at which I could speak to key leaders in the government. I didn't know it then, but God had something very special planned for that strategic meeting.

The first day of training, I was teaching approximately 1,000 Bolivian ministers when my staff passed me a note. Apparently, traffic was stopped outside the building as there were three rainbows overhead, each in perfect circles! I told everyone that there was something unusual happening outside, and we should see it for ourselves. We stepped outside and saw the three rainbows: one was very distinct, the second more out of focus, both appearing to be more white, and the third a colored ring, more like a traditional rainbow. We were awed by the sight and were able to capture it on video.

After the training sessions, we returned to our hotel and saw that the three rainbows had followed us and were directly over our hotel. There was also a gathering of witches protesting, ringing bells, and banging pans. Apparently, the president of Bolivia had called a leadership conference of witches, and those witches were upset at our presence and the rainbows that were following us. Their goal was to speak curses over us, but we were not afraid. We simply rebuked Satan and prayed for the witches to be brought to salvation.

The next day, I attended the breakfast meeting the president had arranged, and because of all the publicity surrounding the rainbows, the meeting was full! My message was simple, "What is God saying? He wants to bring revival to La Paz, Bolivia." I utilized the platform God had given me to share a salvation message, telling those high-level leaders about the miraculous power of God. Our evening healing meetings were broadcast to every Spanish-speaking country in the world, and we saw thousands of people saved and healed. Those three rainbows had a very specific purpose: to draw attention to God and what He wanted to do in Bolivia.

Miracle of Multiplication in Cairo

In 2008, we set up a huge training meeting in Cairo for pastors and leaders. We had Bibles and books for them in their language. We had been praying over the training meeting for months and were expecting mighty miracles for each leader who attended; yet, our expectations were too limited. We had not even begun to imagine the mighty miracle that would take place right before our eyes. We knew that we would have leaders from all over Egypt. We had anticipated about 2,000 total leaders to attend the meeting. Then, just days before the event, we learned that registrations had grown to 3,500. That seemed like a big jump in numbers and we were so happy to have the opportunity to pour into that many Egyptian leaders. But, when the day of the event arrived, nearly 5,000 showed up for the meeting! That in and of itself was not a problem. We were extremely happy to have that many people. The only problem was with the number of lunches we had ordered for the meeting. We had only ordered 3,500 boxed lunches from Kentucky Fried Chicken. When lunchtime came, we had 5,000 hungry leaders, many of whom had traveled very long distances to attend the meeting. We knew we didn't have anywhere close to enough food to feed everyone. That's when the miracle happened. Exactly 3,500 boxed lunches had been delivered and counted. Exactly 3,500 lunch tickets had been handed out before the meeting. But even after all the lunch tickets had been collected and 3,500 boxes handed out, there were still boxes of chicken left. Our team kept passing out boxes of chicken until every leader had been fed. Even after all 5,000 leaders had each received a complete KFC boxed lunch, over 1,200 boxes were left sitting on our tables. We were amazed. God had performed a miracle of multiplication right before our eyes. With the "leftovers" we were able to bless security guards, police officers, neighborhood kids, and the homeless. Everyone near us received a part of that miracle—a KFC boxed lunch.

Bibles for Monks in Tibet

In 2015, I traveled to Tibet for the first time. Over 100 people went with me. Tibet is a Chinese territory where the majority of the people practice Tibetan Buddhism. They have very strict laws governing behavior while you are in the country. You are not allowed to talk to anyone about Jesus, to pass out tracts, or do anything that could be considered evangelism. When we entered Tibet, we were threatened with expulsion from the country if we didn't follow their laws. We agreed that all we would do was prayer walk. It was bitterly cold and hard to breathe because of the extremely high elevation, but everywhere we walked, we prayed that Jesus

---

It is easy to get lost in the numbers or the size of meetings, but it is always the individual that matters most to God. He is adding to His kingdom one person at a time.

---

would be revealed to Tibet.

While we were there, we had the most wonderful, Tibetan guide.

One day, he asked me, "Do you know anything about Jesus?" Do I know anything about Jesus?! I said, "Yes!" He replied, "I would like to know about Jesus." I said, "I have four Bibles in Tibetan" (we had smuggled them into the country). He said, "I want the first one." He then went to the head lama in that area and told him that I had three Bibles in the Tibetan language. The head lama invited us to meet with him. We gave him a Bible, and he said he would read it. My guide ended up getting saved, and I will never forget him. It is easy to get lost in the numbers or the size of the meetings, but it is always the individual that matters most to God. He is adding to His kingdom, one person at a time.

Powerful Healings in Africa

I had a powerful meeting in 2015 in Dar Es Salaam, Tanzania, Africa. We were hosted by a church of 8,000 that had a woman pastor. We saw powerful healings and extraordinary moves of God. Their services were very different from ours. Often, they would take an hour just to cast out demons before their services because they were very aware of the influence of the demonic on the people. In that country, you can't be in a hurry. The services always lasted for at least four hours. But the length of the services didn't stop God. We saw growths disappear, bones replaced, and people saved and filled with the Holy Spirit. It was powerful.

Salvation on the Streets of Mongolia

In May 2018, I traveled to Ulaanbaatar, Mongolia for the first time. I took 75 people with me thinking the response within the country would be fairly small; after all, one-fourth of the population is nomadic. What most people didn't understand at the time was that there was a tremendous revival taking place in Mongolia. Even people on the streets walked up to us and asked us how to get saved. The response was overwhelming. We saw growths disappear and crooked backs straighten out. We also saw people whose eyesight had been so poor that they couldn't read, suddenly able to read without aid. I loved that trip because the people were so open to the Gospel. I can't wait to go back!

We're Going to Stand With You

These testimonies are astounding, and they speak directly to the amazing and powerful God we serve. Lives and nations have been changed as God enabled us to cover the earth with His Word, but it is important to remember that all of it was made possible because of the friends and partners who prayed for us and gave financial gifts to make our ministry possible. There's always a cost to hold the training sessions and healing meetings, and sometimes those costs are higher than at other times. Many

Where there is vision, there is always provision. We must
stand in faith, walk in the vision, and take God at His Word.

years ago, we had two very costly meetings that ended up putting our ministry one million dollars in debt. I remember walking into the board meeting to tell them the news. I thought they would say, "Forget it! Let us off your board, now!" Fortunately, they didn't. I have been so blessed with wise, godly men and women on the board who love and support me. And, in one of the most difficult times we ever faced, they replied, "We're going to stand with you. You were able to see so many people saved at those meetings; that's more valuable than money." I was overwhelmed, blessed, and encouraged by their response! God is so faithful. He brought in the finances to cover that debt like He always does. Some of the time, I don't even know exactly how it all comes in, but it does. Where there is vision, there is always provision. We must stand in faith, stay faithful to the vision, and take God at His Word.

Many times, we do not see the whole picture, but we have to trust God anyway. This happened to me one time in Uganda. I was invited to Uganda by some precious Christians to have a healing meeting. They said, "We will pay all the expenses, and we'll give you $1,500." I prayed about it, and felt I should do it. I traveled to Uganda and held several days of meetings. When we got ready to leave, my hosts said, "We don't know how to tell you this, but we only have $1,000." I said, "That's not a problem at all. I will just sow the other $500." You know God; you just can't out-give Him. Two years later, someone from Uganda gave my ministry the biggest financial gift we had ever received to cover the cost of several big healing meetings! I was overwhelmed with the goodness of God, and deeply touched by the amazing woman of faith who sowed that seed into the lives of people around the world. As I thanked God for the generous gift, He reminded me about the $500 seed I had sown in that country just a few years before. You just never know what God is going to do.

It's not easy to go overseas on mission trips. Many countries make it extraordinarily difficult. The hardest places to get visas are China, Iran, and Pakistan. But I find that the places that are the hardest can also be the

---

. . . I wouldn't trade the privilege of sleeping on a concrete slab with the Chinese underground Christians for anything. It isn't a glamorous life, but it is wonderful!

---

most rewarding in terms of the people's response. When I go overseas, the hunger of the people and what they go through for the Gospel is overwhelming. It makes us American Christians look like whiners. I have dear friends who could be killed at any moment because of their stance for the Gospel. If you are going to minister in other nations, you have to be flexible. You will have to eat things you wouldn't normally eat and sleep in places you have no desire to sleep; but, I wouldn't trade the privilege of sleeping on a concrete slab with the Chinese underground Christians for anything. It isn't a glamorous life, but it is wonderful! I pray that God will allow me to keep traveling and covering the earth with His Word until Jesus calls me home.

Chapter 8

I LOVE MUSLIMS,
AND MUSLIMS LOVE ME

WORDS ARE POWERFUL. WHAT WE say over ourselves, others, and our circumstances—what we confess with our mouth over and over again, has a great impact on our lives and the lives of others. This is true even if we speak those words casually. Proverbs 18:21 says, *"Death and life lie in the power of the tongue . . ."* When you open your mouth, you either speak life, or you speak death; that's why I love to confess the promises of God over my life, family, and ministry every day. As I speak His promises, they are life-giving words that set God's purposes and desires for my life in motion.

One confession I started speaking early in my ministry is, "I love Muslims, and Muslims love me." I said this even before I knew many Muslims. That was my belief; and through the years, I have seen it come true. In the Middle East, I have had unusual favor; my biggest meetings have been in Islamic countries. It is nothing but miraculous that a white, Christian, female, Bible teacher has been welcomed into over 20 Muslim countries. I have even had the privilege of speaking in a mosque, something that is forbidden for even Muslim women to do.

When you open your mouth, you either speak life, or you
speak death. What you confess with your mouth over and
over again, has great impact on you and your circumstances.

My ministry to the Islamic world was birthed in prayer. Inspired by the
life of Freda Lindsay, I prayed for all the countries of the world every day
for a whole year. After that year, when God had me focus my prayers on
about 40 nations, many of those were Muslim countries. When I started
praying for those countries, many people said to me, "You can't minister
in Muslim countries. They don't value women and they will never listen to
you." They didn't consider that God is an all-powerful, prayer-answering
God! James 5:16 says that, *". . . The effective, fervent prayer of a righteous
man* [or woman] *avails much."* And it does!

It is amazing and humbling to me, but Muslims do love me. I love Pakistan.
I am even called the "Mom of Pakistan" by many imams! Whenever I visit
Muslim countries or meet Muslims here in America or on a plane, I am
overcome with love. I feel just like a mother does toward her children; I
know it is a spiritual motherhood that I feel for them. Even when I have
been in very treacherous countries, in extremely dangerous situations, I
have never been overcome by fear. I love ministering in countries all over
the world, but I feel a special calling to Muslim nations. I love Muslims!

In 1978, I wondered, as I began to pray for the Islamic world, *Who is
reaching the Muslim people with the love and healing power of Jesus?* God
stirred in me such a desire to be a part of His solution in the Muslim world.

I have such a love for the Muslim world that I am more likely to pay my way to minister in a Muslim country than to be paid to minister in a non-Islamic country. There was another question that I pondered for years: *How do I reach Muslim people?* My interaction with great evangelists like Daisy and T.L. Osborn gave me the answer to this question; it's through God's miraculous healing ministry.

Healing is the "dinner bell" for the Gospel. When God heals people, that healing sparks faith, and then the Gospel can penetrate their hearts.

Healing, the Dinner Bell for the Gospel

The key to reaching Muslims is very basic: simply demonstrate the healing power of Christ. Stand on God's promises of healing, and you will see God do miracles in people's bodies. Health issues are real everywhere in the world, and that makes our God indispensable. From the very beginning, I saw healing as the bread for the children (see Matthew 15:22–28). God taught me that it is the "dinner bell" for the Gospel. When God heals people, it sparks faith, and then the Gospel can penetrate their hearts. Healing reveals the love of Christ to them in a very special way. It translates the Gospel from the pages of the Bible into their lives and homes, making it alive and practical in the present age.

Health issues are not limited to the poor or underprivileged. People in very high stations in life suffer too. God has used our healing meetings to open doors for me to meet many different leaders of nations. When I meet with them, I make it a priority to pray for their personal healing needs, as well as those of their loved ones. Often, that opens their hearts to the Gospel of Jesus Christ. God has given me very strong faith for healing, and at times even the gift of healing mentioned in 1 Corinthians 12:9. God's healing miracles have impacted entire communities, cities, and countries.

People will open their hearts to you if they know that you genuinely care about them, their personal issues, and individual concerns. For me, I discovered early in ministry that if someone truly realizes how much God loves them, they will respond to the Gospel. There is nothing that shows the love of God in a more tangible way than healing because it requires a very personal touch from God and presents a lasting change. When I was pondering how I should present the Gospel in a closed country, God spoke to me that I should share with them the "God Who Heals." He said, "It is not your name that heals the sick; it is My name. You just present My name; I'll do the healing." My ministry to Muslims started early in meetings in Egypt, but it has continued to this day and become more impactful over time. That trip to Egypt was just the beginning of an adventure throughout the Muslim world.

Ministering in Sudan

In the mid-90s, I had a deep desire to minister in Sudan, but I had no contacts there who could help me get into the country and put a meeting together, which was not abnormal for me. Many times, over the years, God has given me the vision before He has given me the provision, the networking, and finances to do what He has called me to do. After a meeting here in the U.S. where I shared my heart for Sudan, one of our partners reached out to me about a Sudanese man who had connections with the government there. Interestingly, he was a backslidden Christian, but he was still willing to help us cut through the government bureaucracy to get into Sudan. God used him mightily to help us. It took quite a bit of time, but the man was able to obtain permission for us to hold a Christian meeting in Khartoum, Sudan's capital city.

Sudan was not a safe country at that time. The civil war between North and South Sudan had devastated the country for years, and the atmosphere of unrest had also fostered a high level of animosity between Muslims and Christians. I was headed into that extremely dangerous environment and thinking of taking Sarah with me. She had already traveled with me multiple times, but because of the increased danger, I wasn't sure if it was a good idea for her to go. Even though she was 29 years old, I still felt the mothering instinct to protect her. As we prayed about and discussed the situation and the possible dangers involved, we felt that she should indeed go with me. The call of God upon our lives compelled us to go. The fact that the country wasn't open to Christians didn't matter. The fact that the situation was unsafe didn't matter. We had to go where God commanded us to go. We knew that as we obeyed God, He would show His faithfulness to us. So, Sarah and I boldly traveled to Sudan, a place with such a high concentration of extremists that it was sometimes referred to as "the place where Satan sits."

In 1997, Sarah, our team, and I arrived in Khartoum, Sudan, to hold a five-night healing meeting. As part of our mission strategy, before the main evening services, we taught and ministered to the Christian leaders in Sudan, as well as those from other countries who had traveled there for our meetings. In addition to equipping them for the work God had called them to, the ministry time also prepared them to pray for and minister to the people who would attend the services at night. Those daytime meetings were held under a canvas tent. At least the leaders were under the canvas tent. Sarah and I were in the direct sun because the platform wasn't covered by the tent. The temperatures were sweltering as the sun was beating directly down on us. It was a labor of love because the heat made us so uncomfortable, but it was definitely worth it.

Before we started speaking to the leaders, one of the local pastors told us about a 12-year-old girl in his church who had three dreams about Jesus and the sun. When we heard about the dreams, we prayed that everything Jesus wanted to be done in the meetings in Sudan would come to pass. One morning, during a short break in one of the leadership sessions Sarah was teaching, the leaders suddenly started talking loudly with a lot of excitement and animation. Sarah asked the translator what was going on and he told her that a person outside the tent had just seen a miraculous sign. He saw what appeared to be the face of Jesus in the sun. When Sarah told me about it, I knew that it was just like the dream the child had seen before we arrived, and that God had something cooking!

On that particular trip, while the daytime sessions with the leaders were successful, we had numerous challenges with the main healing services at night. Buses that were supposed to pick up the attendees didn't show up. Some of the leaders who had committed to help refused, at the last minute, to attend the evening meetings. Many people had a lot of fear about a large Christian meeting drawing the attention of dangerous Muslim extremists, so the attendance at the first healing meeting was very low. I ignored the numbers and preached as though there were thousands of people in the crowd. The Gospel is powerful, and we saw amazing miracles of healing and salvation.

"They are Seeing Jesus in the Sun!"

The next day, I was teaching on several of Jesus's miracles. Right in the middle of my teaching, most of the people stood up and started running around and shouting. Then some of the people who had been running around fell to the ground. I said to one of my staff members, "Go find out what's happening. I have completely lost the attention of the crowd, and they are not listening to me at all." After just a few minutes he came back and said, "Marilyn, look at the sun! They are seeing Jesus in the sun!" Before that moment, I had not looked up at the sun, but I knew something was happening. Some people said the sun pulsed and flashed, and others said they could see a likeness of Jesus in the sky. As we watched, the people were overcome by what they saw as a miracle in the sky.

I didn't want to lose the opportunity that God had given me to glorify His name, so I loudly proclaimed to the people that Jesus loved them and wanted to be their Lord and Savior. When I asked those who wanted to receive Jesus into their hearts to come forward, over 1,000 people rushed to the platform. I was awed and amazed by God's sovereign work.

God often reminded me that it is
His name that heals, not mine!

Over the next several days, more than 15,000 people came to the evening meetings, and we witnessed hundreds of miracles. One woman took a taxi to the meetings because she was in a wheelchair and couldn't walk. During the meeting, God healed her. She left her wheelchair at the meeting and walked home! People came on stretchers or crutches, and then walked out of the meeting healed. Tumors disappeared, the deaf began to hear, and a blind man received his sight. Those miracles were so encouraging to me. Over the years of ministry, God often reminded me of that night and reinforced the truth that God is never too hot or too tired, and that "it is His name that heals, not mine!"

After the final healing meeting, I found myself wondering about the dreams the 12-year-old girl had seen. She saw Jesus in the sun three times, but we had only seen it twice. Somehow, I knew that we were not done in Sudan. Then before we left, we were invited to the palace of President al-Bashir. At first, I thought we were in trouble for something we had done in our meetings, but that wasn't the case. When we arrived at the palace, we were offered tea and told that we were welcome to return to Sudan in the future. Buoyed by the success of the meetings and the favor of the president, we left Sudan planning to return within a year or two. Little did we know, that it would be 10 long years before we would be allowed back into Sudan.

In 2004, I felt an increased urgency in my spirit to go back to Sudan. We had tried off and on for several years but had never been allowed to go back. As we prayed over the timing, we knew that there had been a number of events in that country that would make our meetings difficult, but we didn't know how to give up. Stephen Kiser, our Executive Director of Global Ministries, agreed to spend whatever time it took to meet with ambassadors and political leaders here in the U.S. and Sudan. Meanwhile, we continued to saturate that nation with our prayers. After three years, Stephen connected with a cabinet member of the Sudanese parliament who was a Christian and a childhood friend of President al-Bashir. He said to Stephen, "I remember when Dr. Hickey came here in 1997. I can still remember that people saw Jesus in the sun. We want to have her back; you will have favor with the palace." It had taken years of overcoming setbacks and intense negotiations between my team and the leadership of Sudan to get back into the country, but a miracle breakthrough was on its way.

Finally, in December of 2007, everything was planned, and I traveled to Sudan to hold healing meetings in a large public stadium in that country. We thought that we had successfully navigated all the problems and had the full permission from the government, but we had a few more surprise roadblocks to overcome. About three hours before the first healing meeting was to start, we were told that a local bishop had turned against us and would keep us from being able to hold the meeting. Shocked, we asked our contact at the stadium if that was true. "Yes, it's true. If he doesn't shut us down, it's an act of God!" Sadly, the man who wanted to shut us down was a fellow believer. We felt stuck. With no other choice, we decided to proceed as if the meeting was still being held that night. As it turned out, the favor of God was greater than the opposition. The vice president of Sudan arrived at the stadium and announced that the meeting could be held. We quickly discovered that his authority and God's power had more clout than the bishop and his government connections. The vice president of Sudan attended the meetings every night, which gave us the ability to ignore the demands of those who stood against us.

During the daytime sessions, I prayed and ministered to 4,000 local pastors and leaders to prepare them to minister with me during the evening healing meetings, and to follow up with the Sudanese people in the weeks and months that followed. That first night, 37,000 people attended, and we saw an amazing move of God that resulted in many people being healed, saved, and set free. The second and third nights, the crowd grew to 45,000 and then 54,000 people. By the final night, 65,000 people attended the meeting, and over 10,000 more, who were unable to get into the stadium, stood outside to listen from the street. Thousands of people were touched by the love and power of God that night. Over 20,000 received salvation and many more experienced the miracle healing of God.

On any given day, the security in Khartoum could be critical. Violence often erupted without any warning or provocation. The normal threat of violence multiplied when we added several nights of growing attendance at extremely powerful Christian meetings. However, during our entire stay in Sudan, the Lord was with us. We made it through our time there without any incident of violence. As we arrived back in the U.S. and I looked back on those meetings, I was so grateful for the thousands of lives that were changed and the miracles and healings that God poured out on those precious people. I was thankful that He strengthened us so that fear didn't keep us from ministering to the people in Sudan. Reflecting on God's faithfulness and protection also helped me move forward into other dangerous countries that were desperately in need of the Gospel.

Lasting Effects of Ministry in Sudan

Another amazing thing about those experiences in Sudan is that I still hear about their effects! In October of 2018, I spoke at a church in Grand Rapids, Michigan. After the meeting, a woman came up to me and told me that she had been at the 1997 meeting in Khartoum, Sudan. She vividly remembers the powerful experience when people saw Jesus in the sun. She got saved that day, and her life completely changed. Not long after the meeting, she immigrated to America with her family. Testimonies like hers always help me think about the individuals in those crowds. The meetings in Sudan were attended by the multitudes, but the impact was felt by individuals. It was overwhelming to me that almost 25 years after the meetings, I was able to meet someone who not only shared those powerful miracles with us, but also experienced salvation and a changed life from a meeting we had fought so hard to hold.

A Gift for the King of Jordan

Fascinated by the name, I had always wanted to visit and minister in the country of Jordan. In 2005, I had the opportunity to travel there and meet with some of the leaders of that nation who were in the highest levels of government. A Jordanian businessman, who I had befriended earlier, arranged a special invitation for me to meet the king of Jordan. That was an almost unbelievable opportunity and I did not take it lightly. As I prepared for that high-profile meeting, I wondered about a worthwhile present to give him. After all, you can't walk into a meeting with a king

> He asked me, "What better gift can you give than prayer?" Wow! It was a light-bulb moment for me.

without a gift; but in my heart, I wondered what type of gift a king would appreciate? I picked out the best gift I could think of and headed to Jordan. When I got there, I found out that King Abdullah II would be meeting with Bill Gates right after he met with me. My heart sank. I immediately reasoned in my brain that whatever Bill Gates could give the king would be far better than my gift! But I took a minute to pray over my heart and to commit the situation to the Lord. It felt like such an important issue to me. Then God asked me a question that entirely changed my approach to the situation and gave me great peace. He asked me, "What better gift can you give than prayer?" Wow! It was a light-bulb moment for me.

When I met with King Abdullah II, I said, "Your Majesty, I love to visit Muslim nations like yours and pray for the sick. Do you know what I would like? I would like the first names of your loved ones who are sick and the name of their illnesses so that I can pray for each of your loved ones by name. I believe that as I do that, God will help them." He seemed very touched by my offer to pray for his loved ones, and he didn't hesitate to give me their names and let me know what healing they needed. This seemingly small act of reaching out to the king opened his heart to me. He was so warm and gracious, and I knew that the "gift of prayer" was better than any other gift I could have given to him. From then on, I had the favor of the king.

Before we left Jordan, we were able to hold a healing meeting in a hotel ballroom in Amman. Two thousand people attended that meeting, and God touched many of them with His love. We saw many miracles and many people gave their hearts to Jesus that night. The favor God gave me with King Abdullah II softened the hearts of people who previously would have been closed to the Gospel. It allowed me to tell them about God's love and see Him change their lives forever.

Meetings in Bahrain, Turkey, and Dubai

A year later, in 2006, we held healing meetings in Bahrain. Once again, I taught leaders during the daytime training sessions and held larger meetings at night. Most of the people who attended the three-day conference were Sri Lankans and Ethiopians. That was surprising to me, but I learned that even though they worked in Saudi Arabia, they lived in Bahrain because the Saudis didn't want the immigrants working in Saudi Arabia to live there. This created a unique socioeconomic dynamic in Bahrain. God is so economical. He never wastes anything we do for Him. Now, after more than 10 years, I still have connections in Saudi Arabia because of the meetings I held in Bahrain. I believe that God will have me minister in Saudi Arabia within the next several years and I am rejoicing ahead of time because I know that God has very interesting ways to get me into difficult places.

Turkey is another one of the Islamic countries that I pray for every day. In 2011, I held a healing meeting in Istanbul, one of the largest and most historical cities in that country. The meeting was in a local hotel, and many Muslims attended. We saw powerful miracles where people were dramatically healed and then accepted the love and saving power of Jesus into their lives. It wasn't a large meeting in terms of numbers, but we had amazing spiritual results.

One of the current popular cities in the Middle East is Dubai, which has more people than any other city in the United Arab Emirates. I sometimes feel that it is over-glorified in the news. To me, it is mostly sand, tall buildings, and shopping centers; but there are also a lot of people from a variety of places, and God loves each of them dearly. In 2000, I took a team with me to Dubai for a healing meeting, hosted by an Anglican church. The Anglicans were the ones who originally took the Gospel to Africa and the Middle East, so I was very excited to work with them. We aired the meeting on closed-circuit televisions throughout the three floors of that Anglican church. After the message, when we were ready to pray for people, we asked everyone who wanted healing to move to the courtyard of the building, so we could lay hands on them and pray for them to be healed. It was powerful and refreshing.

In 2018, we returned to Dubai where we were hosted by a Pakistani church located in a highly populated area. We had many people from different nations who attended the meetings, some even traveling from Pakistan. I preached the first night, and Sarah preached the second night. The people were very open to the Gospel, and they didn't seem to be under any negative pressure from the government. The meetings were wonderful because the people were so open and receptive to the Gospel. The Pakistani pastor who hosted us had previously pastored in Saudi Arabia where the environment had been very different, and Christian meetings had to be held in secret. When I asked the pastor about doing a meeting in Saudi Arabia in the future, he told me that it would be possible to hold secret meetings there, but to hold open meetings would not be safe. Nonetheless, I believe that God wants me to hold open meetings in that country. I am currently working with an imam in Pakistan who has friends who are imams in Saudi Arabia. Once again, it will be exciting to watch and see what God will do!

Meeting with International Leaders
on the Gaza Strip

A trip into the Gaza Strip had been on my heart for years. It is a region that is almost always in the news because of the conflicts between the Israelis and the Palestinians. I wanted very much to visit there to see how I could help the people in that area and tell them about the love of Jesus. I knew that God had given me an important opportunity to get into that area and I needed to walk through that open door.

In 2009, I traveled to Israel, then made my way to the checkpoint that would allow me to enter the Gaza Strip. I was accompanied by Stephen Kiser and Joe Oestreich, our Executive Director of Media and Web. We had all the required paperwork, however, what should have been straightforward permission to enter became rather complicated and drawn out.

We found ourselves standing before the massive brick wall that marks the separation between Israel and Gaza. The vicious twists of barbed wire at the top of the wall were vivid reminders that this was a region where violence often erupted, frequently without warning. The heavily armed guards were vigilant and alert. In my heart, I knew that many people would ask what I was doing there, who did I think I was, and how in the world did I think I was going to make it through the checkpoints and walk into Gaza? But I knew that I was supposed to go into that dangerous and war-torn area with the love of Jesus. Even though my paperwork had been carefully and accurately completed, we were forced to wait for hours to receive permission to be processed through the checkpoints and walk the mile-long, dust-covered road into Gaza.

For some reason, Hamas, the party that rules Gaza, was very worried about bad press. I think they were worried about someone killing me and making a mess in the news. A couple of hours into our wait, they let Stephen in, but they wouldn't let Joe and me in. So, there we were, in the one-mile-wide demilitarized zone in a hut, while Stephen walked through the next barricade and disappeared down the mile of dusty road. I was determined not to turn back. I was going to sit right there until they let me go through. So, I just sat in a chair in that little hut and waited. Joe and I confessed the Word and trusted that God would get us through the bureaucracy.

I'm not sure what changed their minds, unless the sight of an older woman who wouldn't give up was too much for them to overcome. Finally, they let me go through to Gaza. Joe was not given permission to enter, so if I was to go in, it had to be just me, by myself! I walked through the walled-off corridor that was ringed by barbed wire to get to a series of barricades. It was only one mile of barricades and barriers, but it took almost two hours to get through the guarded areas. At each checkpoint, I was met by rigid soldiers who appeared very strict and forbidding. Miraculously, I wasn't worried at all. God gave me peace in the midst of what normally would have been a scary situation. Rather than fear, my overwhelming thought was to get in, so I could see what I could do to help those precious people.

Once I made it through the final barricade, I walked down the dirt road to meet Stephen. The guards took us into a small room. We only had a couple of hours to stay in Gaza, and we weren't allowed to go anywhere else. Yet, we had planned to meet with an imam, a Greek Orthodox minister, and a Christian minister. Miraculously, all three agreed to come together in that small room with Stephen and me. We were able to discuss the needs in Gaza, how we could help the people, and what aid would be most beneficial to them. It was a lot of work and effort for a short meeting, but sometimes it is important to have your feet on the hard ground and claim it for the Gospel. As we walked out of Gaza, shortly after our meeting ended, I knew that seeds had been sown for future ministry in that region.

One interesting footnote to that experience actually happened in the United States shortly after we returned from Gaza. We set up a special dinner for the local imams in Dearborn, Michigan, but they didn't want to attend the meeting because I was a Christian woman. The thing that finally persuaded the 11 imams to attend our meeting was the fact that I had just traveled to Gaza. At first, they didn't believe it, but when they realized that I had been in Gaza, not just heard about it or looked at pictures of it, they said, "She must really love Muslims!" That short trip we took to Gaza opened their hearts in ways that none of my healing meetings ever could. Of course, I did what I always do, I prayed for healing for the imams!

Praise and Worship on Manger Square in Bethlehem

In December 2010, we took a group trip to Bethlehem with about 45 partners and friends. I had been there multiple times and didn't want to miss the opportunity to go there again. That great city is a very special place at Christmastime. We wanted to be a part of a special celebration that was taking place in Manger Square, so we could share the love of Jesus with people in that region.

On Christmas Eve, there was to be a special night of music in the Square. In preparing for the trip, we were told that there would be no speakers allowed on the platform, only singers. We worked for months to get an exception and God, once again, opened a door for me to speak. We told the event coordinators that we would bring an amazing singer with us, Shirley Wilkins, who always travels with us and leads worship on group trips. We said that Shirley would perform if I would be allowed to speak after she sang. Amazingly, the organizers agreed and gave me 20 minutes to speak. In my heart, I thought, *That's a lot of time to change lives.* I was very excited!

*Even when we think that God isn't aware of what is going on
in our daily lives, He wants to be intimately involved with us
every minute of every day.*

Normally, Manger Square is a bustling marketplace, but that night it was bursting at the seams. People were everywhere. They were milling around, buying, selling, haggling over prices, eating, and carousing. The atmosphere was wild, chaotic, and full of energy. By the time the microphone was given to Shirley for her to sing and then to me to speak, the crowd had grown to over 100,000 people in the square, overflowing into all the neighboring streets. International FOX News and CNN were there with their cameras to cover the event. The atmosphere was electric with excitement. Shirley sang, and then welcomed me to the platform. As I walked up to the podium, the Muslim call to prayer came over the loudspeakers. That happens five times each day, and I am very used to it, but that night I cringed inside when it sounded because I knew the call to prayer would cut into my few precious minutes of speaking time. The Muslim call to prayer was so loud that I could not talk over it and I felt myself getting tense and frustrated. I thought, *This will take eight or nine of my minutes, and I only had 20 to begin with!* Then I heard the Lord say, "If you let Me, I can make lemonade from lemons." So, after the prayer call was finished, I stepped up to the podium and declared, "I love the call to prayer because I love Muslims. But I have something special to share with you." Thousands of Muslims cheered. I then shared the simple Gospel. Even when we think that God isn't aware of what is going on in our daily lives, He wants to be intimately involved with us every minute of every day. He quieted my heart and gave me the idea to declare my love for Muslims, right there in Manger Square, to a group of over 100,000 people, many of whom were Muslims. He is an amazing God, and I know that the love of Jesus I shared that night was a seed planted into the lives of those people that will produce a harvest of souls.

Even though the night had been miraculous, God wasn't done. After the celebration in Manger Square, I was invited to attend a private dinner hosted by President Mahmoud Abbas. During the dinner, I was able to present the president with a Bible. Later, as we prepared to leave Bethlehem, I looked back in amazement at all that God had accomplished through a small group of people who were willing to spend Christmas in Bethlehem.

Miracle Healing in Eritrea, Africa

Another country where we saw the strategic impact of God's healing power was Eritrea. Located in the horn of Africa and a neighbor to Ethiopia, Eritrea is home to many extremist Muslims. In April 1997, I traveled to Eritrea to hold healing meetings. Prior to visiting the country, I had coordinated with local churches, and they had recruited people who were prepared to help me pray for the sick people who attended the meetings. When I arrived in Eritrea, I met with the leaders and volunteers of those local ministries to discuss the meetings. I was shocked by what I heard. They had very specific instructions for me: "We don't want you to pray for the sick because that is offensive to Muslims. You can preach the Gospel and pray for them to receive Jesus, but you cannot pray for the sick."

Rather astonished, I replied, "I travel to Muslim countries all over the world, and I've never found that healing is offensive to Muslims. Just the opposite is true; it draws Muslims to Christ when they experience

His healing power." They were unmoved, and replied adamantly, "We don't want you to do that here." I was furious on the inside. I thought, *I'm paying for this meeting. If I want to pray for the sick, I'll pray for the sick!* As always, God is gracious. He spoke calmly to my heart and said, "You can do all things if you have faith in Me. Stay calm!" Then He gave me an idea. I asked sweetly, "Would you let me pray for the sick the first night? If you are unhappy with what happens, I won't do it at all during the next five nights of meetings." They took time to consider my proposition, and I quietly prayed under my breath. Eventually, they agreed.

When we step aside and let God take over, miracles are inevitable.

That night, I prayed, "Lord, You need to show up and show off! It's Your name on the line, not mine." While I was preaching, the Holy Spirit spoke to me, "Ask everyone who has a problem with their wrists or hands to stand." I did just that, and many people stood up. Then I spoke a prayer of healing over them. I had hardly finished praying when a tall man from the audience suddenly ran up to the platform, holding his hand up high above his head while frantically opening and closing his hand. The audience went wild, and their voices grew louder and louder. I asked the lead minister who was with me on the platform to please tell me what had happened. He said with great astonishment, "That man is our nation's number one war hero. During the war, he was shot in the wrist and has not been able to open or close his hand. Now he has received a miracle; Jesus healed him! You need to pray for the sick every night." I was so grateful to God for what He had done and reminded that when we step aside and let God take over, miracles are inevitable. We had five more nights of miraculous meetings where we saw the supernatural power of God heal, save, and set free, thousands of people with His love and mercy.

Building Bridges in Morocco

Morocco was a very different experience for me. The Muslims there practice a different kind of Islam; they are Sufis, the Islamic mystics. They go out of their way to seek spiritual experiences and enlightenment through meditation. I had visited Morocco before but hadn't been able to meet with the Sufis one-on-one.

Then in 2010, I had an opportunity to have dinner with a group of Sufi business leaders in Morocco (all men except for one woman). Their question for me was, "What are you doing in Morocco?" I replied, "I am here to build bridges. I would like to have a healing meeting because in the Koran it says that Jesus heals. I would like to pray for sick Muslims in Jesus' name and see them healed." They were surprised, but they intently listened as I shared many stories about the healing meetings that I had held in nations all over the world, including Muslim countries.

Then, one of the leaders, a man who was in charge of the airline industry for the entire country, said, "Can I ask you a personal question?" I replied, "Yes, and if I can answer, I will." He asked, "When you feel cold about your religion, what do you do?" I was shocked to be asked such a question by a Muslim, especially a Sufi Muslim, as their goal is to foster a personal relationship with God. In that moment of surprise, I felt that God gave me the words to say. I replied, "I have been a born-again Christian since I was 16, and I am now 79. I have dry times. When I feel that way, I read the Bible more, pray more, and try to be around Christians of strong faith to help pull me up. I believe that even when you go through dry times, if you press into God, He talks to you and reveals Himself to you." That exchange broke the ice, and the entire group was able to take turns asking me questions, which I did my best to answer.

> Ministry will never be about the numbers. It is about the individuals and the personal connections that God wants to make with each person.

The presence of the Holy Spirit was very strong, and a bridge of relationship was being built. Then, the Holy Spirit spoke to me and said, "Now, share with each of them a prophetic scripture." So, I asked them, "Would you mind if I gave each of you a promise from the Bible?" They were such sweet people, completely receptive as several of them said, "We would love that!" With their permission, I gave scriptures and prophesied to each one of them individually. The presence of God grew even stronger, and we wept openly as I shared with each one, speaking to their hearts the Word of God for them.

Then, one of the men said, "I know a beautiful love song in our language. Would you mind if I brought a musician in here to accompany me as I sing it for you?" I replied, "I would love that!" The song was called *The Love of God*, and I didn't understand the words, but we all understood the loving presence of God at that dinner. When it was time to leave, we all hugged each other and cried. That experience was such a highlight for me. I didn't have a big meeting in Morocco where thousands of people were healed, but I was given an amazing opportunity to make a heart connection with a group of precious Sufi Muslims. Ministry will never be about the numbers. It is about the individual and the personal connection that God wants to make with each person.

The Underground Church in Iran

I pray for Iran every day. That nation has been in my heart for years. The first time I was able to minister to people in Iran, was via satellite from San Jose, California. I had spoken in a church about my love for Muslims and

213

said, "I believe that God will let me go to Iran and hold a healing meeting." An Iranian Christian in the meeting, Mani, heard me and knew he could help. He approached me and asked, "Would you be willing to share your teachings on satellite television to Iran?" I couldn't say, "Yes," fast enough. I was thrilled! Several months later, I went to a television studio in San Jose and taught the Bible via satellite to a live audience in Iran. Between 600,000 and 700,000 Iranians accessed that Christian satellite station while I was teaching. I was extremely honored to have been able to encourage the underground church in Iran.

After that night, even though I had been able to minister to Iranians by satellite, I had an even deeper passion to go into Iran and hold a healing meeting. Unfortunately, I could not get a visa from the government. For some reason, they would not believe me when I told them that I wanted to go into their country as a tourist! I had heard, "No," from Iran for so many years that part of me thought, *What's the point?* But then a series of events took place that began to unlock that door. When my precious husband died in 2012, he left me his retirement money. One Sunday, I felt such a deep leading in my heart. I felt so strongly that I should give all the retirement money away. The first thing I did was tell my wonderful son-in-law, Reece, who is our rational, logical family member. When I told him what I felt, he said, "I don't know about that. I don't want you to have to live in my basement." We laughed together, but I couldn't get away from the leading in my heart. Finally, after days of prayer, with Reece and Sarah's blessing, I gave that money away. Within days, God put a crack in what had previously been a totally closed door to Iran.

Interestingly, the open door to Iran came through Brazil. I was holding a big healing meeting in Brazil and met a Brazilian who told me that he owned a tour agency in Iran. I told him about my issues with getting a visa, and he said he could work it out for me. It still took a huge amount of prayer to get a tourist visa, even with his connections; but finally, through his tour agency, I was given a visa to Iran. Within months I was on a plane. I remember that stepping out of the airplane onto Iranian soil was a somewhat surreal experience. I had waited and prayed for so long to get there that it was almost hard to believe.

One thing I love is a good cup of coffee and Iran has some of the best coffee in the world! I enjoyed being a tourist and seeing the sites of what was formerly the nation of Persia. Our guide was a beautiful Iranian woman. She took us to the area where Daniel, Esther, and Mordecai's tombs are believed to be. It was such a beautiful and historic area. I was honored to be able to experience a snapshot of biblical history in that ancient country.

We have a misperception that Iranians hate us, but they really love us. They didn't know who I was, but they knew I was an American and that was enough. Through an interpreter, I spoke to several of the women there. They were very warm and friendly, and said that they would like to go to America. They were so curious about us and our country. At one point, I was invited to a Christian's home to eat with his family. We sat on the floor and ate dinner and talked openly about our shared love for Jesus. Unfortunately, some of the men in the government strongly warned the Christians against being around me, so they had to back away.

The government wanted us to stay in a tourist hotel because they didn't want me, a foreigner, to see how bad it was for the people of their country. They did not want us to spend time with any of the regular people. The truth is, the leaders are wealthy, but the people have nothing. The palaces are full of opulent thrones and jewels, but the people live in poverty. The disparity between the wealthy and the regular people was such a sad reality.

Since that first visit, I have only been able to return to Iran once. I haven't been able to hold a healing meeting there yet, but I have not given up. God has helped me to connect with imams in other countries. I believe those divine connections will help to open up an invitation for me to hold a meeting in Iran. I want to partner with an imam who will teach about Jesus from the Koran. Then I will teach about Jesus healing people and demonstrate the power of Jesus by praying for the sick. This dream of my heart is still in process, but I know that God isn't done there yet!

Ministering to Muslims in the U.S.

We have to realize that Muslims are not just "over there," but that many Muslims live here in the U.S. In addition to the desire to minister to Muslims in other countries, God has given me a longing to minister to the Muslims in our own backyard. When I spoke at Bishop Keith Butler's church, Word of Faith, in Detroit, Michigan, I shared that Detroit, at that time, had the highest concentration of Muslims in America. I told Bishop Butler's congregation, "I believe that God could open a door for me to have a healing meeting in a mosque. If He can open big doors overseas in Muslim countries, why can't He open the door to the Muslims in our nation?"

At the time, I thought it was just a statement, not a prophetic word. However, God heard me say it, and He had a plan. A woman in the church contacted me. She had connections with local imams and wanted to help me find a way into a mosque. Eventually, she coordinated a sit-down meeting with Imam Mohammad Ali Elahi, founder of the Islamic House of Wisdom in Dearborn, Michigan, one of the largest mosques in the U.S. I told Imam Elahi how much I loved Muslims and about all the outreaches I had held in Muslim countries. I shared my vision to have a healing meeting in his mosque. Imam Elahi was not argumentative or mean, he was just not interested in my proposal. He said that there was no possibility for that type of meeting to be held in his mosque. He was convinced that it would never work. But with God, we should never say "never."

As I stood up to leave, he asked me, "The next time you are in Detroit,

I would like you to come to my home to pray for my wife and have dinner with us. Would you be willing?" Shocked, I said, "Of course, I would love to meet your wife and pray for you." It was an unusual open door, and I stepped through it. Six months later, I visited Detroit again and spent the evening with Imam Elahi and his lovely wife. The imam shared stories from his life, some of the things he had done as a chaplain in the U.S. Navy in Iran, and the wisdom he felt came from the Islamic community. After about an hour, he asked me to share again what I wanted to do in his mosque. As I spoke about the healing meeting I wanted to hold, he became more and more positive. Finally, he said, "Marilyn, I believe we can do this." The difference was dramatic. It was the relationship that had opened the door.

With God, we should never say "never."

Several months later, I was invited to participate in an interfaith prayer meeting held within his mosque. That was the first time that a woman had been allowed to minister in a mosque in over 1,400 years! I was allowed to speak to a mixed Muslim-Christian audience. My presentation included a video of my outreaches to many Muslim countries, including Sudan and Pakistan. I shared about the miracles of Jesus, and then asked everyone who needed healing to stand up. Many people stood up. After I prayed for them in Jesus' name, I asked each person to tell me if anything had changed in their bodies. Several powerful testimonies were shared, including one from a young Muslim boy who came forward and told me that his eyes had been healed. There was a banner hung at the meeting that the boy had not been able to read earlier in the night because his eyesight was so poor. After prayer, his eyesight improved so drastically that he could read the banner without any struggle at all! Even though his knowledge of Jesus was very limited, he said that night that he believed Jesus had healed him.

I am honored that my faith confession about Muslims has come true. I do love Muslims, and they do love me! My goal, everywhere I go, is to share the love of God in tangible ways. I have been able to travel to over 137 countries, many of which had been previously closed to the Gospel, but God found a way to get me there. I am not done traveling. I know there are many more Muslim countries I will be visiting in the near future, some I have traveled to before, some I have not. As I look forward, I can't wait to meet old friends and make new ones while taking the good news of the Gospel to all who will listen.

Chapter 9

WRESTLING WITH TERROR

HOW DO YOU RESPOND TO obstacles? Do you stand your ground, trusting you will win, or do you back down, believing that the obstacles are too massive to overcome? Most of the time, your level of success in any endeavor is directly related to your tenacity and

No matter the obstacle, we must remember that anything
worth achieving is worth fighting for.

ability to overcome obstacles that block your path. In anything worth achieving, there will be some type of resistance. It can be something basic like people speaking negatively about what you hope to achieve, to doors that won't open, or it can be something more drastic like imminent physical danger or a chasm of financial lack. No matter the obstacle, we must remember that anything worth achieving is worth fighting for. As we walk through this life and pursue our God-given purpose, our response to opposition is crucial. The need to persevere in the face of adversity cannot be overstated; it is imperative. If we cringe at the slightest opposition, we will not succeed. We must fight through challenges and overcome difficulties to accomplish our purpose.

Returning to Pakistan

The truth of these words was underscored as I returned again and again to one of my favorite Muslim countries, Pakistan. I love the people, their clothes, their food, and so much more. It is a country that will always hold a special place in my heart. I have amazing friends in Pakistan and have had some of the most unbelievable ministry successes there. I have also faced the greatest threats to my life and my ministry while standing on Pakistani soil. Yet, I would not trade even one of those negative experiences for anything easier or safer. With God's help and grace, I will continue to go, risking everything I have because I know that people's destinies are dependent on my obedience. I believe that my Lord is counting on me.

When I first started ministering in Pakistan, I didn't anticipate the reception I would receive. I didn't know that God would allow me to meet with presidents, kings, and imams, or that secular and religious leaders would welcome and befriend me. My first, very small and simple trip into Pakistan was in 1995. I didn't know, at the time, that it was the first of many trips into a country where its Muslim leaders would eventually call me the "Mom of Pakistan."

I have never gone to Pakistan to convert anyone. I have gone there to share the love of Jesus and His healing power with the Pakistani people. My goal has always been to help people have encounters with Jesus. He is the "secret ingredient" in any situation. He has poured out miracles and changed hundreds of thousands of lives in Pakistan. The Gospel works! It has made a way for me and prepared the hearts of people on the streets and in positions of power. In the beginning, I didn't know all that would happen. I just knew that I had to take the first step of faith and plan a trip to Pakistan.

I had a heart for Pakistan for years before I had the opportunity to travel there. I prayed over Pakistan daily and confessed that I had favor with the government and with Christian leaders in that nation. In 1994, while I was at our church in Denver, a man who worked with Morris Cerullo's ministry shared with me his desire to help me reach the nations, "If there are any nations that you would like to visit, I can help you," he said. Immediately, I shared my desire to minister in Pakistan. He replied, "Amazingly, a Pakistani pastor who has helped us set up meetings there for other ministries is visiting his family in Denver right now. I can set up a time for him to meet with you."

God can be last minute, but He always makes a way.

The Pakistani pastor met with me, and while he wanted to help me, he was a bit reluctant, saying, "We have not had great experiences with American ministers. Many times, we have worked hard to set up meetings only to have the Americans back out on us. If you want to come, you have to follow through; don't back out!" I promised him that I was committed to ministering in Pakistan, and we began the process. Of course, once people heard that I was planning a trip to Pakistan, we received all kinds of discouraging words. People said, "You are a woman; they won't come to your meetings. And even if you do get a few people to come, they will shoot you!" Despite those not-so-encouraging words, I pushed on, confident that God would make a way for us.

A year later, in 1995, our trip was completely planned to Lahore, Pakistan. However, with only days to go before the meetings started, we were still very far from meeting our budget. I was facing a $30,000 shortfall, but still determined to move forward. God can be last minute, but He always makes a way. The budgeted expenses were quite high because big meetings in big cities are always expensive. In addition to the meetings, we planned to give away books in the native language; the people there had almost no other way to get Christian books. We also planned to provide humanitarian relief in the form of food and clothing to some of the poorest people in the country. We found out a sad fact—not everybody wanted to help us with overseas mission trips. We discovered that fundraising for those types of meetings could be very difficult, but we knew even more that nothing is too hard for God!

God Supernaturally Provides

Usually, as we plan events in one country, we are also executing events in other parts of the world. That was the case in 1995. Shortly before we were due to fly to Pakistan, I had an outreach in Indonesia. On my return trip from Indonesia, I was sitting in the Indonesian airport lounge waiting for my plane, and a man walked up to me and said, "I know who you are." He sat down, and we talked for a few minutes. I found out that he was an Indonesian businessman. Toward the end of the conversation, he asked me, "Are you lacking any money for your meeting in Pakistan?" I replied, "Well, I'm short $30,000." He thought for a minute, smiled a huge smile, and said, "You aren't any longer." At that point, he opened his briefcase, took out $30,000 in cash, and gave it to me. If I hadn't been sitting down, I would have fallen over! It was God's supernatural provision. Miracles like that, along with the faithful support of my friends and partners at home, have made my overseas ministry possible.

After that financial miracle, everything was finally ready for our first healing meeting in Pakistan, but I still found myself dealing with not-so-positive advice from well-meaning Christians. The consensus was that it

---

Over the years, I have learned that the Gospel always bears fruit. When you step out in faith, you will see results.

---

would be foolish to go. "Don't go; they will kill you!" I heard that over and over again. Even a Pakistani man who attended our church told me, "When you stand up to speak and the audience realizes that you are a woman, half of them will walk out. Even worse, you could be killed. There are a lot of radical Muslim groups in Pakistan." I appreciated the love and concern of the people who were warning me because they felt there were very real issues and dangers facing me, but I was determined. I believed that God had called me to Pakistan, so I refused to walk in fear. I just kept saying, "I love Muslims, and Muslims love me."

Over the years, I have learned that the Gospel always bears fruit. When you step out in faith, you will see results. When we arrived in Pakistan for our first healing meeting ever, we weren't sure what to expect. We started with what we knew. We decided to have ministry training meetings during the day to train local ministry leaders, then hold four consecutive nightly healing meetings where we would pray for the sick, share the love of Jesus, and give away books that had been translated into Urdu. We wanted to bless the people and the Christian leaders in that nation. For those first meetings, we fed, taught, and provided lodging for every Christian leader who attended. It was a faith walk, and God came through.

The first night was a hit. The beautiful people of Lahore were open and responsive, and not one of them walked out on me! It was a good thing that they stayed because they were able to witness the healing of a woman who had not walked in over 12 years. I had people place their hands on their bodies where they needed healing, and then I prayed for healing in the name of Jesus. After the crippled woman was healed, she shared her story with the crowd of over 4,000 people. We saw other amazing miracles that night, which greatly touched the people who attended. Word spread quickly and by the next night, there were over 8,000 people at the meeting. That was phenomenal in many ways, but it especially touched my heart since we had been told not to advertise because it would be too dangerous to do so. God was doing His own advertising!

By the fourth night, without any traditional advertising, more than 20,000 people attended the meeting. Thousands of people were healed from diseases and infirmities and set free from demonic torment by the power and love of Jesus Christ. Each night, I taught on one miracle story of Jesus, prayed for the sick to be healed, and then asked who would like the Healer, Jesus, in their heart as their Savior.

God gets mileage out of everything.
He never wastes anything.

The number of people who wanted Jesus, not just as their Healer but as their Savior, was overwhelming to me. Their openness to the Gospel solidified my love for the Pakistani people even more, and it confirmed to me how important Pakistan is to my heart and even more so, to God's heart.

God always has multiple agendas being accomplished at one time. He gets mileage out of everything. He never wastes anything. In the midst of all the healings, miracles, and salvations, I was also given a spiritual son. I did not know it then, but one of the young Muslims in that crowd, a young man sent by the Pakistani government to supervise the event, was Anwar Fazal. Through those meetings, he gave his life to Christ and was called into ministry. Years later, he founded Eternal Life Ministries, which is the largest independent church in Pakistan, with a current but growing membership of over 45,000 people. Since that time years ago, when he received Jesus as his Savior during my first meetings in Pakistan, Pastor Anwar has become a son to me. He is a very strategic partner who has been used by God to help me in ways that I could never have fully known or understood 20 years ago.

As we pray, God will send people who are willing to stand in faith, pray, and financially support us as we do what He has called us to do. After the incredible way God touched people with His healing power and changed thousands of lives in Lahore, I desperately wanted to return to Pakistan. With that desire still burning in my heart, I spoke at Pastor Keith Butler's church in Detroit, Michigan. After the meeting, Pastor Keith, who had been a very good friend of mine for years, asked me to tell him about Pakistan. I shared about the amazing things God had done and the desire I had to return to Pakistan. Most people, even pastors, when they hear about the places I have traveled, the miraculous events that took place, and the other nations where I would like to go respond enthusiastically, "What a great idea! I wish you well," and then they move on. Pastor Keith was different. He said to me, "How can I help?" His question blessed me greatly and allowed me to share the specific needs that had to be met for me to return to Pakistan. Pastor Keith and his church prayed and gave; they ended up giving us much of the support we needed for the second ministry trip. Eventually, I was honored to have Pastor Keith travel with me to Pakistan on two separate occasions.

Second Meeting in Pakistan

In 1997, we arrived in Rawalpindi for our second meeting in Pakistan. While we were there preparing for the meetings, I was invited to be a guest on a local secular call-in radio show called *Good Morning, Pakistan*. I was worried about possibly saying the wrong thing, then having my healing meetings canceled and my visa revoked. The producers told me, "We want you to talk about healing. People will call in with questions about it." For a while during the program, I relaxed and felt like everything was going well as I answered various questions about healing. Then a question came up that I knew was a trap. A woman called in and asked, "Why do you pray for healing in Jesus' name? Couldn't you pray to God in the name of Muhammed or Confucius or Buddha and see the same results?" I took a deep breath, thinking, *Oh no! What do I say?* As soon as the breath whooshed out of my lungs, God gave me the answer. I said, "You know, I

The name of Jesus works! It is difficult to argue with personal experience.

---

don't have any experience praying in the name of Muhammed, Confucius, or Buddha, so I can't tell you. But, I do have a lot of experience praying in the name of Jesus, and I've seen many healings and miracles."

You can always count on the Holy Spirit for wisdom. That answer successfully avoided all the landmines. I didn't insult Muhammed, Confucius, or Buddha. I simply described what I have tried and what had proven to be true: the name of Jesus works! As I have said before, it is difficult to argue with personal experience. In many tough situations, I have been given answers like that. I believe God has gifted me with wisdom that has allowed me to preach the pure, uncompromised Gospel in places that were completely closed to it. We received many testimonies after the program from people who were healed because of what I said. As a result, the crowds at our healing meetings grew.

Those meetings were open-air meetings. We placed mats on the ground and people crowded in as tightly as they could. On the last night in Rawalpindi, we had over 70,000 people attend. A Muslim imam received his sight, and testified, "I'm an imam, and I can see now. Jesus healed me!" A woman had a tumor on the side of her face; after I prayed for the crowd, the tumor disappeared. There were so many healings and salvations that it would be impossible to recount them all.

There's one experience that especially stood out to me on that trip. We hosted a big dinner with the local imams and political leaders in Rawalpindi at the beginning of the week-long meetings we had planned in that city. At the dinner, I was seated next to an imam who was both a religious leader and a powerful political leader. As that was only my second trip to Pakistan, I was incredibly nervous that I would say or do something offensive to the Pakistani culture. However, the imam began the conversation with me in the most unexpected way. "I have terrible pain in my knees," he said. "Would you pray for me?" I was shocked, but I am always ready to pray!

I asked him if I could pray as the Bible instructed, by laying my hands on him and praying in Jesus' name. He said, "I don't have a problem with that." Right there, at the dinner table with our meal in front of us and other conversations going on around us, I put my hand on his arm and prayed for his knees in Jesus' name. He didn't say anything about his knees after I prayed, so I had to trust God that His Word would come to pass. A year and a half later, we returned to Karachi for another ministry trip, and I met him again. "How are you?" I asked. He replied, "I am totally healed. I have not had any pain in my knees since you prayed for me." I knew that God was faithful and moving throughout the Muslim world.

The biggest meetings my ministry has held have been in Pakistan. Remember, over 90 percent of Pakistanis are Muslim. What is it that brings them out to see a Christian woman? It is the healings and miracles that bring hungry people to our meetings. Muslims believe that Jesus heals; it actually says so in the Koran. They believe that Jesus was a prophet, but not the Son of God, as Christians believe. So, the precious Muslim people come to our meetings to be healed. They come in large numbers that defy comprehension, even for those of us who have seen them firsthand.

A Plentiful Harvest in Karachi

The first time we saw 100,000 people at a single event was in Karachi in 1999. The size of that crowd was scary. The people don't want to hurt you, but if you get out into the crowd, they'll crush you without meaning to, just to have you lay hands on them. Each night, the number of people at the meetings multiplied. On the second to the last night, when my team and I crawled into our little car to drive down the single-lane road leaving the stadium, so many people swarmed the car that we were barely able to drive. As we inched our way forward, people started rocking the car back and forth and beating on it with their hands. They desperately wanted to touch us. We eventually made it off the stadium grounds and then traffic opened up. After more than an hour, we made it to our hotel, but we knew we had to do something different on the final night. So, we came up with a plan for a quick, undetected exit. Now, remember, I was in my mid-60s, and the stadium had a nine-foot wall surrounding it. In order to get out before the crowd realized we were leaving, we had our hosts place very tall ladders on each side of the wall. While the pastors were still allowing people to come up and share their healing testimonies on the platform, my team, Sarah, and I snuck out the back. Then we climbed up the ladder inside the wall and climbed down the ladder outside the wall. Ha! Can you believe it? Let me tell you, that was an adventure! No one would believe that I could do it, but there I was, full of the strength and the grace of God. We got into waiting taxis and drove safely back to our hotel.

Those healing meetings were very successful, and the harvest was indeed plentiful. Whenever God wants to take you to another level of influence and fruitfulness, He will introduce someone else into your circle. In 1997, we had connected with Dr. Robinson Asghar, a businessman and evangelist. He served as our Pakistani National Chairman for several years, helping to plan and publicize some of my largest meetings in Islamabad, Karachi, and Lahore. He was an amazing contact who sacrificed so much for us and the kingdom of God.

In 2003, we returned to Lahore, and more than 200,000 people came to hear the message that Jesus loves them and wants to heal them. As always, we saw the faithfulness of God with healings, various miracles, and many decisions for Christ. That was a record-breaker by all accounts, and we celebrated. On our return home to the States, an interesting thing happened. When my Vice President of Operations, Diane Reiter, told several staff members about that miraculous meeting with over 200,000 attendees, one staff member remarked, "Thank God for giving Marilyn such a crowning glory to end her ministry."

And really, that is how many people thought about the ministry that had taken place; they thought it was great, but they also thought that it was the best God could do. In other words, "That was the climax, the biggest event God could put together for Marilyn. Wasn't it a great finale for her ministry?" Those thoughts were perfectly understandable, but I am glad that they were wrong. Very wrong. We did not know that God was not done using me in Pakistan or anywhere else for that matter, and my biggest meetings were still yet to come!

Defying the Enemy in Pakistan

The dangers of ministering in Islamic countries are not exaggerated. In 2005, I escaped a very real threat to my life in Pakistan. We had several nights of healing meetings planned in Islamabad at a stadium that seats over 100,000 people. The day before the start of our meetings, Pakistan's Inter-Services Intelligence (ISI) contacted Dr. Asghar, the Pakistani National Chairman, and Stephen Kiser, and asked them to meet at President Pervez Musharraf's palace. We were not sure what to make of it, but they went into the meeting praying and believing for the best outcome.

Upon their arrival at the presidential palace, Stephen Kiser and Dr. Asghar were briefed on the security situation. Intelligence officials had just arrested 16 members of a 32-member terrorist cell, including several suicide bombers. The arrest happened overnight when the ISI stormed a terrorist compound outside the city and discovered blueprints of the Islamabad Stadium with six large red Xs marked on the stadium, two of which were on the platform. The red Xs were to direct the placement of bombs in the stadium. Also, on the table, they found four pictures that represented the bombs' targets with red Xs over their faces. Those pictures were of me, Dr. Robinson Asghar, Stephen Kiser, and Joe Oestreich. Later, the ISI informed us that the terrorists had taken the photos of the four of us over the previous several days via telephoto lenses while we were there in the city.

Sometimes you hear of dangers to foreigners or missionaries and it feels distant and remote. However, that threat was as real as it gets, and I was the target. Those suicide bombers had taken an oath to kill me and blow up the stadium in Islamabad. President Musharraf and the ISI had to shut down the stadium due to the level of danger to everyone who would attend. The U.S. Ambassador's office was also briefed on the situation, and the consular officers met with us at our hotel to advise us of the seriousness of the danger. He recommended that we leave the country immediately.

I said, "If I die, I die." I released my life into God's hands and entrusted my future to Him.

It was a life-or-death situation. The authorities posted a guard at the door of my hotel room 24 hours a day because they were convinced there would be more attempts on my life. Remember, they only caught half of the cell. There were still 16 men out there who had vowed to kill me. So, for the first time, I began to be truly afraid. I thought, *God, did you call me to be a martyr? What am I here for? Am I going to die in this country?* I walked up and down inside my hotel room, reading the Bible and praying. It was the biggest crisis of faith I had ever had. Yes, I had always known that Pakistan was a dangerous country. I had even faced scary situations before. However, this time was different. I was not facing a theoretical danger; I faced the concrete reality of a specific number of people who had sworn to kill me.

In that difficult moment, as I wrestled with terror and pondered the next steps to take, weighing the consequences, God spoke to my heart as He often does with a scripture. Revelation 12:11 (NIV) says, *"They triumphed over him by the blood of the Lamb and by the word of their testimony; they did not love their lives so much as to shrink from death."* As I read this, I knew I had to make a decision. So, I said, "If I die, I die." I released my life into God's hands and entrusted my future to Him. I met and prayed with Stephen, Joe, and Dr. Asghar, and we all decided that God had given us peace to stay and believe for miracles. If God delivered us from the original bomb threat, then He could continue to protect us. I told my team, "If they take the stadium away, we'll just go to the slums and preach. But please call your wives and make sure they are okay with you staying." Both Stephen and Joe called their wives, prayed with them, and received their support to stay.

Miracles can happen when God's people hear His voice and refuse to run, when they stand firm and believe Him.

Bolstered by the Word, we found the courage to step out of our hotel and dared to defy the enemy. We still had several meetings planned but no venue in which to hold them. I was determined not to be chased out of Pakistan, but we needed provision. With less than 24 hours until our widely advertised stadium meeting was to take place, Father James Shamaun of St. John Vianney Catholic Church stepped forward and offered his Catholic compound in Rawalpindi for us to hold the meetings. The compound included a large cathedral and expansive grounds. We quickly built an outside platform, setting the stage for worship and my teaching, and connected a live video feed for those inside the cathedral.

The meeting was a resounding success; even though we weren't able to advertise it at all, the word got out. We were only able to hold a two-night meeting, but we witnessed thousands of people give their lives to Christ, and many received miracle healings. The compound was filled to overflowing, and people were even sitting on the rooftops of the homes and buildings in the neighborhood that surrounded Father James's property. By the second night, over 40,000 people attended the meeting. After that meeting, the ISI asked us once again to shut down due to growing security concerns. Despite the very real danger, we all felt the presence of God. You see, miracles can happen when God's people hear

His voice and refuse to run, when they stand firm and believe Him. And, as you can see, the radicals were not able to kill me!

More Than 350,000 Hear the Gospel in Karachi

It was not until seven years later, in 2012, that I returned to Pakistan. Over a two-year period, Dr. Asghar helped us put together a meeting in Karachi, which became a huge event. They had such a beautiful welcome for us. We were greeted with flowers at the airport, and there were crowds of people chanting, "Alleluia, Alleluia." That was quite unexpected, but very refreshing after such a long flight to get there. When I arrived at our hotel, I picked up an issue of *Time* magazine that included an article, "The Dark Heart of Pakistan." The article described the radical Islamic groups that had made Karachi "the most dangerous city in the world." It was a little late for danger warnings as I was already in Karachi; but rather than inspiring fear, I felt only peace. I knew that the presence of God was with me and could sense all the prayers of my partners around the world and those from the Christians in Pakistan. We were determined to see God's work done in Karachi!

First on the agenda was a dinner with dignitaries from all over Pakistan, which included pastors, priests, imams, and political leaders. The Federal Minister of National Harmony and Minorities Affairs and Senior Advisor to Pakistan's prime minister, Dr. Paul Bhatti, thanked me for praying for the physically sick, but also for praying for healing from illiteracy, poverty, and terrorism. The Governor of Sindh Province, Dr. Ishrat Ul Ebad Khan, who was very instrumental in securing the required permissions from the Pakistani government for the event, invited me into his home to pray for his family. The trip was off to a great start!

The atmosphere was very cordial and positive. There was a sense that something grand and special was going to happen. I recognized a few people from previous trips. It felt like a homecoming. Some of them approached me to share their testimonies of being healed after I had prayed for them. One young boy brought me a huge bouquet of flowers and said, "This is from my mother and father. My father, Abraham, interpreted for you in Lahore in 2003. You prayed for my parents to have a child and now I am here."

It is extremely important that we give glory to God
for what He has done and reaffirm that there's power
in the name of Jesus.

The general expectation in Karachi was high, and it was very evident in the response of the crowds. The first night we had more than 100,000 people who attended the meeting. The streets leading to the compound had to be shut down as thousands were positioned outside the ground's walls to watch the event on large screens. That was just the beginning, as attendance grew to more than 230,000 by the final night. *The Christian Post* estimated that more than 350,000 people heard the Gospel at those meetings.

The miracles were absolutely outstanding! We always give an opportunity for a few people to share their testimonies, but there is just not enough time to hear everyone's story since the testimony lines are so long. A boy was healed from stuttering, a young girl who was mute began to speak, a little boy, blind from birth, gained his sight, and people began to walk who had come to the meetings on crutches. A man's malignant tumor behind his ear disappeared after the prayer for healing. It is surreal when you stand on stage and hear those awesome testimonies. After they share their story, I always say, "Jesus healed you." It is extremely important that we give glory to God for what He has done and reaffirm that there's power in the name of Jesus.

God was determined to show His awesome power in Karachi, and I was overwhelmed with joy as He did so! What was supposed to be "The Dark Heart of Pakistan" became alive with light. I could have easily allowed my previous experience with the threat of terror to intimidate me and suppress what God wanted to do on that trip. That is not to underestimate the dangers or advocate a lack of precaution. However, I chose to put my trust in an Almighty God, a Merciful Savior, and a Loving Father Who cares more about my personal safety than I do. It had taken us years to coordinate this event, but the harvest we saw with the lives that were changed and the healings that took place, made it worth the wait. Everything that we believed for, God made happen—beyond what we could have hoped or imagined.

Meeting Pastor Anwar Fazal, My Spiritual Son

It is not often that you hear that you have a son whom you have never personally met. I remember the first time I met Pastor Anwar Fazal at one of my conferences. He approached me, beaming with smiles, and very enthusiastically said, "I am your son! I was saved in your first meeting in Pakistan." I was so happy to hear that, but I didn't make too much of it at the time. After all, he was not the only person to approach me at my events with stories of salvation or healing. However, Anwar is a true son, in every way. He has a heart like no other for Muslims to experience freedom in Christ, but beyond that, he has the guts to do something about it. Also, God has blessed him with extraordinary favor with the Pakistani government.

While Pastor Anwar's parents had been Christians and ministers in the Assemblies of God church in Pakistan, he had no personal interest in

God until his salvation experience at my first Pakistani healing meeting in 1995. After getting saved and having a powerful encounter with the Holy Spirit, Anwar resigned his position as a government official and launched a church with four people. It has now grown into a membership of over 45,000, the largest independent church in Pakistan. He is very anointed and has a healing grace on his life.

Anwar is very innovative and does not believe in doing business as usual. In 2006, he launched a Christian television station, *Isaac TV*. It is reaching Pakistan for Christ with many Muslims being changed by this groundbreaking television network. Pastor Anwar felt such a love for and loyalty to me that he made me the president of his network and aired my program daily (dubbed in Urdu) in 72 countries throughout the Middle East, Asia, and Europe, without any cost for the airtime!

It is a blessing when God allows you to see the results of your hard work and sacrifice, and to reap from fields you have wept over and sown into for years. I thought I was stretching my faith when we held meetings in a Muslim country that saw 400,000 people attend. However, when I started working with Pastor Anwar Fazal, it changed everything for me regarding my ministry in Pakistan. He is so well-known there that he is able to open doors and help coordinate relationships that would not have been possible without him.

I had already held several healing meetings in Pakistan with record-breaking meetings each time, but my largest meeting ever was in Karachi in November 2016, hosted by Pastor Anwar. He is a very strategic thinker. He proposed a prayer festival and healing meeting because he knew that labeling it a "prayer festival" would attract people, especially Muslims. He is also a unifier, using his Christian television station to connect the various churches in Pakistan and to massively promote the event.

With my spiritual son by my side, it was time to dream even bigger. I told Pastor Anwar that I wanted to hold an event that had one million people attending, and he said that he could do it. It was going to be my seventh trip to Pakistan. I knew it would be big, but I didn't realize it would be quite that big. What I have realized is that one situation builds on another. The planning took over a year as Stephen Kiser made multiple trips to Pakistan. Not only were we coordinating a one-million-person prayer festival, I planned to meet with imams and minister to Christian leaders while I was there. There were a lot of moving pieces to the event.

The plan for the November 2016 trip was for three of us to travel to Pakistan: me, my executive assistant, and Stephen Kiser. Getting the necessary visas took multiple phone calls and even a trip by Stephen to the Pakistani embassy in Washington, D.C. Somehow, it is always last minute on the visas, and we have to pray in each and every one of them. Finally, we had the necessary paperwork and took the almost 24-hour trip to Lahore, Pakistan.

Pastor Anwar is a wonderful host and goes to great lengths to make sure his guests feel welcome and are treated well. When we got off the plane, we were enthusiastically met by people with large bouquets of flowers who threw rose petals at our feet. There is almost a 12-hour time difference between here and Pakistan, so when we arrived, we were tired and just wanted to sleep, but those precious people had been anxiously waiting for us to arrive. They wanted to take us out to breakfast, so we had to muster our strength and engage.

Every trip to Pakistan has had its own unique stories. I have such extreme favor in Pakistan that I can do things I couldn't do in other countries. One example is the close friendship I have developed with Grand Imam Syed Muhammad Abdul Khabir Azad. The top religious figure in Pakistan, he's responsible for all the imams and Muslims within the country, which involves over 1,000 mosques. Grand Imam Azad brought 300 of the most influential imams from throughout the country to a meeting with me. While there, I was able to pray for tumors, backs, pregnancies, and healing from cancer. Many received miracles that night and stood up to proclaim all that God was doing!

In addition, I hosted over 5,000 Pakistani Christian leaders for two days of intense training and spiritual refreshing. We gave each leader three of my books that had been translated into the native language of Pakistan, Urdu: *Breaking Generational Curses*, *The Names of God*, and *Devils, Demons, and Deliverance*. On any other trip, a meeting with 300 imams and ministering to 5,000 Christian leaders would have been the highlight. However, this trip was so packed, that as powerful and high-profile as those meetings were, they ended up being mere footnotes to the main event.

Prayer Festival in Pakistan
One Million Hear the Gospel

Our main event, the prayer festival, was organized on such a massive scale that to accommodate the people we expected, they brought in 50 acres of carpet to lay down for the people. That's how they fit so many people in one venue; they don't use seats. The people sit cross-legged on the carpet, squishing together to get as many people as possible into the space available. That morning, we went to the venue and prayed over the carpets as they were setting up. We prayed that people would get touched by the love of God and that there would be miracle healings throughout the stadium. There is no way to describe the activity of the workers, and the enthusiasm they had setting up for such a massive event, and the people had not even begun to arrive yet!

You can imagine the security apparatus for such a large Christian prayer festival in a Muslim country with a large contingent of Muslim extremists. Fortunately, God kept us safe throughout this and every other ministry trip we have taken to Pakistan, despite the efforts of the enemy to scare and intimidate us. In the nine times I've been there, there has always been some kind of a threat, with the possibility of being killed—martyred for my faith in Jesus. You have to face that possibility and not let it paralyze you. As for me, I put my trust in God and always moved forward, confident that He called me to that place at that time. And He has always taken care of me.

After over one year of planning, the time had finally come. The actual prayer festival and healing meeting would start at 9:30 p.m. and we were scheduled to depart at 5:40 p.m. to make the three-and-a-half-hour drive to the location. After waiting in the lobby for some time, we were told to go back to our rooms as quickly as possible and wait for a call. We knew something was wrong but had no information as to what was happening. The team gathered in my room and began to pray in the Spirit. There was no fear, only an urgency to pray. We received an "all clear" an hour later, and finally departed from the hotel to drive to the venue.

We found out later that a religious zealot and suicide bomber had detonated a bomb at Shah Noorani, a Sufi shrine in Hub, Balochistan, about 30 miles from Karachi. The Islamic State, ISIL, claimed responsibility for the attack, which killed 52 worshippers and injured over 200 people. Festival attendees were late in coming because the government closed the highway due to the bomb scare, so they had to take alternate routes. It doesn't bother the Pakistani people to start any meeting late. What I have learned is that it doesn't bother them, so it shouldn't bother me. The meeting was scheduled for 9:30 p.m., but it didn't start until around midnight.

It can take a long time for faith goals to manifest, but if you hold fast to your confession, you will see results.

Thousands lined the streets as we made our way to Jinnah Park next to Mazar-e-Quaid, also known as the Jinnah Mausoleum, the national mausoleum and final resting place of Quaid-e-Azam (Great Leader) Muhammad Ali Jinnah, the founder of Pakistan. No Christian organization had ever received permission to utilize those grounds before. That was the evening's first miracle! When we drove onto the grounds, the security team formed a human chain to keep the people back. As I took the stairs up to the stage, I saw the dignitaries already seated on rows of white leather couches. Politicians, police chiefs, and religious leaders of various faiths were present and welcomed, but the main spectacle was the mass of people in front of the stage.

You couldn't really see all the people because there were so many. It almost defied belief, feeling at times like a dream. It seemed unreal. Pastor Anwar's wife, Nida, led worship while the people were still arriving. Finally, Anwar turned to me and said, "Now, we have a million people. Are you satisfied?" I was almost overcome by the impact of that multitude as I said, "Yes, thank you!"

I had been believing for an event attended by one million people for many years. I first started praying for that crazy, out-there number when I started traveling overseas for my first healing meetings (with just a few hundred or thousand in attendance)! It can take a long time for faith goals to manifest, but if you hold fast to your confession, you will see results. Remember, *"He Who promised is faithful"* (Hebrews 10:23). I was amazed at how Anwar knew that there were over a million people, but that was part of the purpose behind the acres of carpet. He knew exactly how much carpet they had laid out and how many people would fit per acre. Amazingly, they believed that many more would have come if the bomb scare hadn't closed the roads right before the event.

Those precious one million-plus people were the guests of honor, sitting cross-legged upon a dusty carpet, invited personally by the Holy Spirit. They sat and listened to me tell of the miracles of Jesus and how the biggest miracle is inviting Him into their hearts. Signs and wonders followed the message as I prayed for those with growths, tumors, problems with their feet and backs, and, in the end, total healing. Testimonies were numerous and remarkable, but due to security concerns, only a limited few were allowed on the platform. Hundreds of thousands of people gave their hearts to Jesus that day, and multitudes of people were healed.

After a high-profile event in such a dangerous area, I always feel relieved that no one shot me.

The Karachi Prayer Festival was the culmination and manifestation of so many years of believing, hoping, and loving; but even as it happened right in front of me, it was hard to believe. When it ended, and we were driving back to our hotel, I felt immense relief. The truth is, after a high-profile event in such a dangerous area, I always feel relieved that no one shot me. However, there's also a sense of nostalgia, as you leave such an intense zone of Holy Spirit activity, knowing that it was a very special moment in history that would never come back again. It was such an honor to have a little part of it, and God showed Himself to be faithful, yet again!

There are times that it is not good for the right hand to know what the left hand is doing (see Matthew 6:3), and it can be advisable to keep some things quiet. However, it is also very important to testify of what God is doing. After the prayer and healing festival with over one million participants in Karachi, we returned to the States and tried to interest the large news networks in doing a special on our ministry in Pakistan. We visited the New York offices of several television channels, including CBS. At the time, we didn't know that CBS had planned to do something called "On-Site Specials," which would be a good fit for our story.

CBS News in Pakistan

Our story caught the interest of CBS. They contacted us a little later and said, "We would like to do something with your story." J.B. Brown, a well-known sportscaster who is born again and Spirit-filled, visited our ministry headquarters in Denver with one of the CBS producers. They toured our offices, met our staff, and told us that they wanted to travel with us to Pakistan to document our ministry there. We didn't know how much Christianity they would allow in the story or what the bias would be in the piece, but we felt that we needed to take a chance. We trusted God and decided to take the CBS camera crew, the CBS producer, and J.B. Brown back to Pakistan with us.

You would think that taking a CBS crew to film my next event in Pakistan would have given us some favor as we worked to get our travel documents from the Pakistani government. However, even with CBS, we had to pray for the visas to come through. But with visas, it's not over until we win.

While Pakistan was not the easiest country to obtain a visa from, our connections within the government have enabled us to successfully secure our visas for previous trips by contacting the Pakistani Embassy located in Washington, D.C. What we realized this time, however, was that by having one million attendees at a prayer festival, we became a target. The government wanted to limit my presence, thus making it much more difficult to secure visas. We went through the same process as always. Our contacts inside Pakistan produced the letters required by the Pakistani Embassy and all the applicable paperwork on our side was submitted; however, the Pakistani Embassy would not produce the visas. They informed us that they were working on them and would decide their status in a few days. After that deadline passed, they said the same thing again, but no real progress was made on getting our visas.

We have experienced this many times. Before we minister in many countries, such as Sudan and Algeria, Stephen Kiser travels to Washington, D.C., shows up at the embassy unannounced, and pushes hard for our visas. Stephen has become an expert at working with obstructionist bureaucrats. While at the Pakistani Embassy, Stephen approached these visas in the same way he always did. He pushed them hard, reminding them of all the failed promises they had given us, only to find our applications in a non-active file at the bottom of the pile. He even had a member of the Pakistani Parliament call the Pakistani Embassy on our behalf. What usually worked seemed completely useless this time. Despite Stephen's best efforts, we had run out of time, as we were due to fly to Lahore, Pakistan in two days. So, on Stephen's last day in D.C., he visited the Pakistani ambassador's office one last time.

This time, God had spoken to him before he left the hotel. These visas were not going to be obtained through strong-arm tactics, even though we were absolutely in the right! So, when he arrived at the embassy, Stephen tried a new approach. He turned up smiling and sharing how much we love Pakistan. They were so surprised at this approach that it completely disarmed them. He told them stories that made the embassy officials laugh, talking about things as simple as their dress, and the Pakistani food that he loved, particularly their sweets. It is very important that you learn to pay attention to the voice of the Holy Spirit; He has strategies that can lead you through the most difficult of situations.

Stephen told me later that he was shocked at how the whole office staff and other people in line started laughing and sharing their own stories. After about 45 minutes, just before the office closed for the day (the last possible day for our visas!), the top official said, "Stephen, we have never had anyone love our country so much and make us laugh so well. You and Dr. Hickey will be a great blessing to Pakistan. The visas are approved!"

It was last minute, but it was just one more instance of how God came through for us as we pursued His agenda.

Two days later, in July 2017, we traveled with the CBS camera crew to Lahore, Pakistan. They spent three days with us, filming the entire experience, including a peace conference that our friend, Grand Imam Azad, held with over 400 imams attending. It was a four-hour event in which the imams talked about peace for Pakistan. I was the only woman there! I spoke last, and God told me what to share. He said, "Talk about Jesus after the Resurrection," because Muslims say that Jesus is the Prince of Peace.

The peace that the good news brings was the perfect subject for the occasion. So, I said, "Jesus is the Prince of Peace, and He demonstrated it after His resurrection. When He appeared to His followers after His resurrection, He said, 'Peace to you,' and then showed them His hands, His feet, and His side. Jesus could only make peace through the shedding of His blood, His death, and resurrection. So, because of His death and resurrection, I have peace to offer others." All the imams clapped for me. The Grand Imam said, "You are the Mom of Pakistan." CBS filmed all of it, using parts of what they filmed in the story that later aired on their network.

Grand Imam Azad invited me, Pastor Anwar, and the entire CBS crew to his house for tea. So, we all sat on the floor, had tea, and talked. After tea, I visited with his wife, and she told me that after I prayed for her spine, which had been totally twisted, she had been completely healed. I am continuously amazed at God's favor and His evident power in Pakistan.

The grand finale of that trip was holding a prayer festival. It was an outdoor event, and it was pouring down rain. Even though I was soaking wet, I couldn't get over how wonderful it was to see the people and to enjoy the miracles and healings that God performed, with many people being touched and healed despite the weather. How could God do that? If you had told me that those things would happen and be documented by CBS, I would have thought you were crazy. God is truly amazing!

On that trip, Grand Imam Azad and I discussed my future ministry in the Middle East. He asked me, "Would you be interested in holding a healing meeting in Saudi Arabia?" I was thrilled! Saudi Arabia is one of the countries on my heart, and I had not been able to find a connection that could help me plan a meeting there. Grand Imam Azad said, "My best friend is the Imam of Saudi Arabia. I can connect you with him." That was even better than I could have imagined!

As we discussed the possibilities, it was decided that we would first hold a peace conference that would bring all religions together. We are planning this event in the near future. After that, I would be able to hold a healing meeting, sponsored by the Pakistani and Saudi Arabian imams. I could never have imagined that God would have put me in such high places with such favor, but He did.

I returned to Pakistan in July 2018. That was more of a personal trip, as I decided to celebrate my birthday with my friends in Pakistan and my spiritual son, Anwar Fazal. I don't like to sit and just eat birthday cake; I like to do something active on my birthday. So, I thought, *What better way to celebrate than to go to Pakistan!* That was my ninth trip to Pakistan, and while I was there, I had the honor of ministering to over 45,000 people at Pastor Anwar's church.

During that trip, I was invited to a personal, family dinner with Grand Imam Azad. One of the Grand Imam's sons will take over for him one day. The other is in business. The men all sit at one table and the women sit at another, but I go back and forth. They let me table hop! The Grand Imam and I are still working to set up peace conferences in both Saudi Arabia and Bangladesh. Truly, Pakistan was the only place I wanted to be on my birthday. Perhaps next year, I will celebrate my birthday in Saudi Arabia!

I have a hard time understanding the level of favor that God has given me, but I have found that if you keep showing up, people will begin to believe that you really care, they start to believe that you love them . . .

and I do love them! I am amazed at where God has taken me in over 60 years of ministry, and I can't wait to see where I go next. Wherever God takes me, I know that it will be beyond my wildest imagination.

Chapter 10

DON'T BE BURIED WITH THE MANTLE

WILL THE WORLD FEEL THE impact of your existence? Will it matter that you were here? Will your life be deemed a critical part of someone else's success? As we live life, it is important to think and act beyond our immediate and selfish needs and desires, and live with our minds on others and generations yet to come. Learning to think beyond ourselves and be eternity-minded is a constant battle that we must win. A critical part of true success is the imprint we leave on other people. This means that we must multiply not just our efforts but ourselves in others. To make a significant impact, to be a person of immense influence and leave a legacy, we must be generation-minded and build structures and systems for tomorrow. The foundations we lay for future generations allow them to go farther than we did and ensure that our legacy will last.

You have a rich spiritual inheritance from God. Every promise in the Bible and every successful method for ministry is yours for the taking. This part of my story is meant to help you do just that. If you learn strategic lessons from my life, you can walk in greater success and anointing than you ever thought possible.

I fully expected to retire well before my 80s. However, my passion for souls has not diminished, and God's calling and anointing on my life have stayed strong. In fact, I have seen bigger crowds, greater miracles, and more people reached for Christ in my 80s than I saw when I was younger! Even though I am still traveling and ministering all over the world, I am also very aware that I have an important obligation at this stage of my life to pass on my knowledge, experience, and anointing to the next generation.

A critical part of true success is the imprint we leave on other people.

The Lord dealt with me a couple of years ago and said strongly, "Don't be buried with your mantle. Pass it on." That's when my passion for mentoring greatly increased. Although I had mentored Sarah and Reece for years and had impacted other people throughout my ministry, I had never taken mentoring as a mandate from the Lord. When we read 2 Kings, we see that even though Elijah threw his mantle to Elisha, Elisha was buried with his. After he was buried, they threw a dead man on Elisha's bones, and the dead man came back to life (see 2 Kings 13:21). Unfortunately, there was a lot of power buried in that grave. After God told me not to be buried with my mantle, I began to make a concerted effort to pass my mantle on to as many people as I could. I am intentional about pouring into other people, including young leaders who will impact their generation and the world. My heart is to see people in the Word and effective in the areas to which they are called. To that end, I am devoting more time to developing leaders and mentoring individuals. I also put together a five-volume mentoring series with over 50 hours of life-changing teaching and strategically written journal pages to correspond with each teaching. I refuse to take my mantle to the grave.

You can also receive mantles from more than one person and then see God add to those mantles a unique anointing that He has for your life. It is not about one specific person; it is about each of us doing all that God has called us to do.

The traditional understanding of the "mantle" is the anointing on someone's life that is transferred to someone else. The anointing is the supernatural giftings or skill sets that God gives to a person, so they can complete the assignment He has for them. We see this in the lives of Elijah and Elisha, Moses and Joshua, and Aaron and Eleazar. Their mantles were passed down at the end of their ministries. However, it is important to expand our understanding of what the mantle is. Mantles come in and through many avenues: teachings, relationships, connections, anointings, processes, and strategies, to name a few. You don't need to wait for someone to die to receive a mantle. It also isn't necessary to have someone lay their hands on you for you to receive it. You can also receive mantles from more than one person and then see God add to those mantles a unique anointing that He has for your life. It is not about one specific person; it is about each of us doing all that God has called us to do.

My daughter, Sarah, and her husband, Reece, are running with their mantles and making great waves here in the U.S. and internationally. They were called into ministry years ago and have continued to grow in their impact and influence that change lives every day in our community and around the world. My son in the Lord, Pastor Anwar Fazal, also took hold of the mantle and ran with it. Today, he has the largest church in Pakistan, owns a television network that broadcasts the Gospel throughout the

Middle East, and is making an enormous impact on the world. For years, Greg and Jean Metcalf have partnered with my ministry, traveled on group trips, and attended conferences with me. They have become very successful in business and ministry as they seek to honor God in everything they do. At an early age, Chantell Cooley, a young woman whose family struggled with financial lack, grabbed hold of my teachings on confessing scripture and added that discipline to her daily life. God used that habit to break the spirit of poverty off her family and catapult them into success. Today, they own two universities, and God uses them in powerful ways to increase His kingdom. Many of the men and women who have traveled with me on group trips and ministered with me around the world have also grabbed ahold of my mantle and are being mightily used by God in their families, businesses, and ministries.

There are so many men and women throughout my life and ministry who have caught my mantle and run with it. This is not because I am anyone special—it is because God wants to use each of us to change lives. Anything He gives us, He wants us to pass on to other people. If you believe it, you can catch the mantle right now, run with it, and do greater things than I have ever done.

Word to the World College

Another way God enabled me to empower others was through Word to the World College, which was my ministry's Bible college. I had been traveling internationally for several years, and often ran into people looking for training. I had a very strong desire to equip people to get in the Bible for themselves and to equip them to fulfill their calling. To meet that need, I started the Bible college. We utilized Sunday school classrooms and set up dormitories at our ministry headquarters. God brought us students from all over the world. My goal was not just to teach the Word, but also to prepare people for ministry.

Word to the World College was a two-year, fully accredited Bible college committed to taking God's Word to the world. It was another way of fulfilling the mission God gave me to "cover the earth with the Word." We weren't a large college. We had between 100 and 150 students at the peak of our enrollment. But when I asked God about the size, He told me, "It's not about how big it is; it's about what it does. It's about the people who graduate from your Bible college and what they do to impact the world for Me." Planning, developing, and implementing the Bible school was a great experience. Over the years, our students have planted churches throughout the world, and many of those students are still serving in full-time ministry today. Periodically, some of the students return to Denver to spend time with us. Even after several years of no longer having a Bible college, we still feel like a big family, and I am so grateful that the fruit from that part of our ministry continues to grow and produce more fruit.

After we closed the Bible college, God gave us additional ways to develop leaders through domestic and international training seminars and conferences. Also, I spend several days each month mentoring individuals who are serious about being used by God in ministry or business. I want to impart every ounce of wisdom and experience that I possess into the next generation.

Mentoring Future Ministers for Christ

Sometimes I mentor individuals in my home. As my schedule allows, I invite individuals or groups of two to three people to spend part of a day with me. I listen to them, speak into their lives, and answer their questions. Then, I have a friend join us and together we anoint them with oil and pray for the miraculous to be made manifest in their lives and ministries. Additionally, we give them an opportunity to sow into our ministry because we know the value of sowing. We believe that as we have poured into their lives and they have sown into our ministry, the harvest for both of us will be abundant.

My mentoring approach includes an emphasis on both the Word and the Spirit. I always look at each person as an individual and ask, "What is your greatest need? How can my experience help you?" Many people have settled for a small vision, so I work with them to expand their vision. It is surprising how simple and practical some of the mentoring can be. I minister to people who have huge churches, but they don't know how to command an audience. So, I work with them and have them practice preaching to me. Many people don't know how to lead someone to Christ, do an altar call, or pray for the sick. I try to help them develop those skills.

Mentoring brings you face-to-face with the messy parts of life. I went through messy things and I don't give up on messy people. I'm not ever going to do that. I confront them; I don't compromise, but I don't give up on anyone. People didn't give up on me. There was a time when, if you had seen me, you would have wondered, *Come on, is she really called?* At that time, I wouldn't have known whether I was or not. I needed mentors, and I believe that through the mentors God gave me, He equipped me to do His will and prepared me to pour into others.

Whether I am training a Bible class or mentoring individuals, I endeavor to impart the following five strategic lessons. I learned each lesson through years of challenging life and ministry experiences.

Five Strategic Lessons of Life and Ministry

Strategic Lesson #1
Embrace the Process

We must understand the importance of process. The theme in the early years of my ministry was "the process." I didn't start my ministry and instantly begin airing on television to billions of people. I had to go through a lot of in-between processing. Processing isn't fun, but it is necessary. That is the way God does things. Many people want to jump from "here" to "there" and avoid the hard work of going through the process, but that isn't realistic. My process started with home Bible studies. I wasn't unhappy with the studies or trying to move beyond them. My ministry grew slowly and surely until I began to teach on radio and then on television. I didn't short-circuit the process.

To make a lasting impact for the kingdom of God, we must walk through the process with faith and trust God even when circumstances don't line up with the things He has promised. But that is not all. We must be willing to do a lot of hard work. Getting up at 4:00 a.m. to catch a plane, going without sleep in order to sneak in and minister to an underground church in China, and investing hours upon hours of study in preparation for one 30-minute television program, are examples of the highly necessary and often difficult work that was a part of my process. And there are no short-cuts through the process. I meet people all the time who want a big global ministry, but they won't even walk across the street to witness to a neighbor. If we try to shortchange the process, we will fail to develop the tenacity, resilience, and faith we need to do what God has called us to do.

Settling for a "good idea" rather than pursuing a "God idea" can short-circuit the process and cause us to fall short of God's best. I did this when I tried to get a group of people from our church to help me with home Bible studies. I thought, *I need to get a group of people to help me lead these.* It was an idea that came from my own brain, not from God. It was a "good idea" but not a "God idea," and it failed miserably. The potential leaders were willing, but they didn't have any training, so the groups didn't do well. In fact, no one wanted to go to their groups. Therefore, they quickly dropped out. We must take every idea and pray over it until we know if it is something God is telling us to do. If it is part of God's process for us, He will give us peace in our hearts to implement the idea.

"I am a servant. That's what Jesus is. You don't get any higher than that."

When we are in the process with God, we must stay humble. Our ministries cannot be about our titles or how important we appear to others. For instance, people often ask me, "What should I call you? Should I call you Dr. Hickey?" Even though I have an honorary doctorate, that's not something I am comfortable with using, unless it's overseas and helps me get into places with the Gospel. So, when they ask me my title, I say, "I am a servant. That's what Jesus is. You don't get any higher than that." One especially humbling experience took place at an Assembly of God Church in Burlington, New Jersey. It was very early in my ministry, and the pastor had asked me to speak at his church after hearing my radio program. He was a little caustic in his words to me, and when I asked him how long he wanted me to speak, he said, "As long as you are anointed, after that, sit down." He also told me that he would tell me to sit down if I was still speaking after I was no longer anointed. As I was speaking my message, I saw a man at the back of the church, sitting in a wheelchair. I stopped my message and said to the man, "God wants to heal you. You are going to walk. Get up from your wheelchair, in Jesus' name." The auditorium grew silent, and the man just looked at me, so I said it again, even louder. I ended up telling him to get up and walk multiple times before the assistant pastor finally walked over to me and whispered, "Marilyn, the man doesn't have any legs!" By that time the pastor was laughing, and my heart was sinking—what a humiliating experience. I could have crawled in a hole. Instead, I swallowed my pride and finished speaking my message. Over the years, that pastor has become a really good friend of mine, and I am forever grateful for that humbling experience. Later, when I prayed about it, God didn't rebuke me for missing it. He spoke to my heart and said that if I would continue to walk in faith, I would indeed see people healed by Him and come out of wheelchairs.

Another part of embracing the process is recognizing the value and importance of the physical body God gave to each of us. We must invest in our physical health as much as we invest in our spiritual health. During most of the years of my ministry, I maintained a very consistent daily routine. After my morning devotion time, when I prayed, memorized scripture, and confessed the Word, I spent 30 to 60 minutes exercising. I didn't do that because I loved to be sweaty! Exercise was never interesting to me for its own sake. I took that time to focus on exercise because I was determined to have a long and healthy life. I am 88 years old and still going strong. I know that God has energized and equipped my body, but I also know that I am responsible to do my part. We must exercise and watch what we eat. Healthy eating habits may be hard to start, but once we see the increased stamina, energy, and strength in our bodies, those habits won't be difficult to maintain.

Strategic Lesson #2
Put God's Word First in Your Life

I desperately want you to have a passion and a hunger for the Word of God. We can only be successful if we prioritize the Word. We all know that we have to eat for our bodies to survive, but do we know that we have to eat spiritually? We have to read, memorize, and study the Word of God to survive spiritually and have success in life. Each of us should have a Bible reading plan. If we don't, we won't consistently read through the Bible. If we fail to plan, we plan to fail! The plan I follow allows me to read through the Bible twice each year. There are plans that help you read the whole Bible or just the New Testament in one year. Pick one and stick to it. God teaches us wisdom in the secret place (see Psalm 51:6). He does that through His Word. If we read the Bible, the Bible will "read us." God will take the truth of the Bible and make it wisdom in our lives. What we read is used by God to give us wisdom that we can apply to our lives, but this only happens if we do our part. We must read the Word of God!

If we fail to plan, we plan to fail!

Every morning, after I pray and read the Bible, I spend time memorizing the Word. I have done this for almost 50 years. When I started, I would memorize one scripture a day. After a while, I was able to memorize two to three scriptures a day. Eventually, I could memorize 15 verses a day. Many times, we limit ourselves by thinking we can only memorize one or two scriptures, but I am convinced that the Holy Spirit will help us memorize many more than that. I don't memorize scriptures so I can brag about how many books of the Bible I have committed to memory. I do it because memorizing and speaking scriptures brings life to my mind, spirit, and body. It also gives me a repertoire of scriptures inside my heart that the Holy Spirit can use to minister to me and others when we need it most. We must memorize the Word of God!

Joshua 1:8 (NIV) says, *"Keep this Book of the Law always on your lips; meditate on it day and night, so that you may be careful to do everything written in it. Then you will be prosperous and successful."* I have a list of scriptures in my phone that resonate with me. I update them periodically and confess the whole list every morning as I drink my coffee. It is okay to personalize the scriptures as we speak them. One of my favorite scriptures is Galatians 2:20 (NIV), *"I have been crucified with Christ and I no longer live, but Christ lives in me. The life I now live in the body, I live by faith in the Son of God, who loved me and gave himself for me."* I personalize that scripture by saying, "I am dead to sin; I live by faith in the Son." When I travel overseas, I work to get in sync with the local time as soon as possible, so I can continue to keep my routine of confessing the Word. For me, it is not an option to let the Word go, even for a few days. You see, that is how God started everything. He created the entire world with the Word. If we want to see miracles in our lives, we must speak the Word instead of the problem! There is always a promise that God has given us that is an answer to our problem. If we trust the promise more than the problem, we will see miracles. We must speak the Word of God!

Our words really do matter. Besides confessing the Word during our devotional time each day, we should make sure that the truth of the Word is reflected by what we say about our health, our life, our children, etc. In my 20s, I was a teacher, and that took a lot of energy. Every time Wally came home, he would ask me, "How are you doing?" Invariably, my response would be, "I'm so tired!" I was confessing my circumstances, and not the truth about the Word; I was stuck in a cycle of exhaustion. I didn't begin to feel more energy until I realized that my energy and strength come from God, not my circumstances. Then I began speaking the opposite of what I was feeling. I developed the discipline of watching my words and speaking life over my body, mind, and spirit. It made such a difference in my life. I truly have more energy now, at 88 years old, than I had when I was 20. Our words must line up with what God says about us!

Strategic Lesson #3
Pray as if Your Life Depends on it, Because it Does

I have seen indisputable evidence that prayer works, and that praying people succeed. Our level of effectiveness and power in life and ministry is directly proportional to the amount of time we spend in prayer. Praying and having intimacy with God is the foundation of a fruitful life. I saw this firsthand in my relationship with Dr. Yonggi Cho. He had a great passion for prayer which led him to pray for at least four hours every day. The results were incredible. My goal is to always press into God, seek Him, and make my time with Him the first priority of each day. It also helps me to hang around people who love to pray. The more they pray, the more I want to pray, and the more I pray, the more I want to pray!

Our level of effectiveness and power in life and ministry is directly proportional to the amount of time we spend in prayer.

Strategic Lesson #4
Implement Wisdom in Life and Relationships

We need wisdom every day. James 1:5 says, *"If any of you lacks wisdom, let him ask of God, who gives to all liberally and without reproach, and it will be given to him.*" We need wisdom in relationships, circumstances, and every area of our lives. Throughout my life and ministry, there have been times when I had no clue what to do. God doesn't want us to be clueless. He wants us to have wisdom, and He promises to give it to us.

If we want to be wise, we must be flexible. If we try to bend something that is stiff, it may break. It is the same way with us. Life is always changing, and many people fight that change. If we let ourselves become ruffled and irritated by every change that comes our way, we will live a life of turmoil; instead, become flexible. When I first ministered in Ethiopia, I was told that I would have to wear the customary thin cotton clothing if I expected the people to listen to me. I didn't want to wear that outfit, but I knew it was the wise thing to do, so I did. Then when I was preaching, if I started to use a word that the people wouldn't understand or one that would be offensive to them, my interpreter would say, "Don't use that word, use this word instead." I could have dug my heels in and decided I didn't want to change my words, but that would not have been wise. I had successful meetings with lasting fruit because God gave me wisdom and helped me to be flexible.

It is also wise to forgive quickly and refuse to carry an offense. Dealing with people at an intimate and personal level requires an abundance of grace. We can pour our lives into people, and they can turn around, walk out on us, and forget how to spell our names. Rejection and ingratitude are very real, and we must have wisdom to forgive and walk in love. During the very first charismatic conference at which I spoke, they received a love offering for me and told me they would send it to me after I got home. Seven days went by, and I didn't receive anything in the mail, so I called and asked them about it. They said, "We are sending it." Another week went by, and still, nothing had arrived, so I called again. They said, "We are sending it." When the third week went by, and I had still not received the check, I called again, and they said the same thing. I started to develop a negative attitude and entertain offense, but the Lord spoke to me and said, "If you sow it, you can get a harvest." As I prayed about His words to me, I knew He was telling me not to take offense but pray and "give the offering" into that church and then He would bless me. I forgave them for receiving an offering but not sending it to me. I prayed and told the Lord that I was "giving" that money to them. God had given me wisdom to avoid offense and keep my heart from becoming angry and bitter. I have never regretted that choice.

If we walk in wisdom, God will take what looks like a disadvantage and turn it into an advantage. I have seen God use "disadvantages" in ways that turned out to be the best thing for the people involved. When I started in ministry, women were not allowed to speak from the pulpit. It seemed like a huge disadvantage, but God gave me the wisdom to accept the fact that He had made me a woman and that I could trust Him to make it an advantage. Then, when I wanted to get on radio, the men who controlled the programming said that they didn't want women on their radio station. God gave me wisdom in the form of a question. I asked sweetly, "Oh, do

> When the day is done, and the dust settles, we must ask ourselves if we have revealed the love of Christ to the people we met that day. That is the ultimate test.

you have something against women?" I think that scared them and they ended up allowing me to speak on the radio. In all the Muslim countries to which I have traveled, being a woman could have been seen as a disadvantage, but for me, God turned it into an advantage. Nine times out of ten, they underestimated me. They looked at me as a stupid woman, and they were convinced that I couldn't do anything to hurt anyone. God used that to open the door for me to share His love and healing power.

Now that I am an old woman, it is even more advantageous because they see me as even less of a threat. We have a choice. We can focus on our disadvantages, or we can trust God to turn them into advantages. Let's use wisdom and trust God to do that more and more.

If we are wise, we will love people. We cannot just say we love people. We must ask God to give us a genuine love for people that causes us to really walk in love with them. In whatever we do, the love of Christ must be the foundation, the center, the ultimate objective. When the day is done, and the dust settles, we must ask ourselves if we revealed the love of Christ to the people we met that day. That is the ultimate test. If the love of Christ was revealed, we have succeeded. As a pastor's wife, I had plenty of opportunities to pass or fail this test.

One time I remember miserably failing was with a lady in our church who was a counselor. Wally and I had helped her to get started in her ministry and had sent multiple people to her for counseling. Then we found out that she was saying negative things about us to people in our church. Her actions hurt my heart; I was wounded and offended. I couldn't believe she would make up lies against us, and I wanted to tell her off! Whenever I saw her at church, I would turn and walk the other way. I thought, *I don't want to go anywhere near her.* My attitude was ugly, and I wasn't walking in love. Then she called me and asked me to go to lunch with her. I didn't want to go, but God spoke to my heart and told me, "You take her to lunch." That was a double insult. Not only did I have to spend time with her, but I also had to pay for it. I didn't like it, but I knew I had to obey God. When we met at the restaurant, the first words out of her mouth were, "Marilyn, I want to apologize for how I have treated you. I have said ugly things about you, and I am sorry. Would you please forgive me?" You could have knocked me over with a feather. I was shocked. That day I forgave her, and God began a healing process in my heart; but before that moment, I had failed to walk in love.

If we are wise, we will avoid comparison because it makes us dissatisfied with our lives. If we find ourselves tempted to compare our lives with others, we must look to God. He is the only One to Whom we should compare ourselves. It can be hard, but if we can keep from being infected with a spirit of criticism, comparison, and competition, we will be more content and satisfied.

First Corinthians 1:30 says, *"Christ Jesus, became for us wisdom from God."* There may be 100 times each day that we need to ask God for wisdom. He never gets tired of us asking for wisdom, and He is always faithful to give us the wisdom we need.

Strategic Lesson #5
Give Generously

"For God so loved the world that He gave His only begotten Son, that whoever believes in Him should not perish but have everlasting life" (John 3:16). God loved, so God gave. We too should give.

It doesn't matter how broke we are; we can always find a way to give something to someone.

There is power in giving. We can give time, money, love, compassion; really, we can give a lot of things. It doesn't matter how broke we are; we can always find a way to give something to someone. If we didn't have any material possessions at all, we could still pray for someone and show compassion and kindness. Even when we are extremely busy, we can find a few minutes in our day to be a blessing to someone.

God will give us creative ways to sow into people's lives. One time, my friend Rick, who is a pastor in St. Louis, desperately needed $70,000 to finish paying for his sanctuary. I didn't have the money to give him, but I called him and offered to help. I said, "Rick, I will come and help you raise the money. I want to help you. Just pay my expenses; I don't want an honorarium." I flew to St. Louis and was getting ready to speak in his church when something very supernatural happened.

I was in the sanctuary, on the front row, praying, "Oh, God, help me with this. I want him to get the money he needs." Just then, a woman tapped me on the shoulder. She said, "I'm Joyce Meyer, and this is my husband Dave Meyer, and we're thinking of going on the radio with our ministry. We know you are on the radio; would you mind praying for us?" I am so blessed that I had the opportunity to pray for Joyce and Dave that day. I had gone there to be a blessing to my friend, Rick, but I received an even greater blessing. Joyce has a truly supernatural ministry and is mightily used by God. For decades now, she has been a partner with my ministry and a true friend to me.

Leaders, no matter how accomplished they are, go through moments and even seasons of disappointment and rejection. The strain of life and ministry can push you to the brink. If you aren't careful, you can come to the end of yourself, wondering if it is all worth it. How do you find the strength to keep moving on, to keep fighting against enormous opposition, when every fiber of your being is screaming, "Give up!" I have found that during those times, it is best to find someone to whom you can generously give love, financial blessing, or prayer. One of the times I wanted to totally give up was during that season I shared about earlier when I had parasites and wanted to die. That would have been the most extreme form of giving up. Instead, God told me to give. He told me to call 10 people every day who were sicker than I was and pray for their healing. I thought, *God, that is impossible. I can't do it.* Still, each day He gave me 10 people to call, and I would call them and pray with them. God also told me that I had to be totally positive while I was on the phone with them.

That was extremely difficult. I could not complain about how badly I felt. I could not comment on how sick they were or how drastic their physical condition appeared to be. Many times, those were very short calls because it was hard to find positive things to say! In those cases, I prayed and then quickly said, "Goodbye." But by giving to them through the phone call and prayer, even when I felt that I had nothing to give, God changed me and put me in a place to receive total healing.

Embracing the process, putting God's Word first, praying as if my life depends on it, getting wisdom, and giving generously are the five solid foundations of my life and ministry. My prayer for you is that you will learn them too, and in doing so, you will walk in all that God has for you.

Even today, at 88 years old, I continue to tell people around the world about the love and healing power of Jesus Christ. I still travel several times each month and many times my travels take me halfway around the world. Years ago, when I looked at my future and the important generations yet to come, I didn't think I would live this long and be so active. When I was in my early 70s, a man in my church asked, "When do you think you will retire?" I said, "Probably at age 74." Of course, I didn't retire then. So, he asked me again a few years later, "When do you think you will retire?" I said, "Well, maybe at age 77." I didn't retire at that time either! I never thought I would have my biggest meeting, with over one million people, when I was 85. That was surprising to me. I finally stopped making five-year plans for retirement because every time I considered retirement, I thought, *That is stupid. You feel great, you are still called, and there are still needs in the world.*

My goal is to keep giving back as long as I have breath. This book is just another way for me to share my life with other people, pass on my experience, and mentor future generations. My prayer is that reading the story of my life has inspired, encouraged, and convinced you that with God: IT'S NOT OVER UNTIL YOU WIN!

Acknowledgments

How do you capture anyone's life in a few pages and do it justice? How do you sort through memories and moments and miracles? Though the memories and moments are mine, I could not have written this autobiography without the significant help of some very special people. I am deeply grateful to Nancy Buckner for her wisdom and passion to research every part of this project and fill every gap along the way. This book would not have been written without Nancy's vision for the project, attention to detail, and diligence in prayer. I was privileged to work with Michelle Ofori-Ansah, whose talent and experience allowed her to skillfully draw out the long-past history and intricate details of my life. I appreciate Diane Reiter who watched over this huge project to bring it to pass. Her wisdom and leadership were indispensable. In addition to overseeing my ministry as Vice President, she became my editor. She worked tirelessly with Bobbie Sartini, Tahnya Abraham, Becky Reid, Joe Oestreich, Patsy Rosales, and Karen Zirger on major rewrites and seemingly endless edits, but still managed to meet deadlines without compromising the integrity of the project. Her spirit of excellence inspires me. I am grateful for Ruth Haugen, Michael Riedy, Dustin Groeneman, and Tatyana Yaremkiv, whose creativity and tenacity were instrumental in the design and promotion of this book. I am also grateful to Stephen Kiser. Reaching the nations to which God called me would not have been possible without him—the hand in the glove. I am in awe of my dedicated staff and thank God for them every day as they continually use their gifts and talents to *Cover the Earth with the Word*. They are the best! And, to the creative team at Inprov, whose guidance has helped me to reach more people in more places, I am eternally grateful. I thank God for the story I have lived to tell and for those who have helped me tell it.

—*Marilyn Hickey*

Endorsements

Robert Morris—Founding Lead Senior Pastor of Gateway Church, Southlake, TX, bestselling author of *The Blessed Life*, *Frequency*, and *Beyond Blessed*

> In her new book, *It's Not Over Until You Win*, Marilyn Hickey shares her story of a life deeply rooted in the Word and prayer. She details the numerous times God has saved her from seemingly impossible situations only to come out victorious. This book will encourage and inspire you in your faith as you believe God for miracles in your own life.

T.D. Jakes, Sr.—Pastor of The Potter's House of Dallas, author, and filmmaker

> Marilyn Hickey has left an indelible impression on my life and millions of others. Her riveting story, coupled with her tenacious fidelity to God's Word, blazed a trail that could not be ignored. *It's Not Over Until You Win* is now going to fuel the next generation with faith and fire! You simply must read her thoughts, stories and reflections!

Benny Hinn—Pastor, Evangelist, and author of bestselling books, including: *Good Morning Holy Spirit*, *Prayer that Gets Results*, *Blood in the Sand*, and *Lamb of God: Yesterday Today & Forever*

> Marilyn Hickey and I have been dear friends since the early 70s, when we met in Buffalo, NY through a mutual friend, Pastor Tommy Reid. Throughout all those years Marilyn has been a very powerful and courageous minister of the Gospel, and in my opinion the greatest Bible teacher on planet earth. My dear friend, Marilyn Hickey,

with her dear husband, Wally, who is in heaven now, established one of the greatest churches in America in Denver, Colorado, and her television ministry has affected millions. I have met so many leaders worldwide whom she has greatly impacted for our precious Lord Jesus. Marilyn still continues to amaze so many of us, traveling and preaching the Gospel with demonstrations of the Holy Spirit in many nations, including Muslim nations such as Pakistan. I am amazed as I watch her travel, still going strong. I pray the Lord will give her many years of ministry and health, as she continues blessing the nations with the Gospel. I am proud to call myself her friend.

Chantell Cooley—Co-founder of Columbia Southern University, author of *Stand on the Word* and *Winning the Game of Life*

This book will challenge you to pursue the Word like never before. Marilyn's life story shows her practical and thorough revelation of speaking the Word and will inspire you to believe what the Word says about you. When I took her incredible teaching and applied it to my life, I experienced breakthrough and victory. You won't be able to put this book down because it is key to your success!

Daniel Kolenda—Evangelist, CEO of Christ for all Nations

There's no one like Marilyn Hickey! For decades, she has been a voice of wisdom and encouragement to millions of people. She is an accomplished author, inspirational teacher, powerful minister, and a modern-day expert on the Word of God. She is known as a woman of great faith, who believes, "God can do anything!" Marilyn's autobiography, *It's Not Over Until You Win: My Lifetime of Experiencing the Miracles of God*, is a treasure box. It is full of miraculous testimonies and amazing stories of her incredible life of adventures with her best friend, the Holy Spirit! I know your faith will grow as you journey through the pages of Marilyn's story, and believe you will be inspired to follow her lead and step out into all that God has planned for your own victorious life!

Evon Horton—Pastor of Brownsville Assembly, Pensacola, FL
Marilyn Hickey has spoken into my life and ministry for over 33 years. No one has impacted my ministry as much as she has; literally changing my life and ministry through years of teaching truth, imparting wisdom, and inspiring faith in me. As Marilyn talks about her journey, you too will be encouraged and challenged. This is an amazing book that is sure to lift you up and draw you closer to the Lord. I know that God will do something amazing in your life as you read this book.

Ginger Lindsay—Christ for the Nations Board Vice Chairman
Author Marilyn Hickey is truly a "Mother of the Faith" and a "Woman of the Word of God" who was honored by Christ For The Nations with the Freda Lindsay Award. Her story is compelling and inspires the reader to be aware of God's love for the one who feels unlovable and who questions their purpose for living. I recommend you read this book as a devotional each day, so you can learn how Dr. Hickey became such an incredible woman of influence all over the world; and find out how you, like her, can fulfill your purpose for God.

Greg Mohr—Director of Charis Bible College, Woodland Park, CO
I am blessed to know Marilyn Hickey and to have had the opportunity to be touched powerfully by her life and ministry for years. I know that you are going to be blessed by reading her autobiography, *It's Not Over Until You Win*. As you read, you will be encouraged to be the winner God ordained for you to be and you will receive from her wisdom and anointing.

Guillermo Maldonado—Founder of King Jesus International Ministry

Marilyn Hickey is a pioneer in the Kingdom of God. She is an anointed teacher of the Word that is powerfully used of God to build the body of Christ. Also, she has a strong evangelistic anointing and boldly preaches the Gospel in the United States and around the world, with the demonstration of the supernatural power of God through miracles, signs, and wonders. Marilyn has been in full-time ministry for many years and continues to travel extensively and to impact countless multitudes. I wholeheartedly recommend her new autobiography, *It's Not Over Until You Win: My Lifetime of Experiencing the Miracles of God.* Not only is it packed with wisdom, revelation, and testimonies of miracles, it is deeply inspiring and will activate faith in believers and leaders alike to walk in the power of God in their own lives to reach their potential and fulfill their purpose. Beyond the excellent and relevant content of Marilyn's book, I can also testify to the substance of her character as she is my dear friend. Marilyn is a true and mighty woman of God, that my wife and I love and respect. She is genuinely a gift to the body of Christ!

James Goll—Founder and President of God Encounters Ministries, Franklin, TN

Over the years and generations, God has raised up champions of faith. Marilyn Hickey is not only one of those champions but is a hero of many of them. Marilyn has a long shadow of Jesus's power, presence, and supernatural touch of God that will encourage you as you read about her life and legacy. You will receive encouragement, faith, hope, and love as you read, *It's Not Over Until You Win.*

Joan Hunter—Author, healing evangelist, and TV host of *Miracles Happen!*
What a treasure you hold in your hands! Marilyn Hickey's life
and ministry have spanned several generations and almost every
media format, all five-fold ministry positions, and has covered the
earth. From the Great Depression and the Greatest Generation
to Millennials, from the beginning of the Healing Revivals of the
mid-20th century and the Charismatic Movement of the 1960's and
1970's until this very day, she has been at the forefront of Kingdom
life and ministry. Anyone interested in ministry can learn from her
experiences, but I strongly recommend that everyone in ministry,
especially all women, read this book and allow Marilyn to guide
you to maturity. I have personally known her for over 40 years and
I assure you that her autobiography will greatly benefit you for years
to come.

John Bates—Author of three books, including *Inner Hearing*, Senior
Leader of Freedom Fellowship International, Waxahachie, Texas;
www.johnbatesministries.com
Steve Jobs, co-founder and former CEO of Apple Inc., said, "Your
time is limited, so don't waste it living someone else's life." Marilyn
Hickey has chosen to live her best life. We can all learn from her
unswerving dependence on God and His Word. It was in the mid-90s
that I sat in a large healing rally for the leadership of the Assemblies
of God in Springfield, Missouri and heard her deliver a powerful
sermon on signs and wonders. At the conclusion, she paused
and then declared God was going to heal warts and growths. My
sensibilities were rattled! "How undignified," I mused. I was then
reminded of a wart I previously had removed by a dermatologist,
no less than three times. I humbly stood for prayer and two weeks
later it had disappeared, never to return. There were MULTIPLE

healings that night, as are common in her meetings. Throughout the years, she has continued to shake out any religiosity in me. Stories like mine circle the globe regarding this powerful international speaker. I have watched her interact with world leaders and I have seen her with common beggars. She treats everyone the same, with the utmost respect. I am so happy this book has been written. You will be greatly encouraged and lovingly challenged as you read the powerful life story of this industrious trailblazer.

Karen Wheaton—Founder of The Ramp, Hamilton, AL

As you journey with Marilyn through the pages of her life, you will understand why her teaching has made such a deep impact on the world. She has lived her message, proven her faith, fought her battles ... and won. Learn how to keep contending for your win from one of the greatest teachers given to our generation.

Mark Chironna—Church on the Living Edge/Mark Chironna Ministries

In our culture, we tend to refer to someone whose life has consistently been marked by extraordinary accomplishments as a "legend." While some people are a "legend in their own minds," others are genuinely deserving of the recognition and honor and the appellation, "legend." For me, Marilyn Hickey is a "living legend." She has been a staple and a constellating figure in my own personal journey. Her iconic, "Let Jesus live big in you" has remained imprinted on my heart for my entire journey since my conversion to Christ. You hold in your hands, more than a new book from her pen. This is the story of a life well-lived for a Savior Who loves an entire world, and a woman who won't stop until the whole world knows it, even those who appear to be enemies of the Gospel. I have found that even those who oppose Marilyn at first are won over by her graciousness and incurable confidence in Jesus. *It's Not Over Until You Win* is a gift to all of us. May it be read far and wide, and may Marilyn's well-lived life for Jesus, inspire you to "let Jesus live big in you," so that you too can discover how Jesus always causes us to triumph, so you don't stop until you win.

Mark Rutland—President Oral Roberts University, author of *David the Great*
Marilyn Hickey's new book is, on the one hand, a moving and honest memoir. On the other hand, it is an adventure story that awakens the dozing soul, that makes you want to get up out of life's easy chair and actually do something for God. If you do not want to be moved, stirred, or challenged, stay away from this book. I tell you in all sincerity, this book is dangerous.

Patricia King—Founder of Patricia King Ministries and co-founder of XPmedia.com, host of Patricia King Everlasting Love TV
I am so blessed to be able to recommend Marilyn Hickey's amazing autobiography, *It's Not Over Until You Win*. I have spent hours listening to this woman—so full of the Spirit, so full of joy, so full of hope, and so full of the Word. The foundations she laid in my life through years of line-upon-line, precept-upon-precept Bible teaching have changed the way I walk before the Lord. As you read this book, it will be like sitting at the feet of a great mentor or of a seasoned general. You will be infused with faith and glean treasures of gold.

Richard Roberts—Chairman and CEO of Oral Roberts Evangelistic Association

From miracle to miracle to miracle . . . that's the life story and testimony of a true woman of faith. Marilyn Hickey's autobiography will not only inspire you but will give you priceless steps of how to live your own life of miracles.

Roberts Liardon—Founder of Embassy Global Network, author, church historian

One of the most revelatory teachers of the Word of God is a woman named Marilyn Hickey, and it turns out that she has lived and continues to live an extraordinary life. As a church historian, I love this book! As a minister of the Gospel, I am so grateful that God put Marilyn in my life at a young age and that she is still here to teach, inspire, and encourage me. Marilyn has always utilized Christian media, encouraging many to read through the Bible every year with her, as well as teaching the value of memorizing Scripture and meditating in the Word. I continue to receive tremendous revelation from her. Today, she is long past retirement and is still going strong, even traveling to dangerous parts of the world to hold crusades. She has never quit! Thank you, Marilyn, for being such a great role model, ministering with the utmost integrity and the power of God. Your life is proof that, in Jesus Christ, *It's Not Over Until You Win!*

Sharon Daugherty—Pastor of Victory Christian Center, Tulsa, OK

What an inspiring book! Marilyn allows you to see into her various life experiences of difficulty, trauma, danger, depression, and even suicidal thoughts. Then she shares the overcoming power she found in her relationship with God and His Word. She shows how the people in our lives also influence us in winning over situations we face. This book is right on time to help so many who are struggling in life.

Taffi Dollar—Pastor, World-Changers Church International; Founder of WCCI Women's Ministry and Prestige Ministry

Marilyn Hickey gives a heartfelt glimpse into her life and ministry in *It's Not Over Until You Win*. Reading the book is a journey in itself: a journey which unveils her as a woman after God's own heart, a woman who happens to have a heart for people, as well. This biographical journey is both humorous and engaging, and you will be blessed by her transparency.

Dr. William M. Wilson—President, Oral Roberts University

There is simply no person on earth like Marilyn Hickey! I am so pleased and excited about her new book, *It's Not Over Until You Win*. This behind-the-scenes journey with Marilyn around the world and through life's challenges will inspire, empower, and motivate you. If God can open these amazing doors and pour out His miraculous power for Marilyn, then imagine what He can do for you!